The Manager's Tale

The Manager's Tale

By Hugh Mackay Ross

Watson & Dwyer Publishing Ltd.
Winnipeg, Manitoba

Watson & Dwyer Publishing Limited
232 Academy Road
Winnipeg, Manitoba R3M 0E7

Canadian Cataloguing in Publication Data

Ross, Hugh Mackay
   The manager's tale

   Sequel to: The apprentice's tale
   Bibliography: p.
   Includes index
   ISBN: 0-920486-34-7 (bound); 0-920486-30-4 (pbk.)

1. Ross, Hugh Mackay. 2. Hudson's Bay Company -
Biography. 3. Fur Traders - Prairie Provinces- Biography.
4. Fur Trade - Prairie Provinces - History - 20th Century.
I. Title
FC3376.1.R688A32 1989   971.2'03'0924   C89-098091-8
   F1060.92.R688A32 1989

The publication of this book is
supported by grants from the
Canada Council and the Manitoba Arts Council

Bound and Printed in Canada
by Hignell Printing Limited, Winnipeg

DEDICATION

To Jane:
The fair, the chaste,
the unexpressive she!

ACKNOWLEDGEMENTS

Following the publication of my first book *The Apprentice's Tale*, I received dozens of letters and phone calls. Some were from men who had served under the same conditions and during the same time span, all recalling, with great relish, their time with the Hudson's Bay Company. Others were from complete strangers, who either knew the area depicted at the time, or whose friends or relatives were mentioned in the book. I thank them all for their kind remarks.

The one question they all asked was 'Did you keep a diary? How can you remember everything so clearly?' No. I didn't keep a journal but, as anyone my age will verify, I suppose we remember things that happened long ago more clearly than we do today's events. In fact, I can never recall how many grandchildren I have unless I do some figuring.

But, being fallible, many things in this book had to be verified and checked for accuracy. For reading this manuscript and giving invaluable suggestions and recommendations, I am indebted to Shirlee Anne Smith, Keeper, Hudson's Bay Company Archives. For their able assistance and infinite patience, I am also indebted to Alex Ross and Judith Beattie of the Hudson's Bay Company Archives, Provincial Archives of Manitoba.

I wish to thank Don Ferguson, former Personnel Manager, Northern Stores Department who allowed me to borrow all the copies of the *Moccasin Telegraph*, staff magazine of the HBC, covering the period 1941-71; Kent Gibbons, Research Assistant, *The Beaver* magazine, for supplying histories of the posts; the staffs of the *The Beaver* and *The Moccasin Telegraph* at Hudson's Bay House; The Venerable W.J. Rowe, Archdeacon of Prince Albert, the Anglican Church of Canada for historical background on Stanley Mission Church; Father Mathieu, Portage La Loche and Father Darveau, Brochet.

My gratitude to the late Eric W. Morse, M.A., F.R.G.S. and to Major General N.E. Rodger, Vice-Chief of General Staff, Canadian Army (Rtd.) for permission to quote from their letters; and to Wayne Runge, Fur Administrator, Saskatchewan Parks and Renewable Resources, Prince Albert, and Rene Baudais, Pilot *par excellence.*

A special thanks to all my old Company friends for sharing their memories with me: Tom Scurfield, Des Pitts, Wulf Tolboom, Harry Borbridge, Bert Swaffield, Mac Watson, Victor MacKay who now lives at Geraldton, George Fleming (Calgary), Bob Campbell (Grande Prairie), and to Bob Middleton and his wife Nancy (Victoria). Also, my thanks to Steve Preweda, Store Manager, Hazelton; Owen Kingston, Store Manager, Brochet; Douglas Mousseau, Manager, Portage la Loche, and Iris Harris, now retired and living in Winnipeg.

But most of all, I am indebted to my wife, Jane, who typed, corrected, and edited this manuscript and turned my oft-incoherent dictation into smooth, flowing prose. Without her constant help and encouragement, this book could not have been completed.

Hugh Mackay Ross
Winnipeg, Canada
February 1989

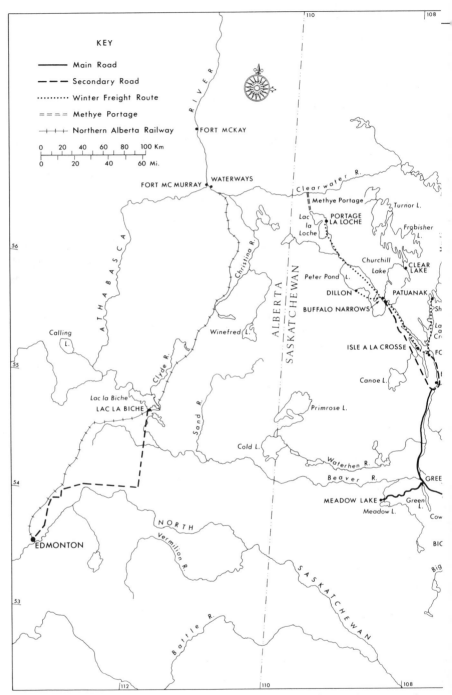

KEY

Main Road
Secondary Road
Winter Freight Route
Methye Portage
Northern Alberta Railway

0 20 40 60 80 100 Km
0 20 40 60 Mi.

In 1950 the Hudson's Bay Company gave me permission to change the names of certain posts to conform with local usage. Lac du Brochet became Brochet; South Reindeer Lake became Southend; Pine River changed to Patuanak and Lac la Ronge

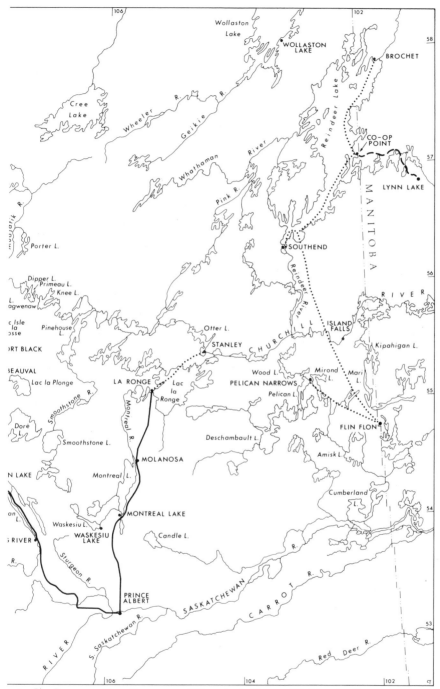

to La Ronge. Also there are different spellings of Isle a la Crosse. Now Ile-a-la-Crosse has been officially accepted as correct. During the 1940s and 1950s, the Company's official usage was Isle a la Crosse, and this I have used throughout.

Ross's Travelling District Office

CONTENTS

MAPS

Maps by Caroline Trottier.

Photographs are from the Hudson's Bay Company Archives Photograph Collection, Provincial Archives of Manitoba, unless otherwise credited.

Rupert's Land

By the Charter, the Company was granted the 'sole Trade and Commerce of all those Seas Streightes Bayes Rivers Lakes Creekes and Soundes in whatsoever Latitude they shall bee that lye within the entrance of the Streightes commonly called Hudsons Streightes together with all the Landes and Territoryes upon the Countryes Coastes and confynes of the Seas Bayes Lakes Rivers Creekes and Soundes aforesaid that are not actually possessed by or granted to any of our subjectes or possessed by the Subjectes of any other Christian Prince or State'.

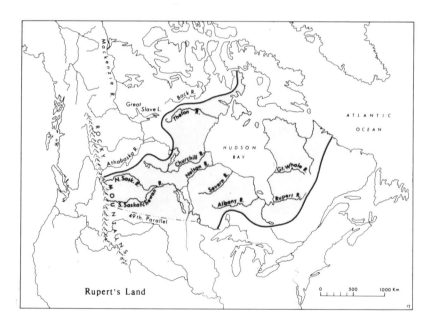

Rupert's Land

INTRODUCTION

Histories of the Hudson's Bay Company have been written by writers more able than I. Some have been good; others, in my view, not so good. This book is not a history, nor am I an historian. My account of my years as district manager is perhaps a stitch in a vast and complex tapestry created by Company men and women over a span of three hundred and twenty years.

In this preamble, I step out of my niche as narrator to comment on the role of the young apprentice clerks who carried the business of the Company forward in distant places, and to fill in some of the relevant background of the Fur Trade Department as it was in 1941.

In 1870 the Company negotiated the sale of Rupert's Land -- all the land around the rivers flowing into Hudson's Bay, as described in the Company's Charter, granted by Charles II in 1670 -- to Canada for the sum of £3,000,000. It retained title to the lands surrounding each trading post, large acreages around such main posts as Fort Garry and Fort Edmonton, and one-twentieth of each township settled within the Fertile Belt.

The impressive total of lands received in the Fertile Belt was 7,000,000 acres, and starting in 1905, the Company retained the mineral rights when selling land.

At first, settlement onto western land was slow but after the completion of the Canadian Pacific Railway, it picked up. A vigorous advertising campaign sponsored by the federal government under Clifford Sifton, then Minister of the Interior, and the Canadian Pacific Railway was carried out in central Europe. Between 1898 and 1913, streams of immigrants mainly from Russia and central Europe poured into the western prairies. In 1874 the Hudson's Bay Company established a Land Department to handle the sale of the farming land it owned. Land was a valuable asset, providing more profit than the Fur Trade

Department. It was believed in high places that the future of the Company depended on land rather than on fur.

Northern posts were allowed to fall into decay from lack of attention to repairs and replacements. Household furnishings were supplied at the very minimum cost. Because of the poor living conditions, few white wives of post managers were prepared to live in the North. Most traders married natives or half-breeds.

Because of the remoteness of some posts, inspections were few and far between. District managers or inspectors were able to visit each post no more than once a year. Stocks were allowed to build up in order to have goods on hand to keep trappers from selling fur to the free traders, and trapping advances increased yearly to the point where they were uncollectable. In short, the fur trade had not yet progressed from the nineteenth century.

In 1923, Mr P.A. Chester joined the Company as an assistant accountant on the staff in London, England. The following year he was sent to Canada to review the Company's accounting system. He was appointed Chief Accountant, Winnipeg Head Office in November 1925, and in October 1930 was named General Manager of the Company for Canada.

Mr Chester supervised the Fur Trade Department from the time of Commissioner Ralph Parsons' retirement in 1940 until R.H. Chesshire was appointed manager in 1942. He became a member of the London Committee and Managing Director for Canada on August 29, 1946. His job was to bring the fur trade into the twentieth century and he went about it in a methodical way. It was his belief that to keep a good man in the North that man must be provided with a comfortable home to which he could bring his wife, and a modern store to work in. A comfortable home meant a house with hot and cold running water, central heating, electric lights and an indoor flush toilet. A contented wife meant a happy husband who would do a better job for the Company.

John Watson, an architect, was hired by the Company to draw up the necessary plans, and gradually new buildings began to appear throughout the North. With the advent of the war in 1939 and a shortage of building materials, this program was slowed down but was completed immediately after the war.

Staff health was another of Mr Chester's concerns. All staff at the posts, including wives and families, were required to undergo a medical and dental examination every two years when they came out on furlough. The Company paid for the examinations, but the dental work, using a dentist of their choice, was the individual's responsibility. Before returning to a post, a clearance examination by the Company-appointed doctor and dentist was mandatory. The first Company doctor in Winnipeg was Dr Kitchen, and the first dentists, Drs Garvin, Johnson and Brown.

Dr F.F. Tisdall and Dr J. Harry Ebbs, later assisted by Dr Elizabeth Chant Robertson and Dr T.G.H. Drake, were nutrition experts engaged to study the diets of the post staff. During the winter of 1941-42, everyone was required to keep a record for one month of all meals and snacks taken. When analyzed, the results were anything but satisfactory. As a result a supply of vitamin tablets were sent to each post to be taken daily by all members to augment their diets.

Special requisition forms for mess purposes were drawn up containing enough supplies for a completely balanced diet for one year. Sufficient choices were given in each category to satisfy every taste and included a special meal of Hormel canned whole chicken for Christmas and a canned ham for Easter, and all the usual holiday trimmings. These were shipped separately, charged to expenses and were not to be mixed with the stock for sale. Allowances were made for posts such as Waterways, Alberta that had regular access to supplies of fresh fruit, vegetables and meat, but for inland posts and bachelor managers, these supplies were a godsend. Managers could order any special delicacies they preferred.

A story is told of one post manager whose progress, post by post, from the Arctic down the Mackenzie and Athabasca Rivers, could be traced by the quantities of Nairn's Oatcakes and Crosse & Blackwell's Herrings in Tomato Sauce left unsaleable on the store shelves after his departure.

All the houses were completely furnished and a booklet issued listing minimum quantities of household items. These were checked by the district manager yearly, in co-operation with Miss

Jessie Bacon who was brought to Winnipeg from the Toronto buying office to handle the operation.

In 1940, salaries were changed from an annual wage with board supplied to a gross monthly salary with a fixed monthly deduction to cover mess. The change was made in part to comply with income tax regulations. There had always been a retirement pension scheme but it was paid from a fund set up by the Company and no contributions were required from the employee. After the war, this was changed to a compulsory plan with both parties contributing a set amount. Some post staff objected. Up until then, all post staff retired at the age of 60. The retirement age for staff in the retail stores, however, was 65, so the retirement age covering Fur Trade and Retail Departments was standardized at 65. Some of the old-timers who had been planning for and looking forward to retiring at 60 objected to the additional five years and the change in the pension scheme, and they were allowed to stick to the original plan.

The history of the hiring of apprentice clerks is of particular interest to me, having come in as an apprentice myself, at age 18 from Rothes in Scotland.

For the first hundred years or so after incorporation in 1670, the Company had only a few trading posts in Hudson's Bay, and so required very few apprentice clerks.

These young men were hired in the London area. It is interesting to note that an entry in the Minute Book of the London Committee dated March 8, 1683 reads, 'Captain Simson againe appearing and declaring his intentions for going to Scotland, was desired to use his endeavours to procure ten or twelve able young men twixt twenty and thirty years of age to serve ye Company in Hudson's Bay.'

There was a great need for labourers and tradesmen of all kinds at the forts and this need was supplied by great numbers of men from the Orkney Islands. For two centuries Orcadians played a major part in the development of the fur trade. They were picked up each year by the Company vessels at Stromness in the Orkney Islands en route to Canada. In 1798, sixty-three Orcadians -- one

apprentice clerk, forty-five labourers and seventeen tradesmen --
left Stromness for Hudson Bay.

Most of the men worked for the Company for ten or twenty
years, saved their salaries carefully and then returned to Orkney
where they purchased farms and were comparatively well off.
Some of them stayed on in the service and, by sheer hard work and
ability, made their way up the ladder from labourers to clerks and
ultimately, managers of posts. A few attained commissioned rank.

After the union with the North West Company in 1821, more
Scottish names began to appear on the lists of employees, possibly
because of the hiring of friends and relatives of the North West
element. In 1857, in his evidence to the Select Committee on the
Appointment of Apprentice Clerks, Edward Ellice said, 'I took
great care in former times to send out the best men we could find,
principally from the north of Scotland, sons of country gentlemen,
clergymen and of farmers.'

The difference between officers and men was great, and with
few exceptions, only by beginning as an apprentice clerk could a
young man hope to climb the ladder of promotion. In the new
country this created hardship for the half-breed sons of employees
and George Simpson created for them a new rank -- postmaster.

Hiring apprentice clerks in the Old Country went on in a
desultory fashion, interrupted from time to time by wars and
depressions. The Company maintained an agent in the northeast of
Scotland, a fertile recruiting ground. In 1910, he was A.E. Milne,
an Aberdeen solicitor. He hired J.W. Anderson who sailed from
Peterhead on the S.S. *Discovery* in company of two others bound
for Charlton Island. That same year eight other clerks sailed from
London for York Factory aboard the Company ship *Pelican*.

In the depression years of the 1930s, recruiting was confined
to Canada by government request. R.J. Campbell, a Winnipeg boy
hired in 1933, was one of twelve selected from 900 applicants. His
monthly salary was $20 per month plus room and board but I
understand that for a short time this starting salary was cut to $15
per month.

After World War II, J.W. Anderson, seconded from his job as
Manager, Eastern Arctic Division, made annual trips to Scotland

on recruiting drives. He addressed high schools and academies and showed a film depicting the life of a fur-trade apprentice clerk. I still have two postcards he mailed to me in October 1951. One reads 'En route to Elgin, I called in at Rothes and had a delightful, if short, visit. Your mother bids me tell you I had a dram of Glen Grant. Your folks in fine spirits. Why you should exchange the famous Speyside distilleries for Shea's Brewery in Winnipeg is more than I can fathom. The "romance of the fur trade", I guess.'

The second reads, 'At a meeting at Forres Academy yesterday, the Rector, A.B. Simpson [my former headmaster at Rothes] introduced me by telling the class of 'two famous men of the Hudson's Bay Company'. One was Lord Strathcona, the other was Hugh Mackay Ross. The Rector had some nice things to say about you and, you may rest assured, I had some too. So we both outshone ourselves saying 'nice things about Hugh Ross'. J.W. loved his little joke.

Sometime between 1938 and 1949, the apprenticeship system was abandoned. On June 14, 1949, Victor MacKay signed on in Scotland as 'clerk' for a two-year period at a monthly salary of $80 less $25 board and lodging. On 2nd July, 1957, George Fleming was hired as a 'trainee' for three years at the starting salary of $150 per month, less $50 room and board.

The large turnover in staff always worried me -- not only in my district but throughout the fur trade. As an example, I came out in 1930 in a group of forty-four apprentices. By the mid-1950s there were, to my knowledge, only seven of us left: Don Wilderspin, Graeme Beare, Dick Howell and I were District Managers; Tommy Thomson was a department manager in Winnipeg Merchandise Depot and W.M.S. McLeod was a post manager. Matt Cook was transferred to Bay Stores Department. Only one -- Bill Calder -- has died and is buried at Iglulik.

In the early 1970s, Robbie Knox came out from Turriff, Aberdeenshire as one of a group of twelve. Ten years later, he was the only one still working for the Hudson's Bay Company.

There doesn't seem to be any particular pattern to explain the turnover, although many who had completed their five years' apprenticeship in the Arctic did not come back after their six-month holiday in Scotland. Some just got plain homesick -- and I knew all about that -- and returned to the Old Country as soon as they could. Some got married and found their wives couldn't stand the isolation. Many obtained jobs either with free traders or outside firms, or went into business for themselves. Some were employed by the Department of Indian Affairs as Indian agents, or with other government departments. Their Hudson's Bay Company training stood them in good stead and made them naturals in finding jobs elsewhere. A lot of Canadian boys just could not stand being away from the bright lights of the city.

In a recent letter from Grande Prairie, Mrs R.J. Campbell says, 'My husband, Bob, joined the Company in 1933 and spent eighteen years with them before we went into business for ourselves. Bob often refers to the Company as his "university". It taught him bookkeeping, merchandising and the control of debt.'

Victor MacKay, after serving three years in the British Army, joined the Company in 1949. Born in Rosyth and educated in Dunfermline, Scotland, he served his apprenticeship in Saskatchewan, and later became manager of such posts as Green Lake, Stanley, La Ronge, Churchill, Inuvik and Red Lake. Yet he left in 1973. His great love was flying and Vic was one of the first post managers to buy his own private plane. He is now manager of the airport at Geraldton, Ontario. He tells me, 'Actually it was my business background and aviation experience that got me this job.'

George Fleming from Keith, Scotland, was the son of a Colonel in the British Army who lost his life in North Africa during World War II. A product of Gordonstoun School, he joined the Company on 2 July 1957 and, after serving as a trainee at various posts in Saskatchewan, he became the manager of Patuanak and then Stanley. He resigned from Stanley in December 1962 to go into partnership with Pat Campling, taking over the management of Red's Camps -- a fishing operation run by Red Boardman, a local La Ronge man. Later George went on his own and built Hatchet Lake -- originally a fly-in outpost from La Ronge -- into one of the finest and best-appointed fishing lodges in northern Saskatchewan.

I liked the tall, tow-headed Scot the minute I met him. He had the weirdest laugh I've ever heard and I have always called him 'Wee Geordie' after the hero of a film made in Scotland, starring Bill Travers. His mother came out from Scotland to visit him in 1961. In George's words, 'She arrived in a Cessna 180 full of groceries, sitting on a case of Carnation Milk. Mother stepped out onto the float, looked around and remarked, "What a God-forsaken place". And we looked upon Stanley as being the most picturesque post in Saskatchewan!'

Whether his mother's impression had anything to do with George's decision to leave the Company, I don't know. But he is now busy and happy doing what he loves, running his fishing lodge near the border of the Northwest Territories.

There is a traditional belief that the best apprentice clerk is a Scotsman, preferably from Buchan -- that part of northeastern Scotland that bulges into the North Sea -- with a coastline stretching from Aberdeen via Peterhead and Fraserburgh, round to Banff and even as far as Inverness. This may be true but, like the universal image of Scots being tight-fisted, I suspect that most of the men who nurture this tradition originated from that part of Scotland themselves.

A story is told of how the masters of the Hudson's Bay Company supply vessels obtained apprentice clerks. Anchoring off the Scottish coasts, small boats were sent along the shore to set out traps. These traps, each carefully attached to a rock, consisted of quart-size jars, slightly narrowed at the neck and half-filled with choice oatmeal. The boatmen then concealed themselves and watched as the young fellows drifted down to the shore to investigate. Finding the oatmeal in the jars, most of them grabbed a handful and gleefully raced home with their unexpected bonanza. And they were allowed to leave unmolested. But there were always two or three who grabbed such a large handful that they were unable to extract their fist from the jar, unwilling to let go of their prize. These were the lads who were signed on as apprentice clerks!

I must admit to partially accepting both these stories and I always tried to get a few of the Buchan lads for my district when a fresh bunch of trainees arrived in Winnipeg.

Be that as it may, I strongly believe that good men are where you find them. Any number of first-rate staff came from the City of Winnipeg, and a farm boy from the Prairies needs to take a backseat to no one. He is honest and trustworthy and is no stranger to hard work. I know. I had several of them in Saskatchewan District.

I have often been asked the question, 'If you had your life to live over again, would you still work for the Hudson's Bay Company?' My answer is always the same. Yes. If conditions were the same as they were in 1930. At that time, there was an aura of romance about the fur trade. We were fur traders, not storekeepers. We travelled by canoe and dogsled and we mainly lived off the country.

I was in charge of Grassy Narrows for two years and had one visit by a district manager. During the four years I was in charge of Temagami, I had only two visits. I was trusted to use my head and make my own decisions.

Nowadays, everything is modernized. Travel is all by aircraft or snowmobile and the paddle has given way to the outboard motor.

No longer are there fur trade posts, but instead 'Northern Stores Merchandise Units', all in touch with their district office by telephone. There are specialists to assist you with accounts, credit control, merchandising and display.

The romance is gone. I do not think I would like that.

Hugh Mackay Ross
Winnipeg, February 1989

PART I

Store Manager: Waterways, Alberta

Everyone who has travelled 'down north' has fond memories of the Muskeg Limited. Until commercial flying came into being and airfields were built at key points down the Mackenzie River, every passenger going north travelled aboard it. From the time of its construction in 1924 until the early 1940s after the Alaska Highway was built and an extension named the Mackenzie Highway pushed forward to Hay River on Great Slave Lake, every pound of freight consigned to the North was hauled by it.

The Muskeg Limited was a mixed train operated from Edmonton by the Northern Alberta Railway; it ran approximately 300 miles northeast to its northern terminus -- Waterways -- on the banks of the Clearwater River a few miles from Fort McMurray. Every Tuesday morning about 8 a.m. the train pulled out from Edmonton and rattled, clanked and swayed its slow way north past Lac la Biche, Chard, Cheecham and Anzac arriving at Waterways station about noon the following day. It left on its return to Edmonton at 5 p.m. on Friday, arriving anytime late Saturday afternoon.

Travelling through farming country as far north as Lac la Biche, it stopped at every station, siding and habitation: sometimes a short stay to drop the mail and a few small freight shipments and, at other times, a long delay while one or more freight cars were switched to a siding. Beyond Lac la Biche we even stopped at places where there were no visible signs of human occupation to allow native families to get off -- complete with dogs, sleighs, canoe and children: trappers en route to their hunting grounds.

Tacked on behind a seemingly endless string of assorted freight cars was a daycoach, a baggage car and a sleeping car. Presiding over the sleeping car was the genial porter, Len. He was a fixture on the train, known to everyone in the North. I don't think I ever saw him without a white flashing smile on his strong, chocolate-coloured face. He took my family in hand and soon had the two girls perched safely on a newly made-up bunk. 'I'll be around if you need anything, Ma'am. You just ring the bell for me.'

'Len, is there somewhere we can heat up a bottle of milk?' asked a worried Bea.

'You give me the bottle and I'll take care of it.' He looked down at the girls playing quietly on the bunk. 'I think I'll rig up something along the side of the bed so the kiddies won't fall out if the train should lurch suddenly.' He took the bottle and, as he opened the door into the corridor, smiled and said, 'I'll let you know when the dinner bell goes and keep an eye on the little ones while you eat.' As he quietly closed the door, Bea whispered, 'What a wonderful man.'

And that was how everyone who travelled the Muskeg Limited thought of Len. He had a prodigious memory and never forgot a name. If somebody at Waterways or Fort McMurray wanted something special from the big city, they just asked Len and on the next trip he would bring the item along with the bill showing the purchase price in Edmonton. He was in particular demand in the early spring, bringing bedding plants for enthusiastic gardeners.

This then was the train my wife Bea and I and our two daughters -- Barbara, aged two and a half, and Jennifer, one year -- caught on an early October morning in 1941. We had been enjoying a quiet holiday with Bea's parents in Winnipeg, having come in from Temagami, my post in northern Ontario. Then an unexpected summons had come from Hudson's Bay House the previous Friday afternoon. I was instructed to proceed to Waterways immediately to take over from Tom Lindley who was being transferred to Montreal. There wasn't even time to return to Temagami to pack up our personal belongings. That would have to wait until the following spring. The fact that the Company had built a brand new house at Waterways, with an indoor toilet and hot and cold running water was an added inducement to my accepting the post.

We took the Transcontinental the next day to Edmonton and put up at the Corona Hotel which was used by the Company for all its transient employees. The following Monday, I went down to the Western District office to meet my new boss and get his

intructions, but since the district manager, Chief Factor John
Bartleman, and his inspector, Bruce F. Clark, were out in the
country, Mr George Pendleton, the accountant, gave me the railway
tickets and a letter of introduction to the post manager.

Tom Lindley met us at the station. He arranged for our luggage
to be removed from the baggage car and instructed the porter to
have it delivered to the hotel. Bea looked at me with a puzzled
expression. 'Why are we going to the hotel? I thought we were
moving into a brand new house. That's what we were told in
Winnipeg.'

Tom looked a little sheepish. 'I know. Winnipeg office thinks
the house is completed but, in fact, it won't be ready for another
week or ten days.' 'What's the problem, Tom?' I asked. The two
girls were both tired and fractious; Barbara pulled on my hand and
Jen rubbed her eyes. 'I don't really fancy spending a week in a
hotel with two babies.' We reached the hotel, stopped at the door
and waited for Tom's reply.

'Let's get you and the children settled in. Then we can have a
coffee and I'll give you all the sordid details.'

Joe Doyle, the hotel proprietor, was a huge, genial Irishman
who looked more like a heavyweight boxer than an innkeeper. He
and his wife welcomed us and made us feel right at home. The
rooms were clean and well furnished and the dining room had a
reputation for serving good meals. Unfortunately our rooms were
almost directly above the beer parlour and we found that until it
closed, it was impossible to get any sleep. The noise was especially
hard on the girls. I couldn't see remaining in the hotel for another
ten days.

Over coffee, Tom told us about the house. 'Look, the
contractor is a local man named Louis Mercier. He's a good
workman and has built several stores and houses for the Company.
Unfortunately, your new house is quite close to the beer parlour and
Louis...well, Louis likes his beer.'

I went along to the store the next morning to meet the staff.
Besides Tom, there were three female assistants -- two local
married women and a girl named Kay Gangstad who was
permanent staff. There was also an apprentice clerk whose name I

The Hudson's Bay Company's dwelling house at Waterways, 1942. The Ross children -- Barbara, 3, and Jennifer, 18 months -- play at the gate.

can't remember because within three weeks he was transferred. A local boy, Peter Bromley, delivered groceries after school and did chores on Saturdays.

Tom looked at me anxiously. 'You don't look like you slept very well.'

'I didn't. None of us did,' I growled. We were supposed to start taking the change of management inventory immediately but I asked Tom to excuse me for an hour or so and asked directions to the new house. I wanted to have a talk with the contractor.

Louis Mercier was a very likeable Frenchman and while we later became good friends, I gave him little cause to like me that morning. He showed me around the house and I asked how much work was still to be done. 'There's not too much left to do now,' said Louis. 'The rest shouldn't take more than a week or two.' He hefted a bottle of beer, drank half of it down and wiped his mouth with the back of his hand.

I put it to him straight. 'Mr Mercier, Winnipeg office is under the impression that this house is ready for occupancy. It should have been finished a week ago.' Louis began listing the multiple things that had delayed him and finished his beer, quite casually. Obviously he had faced irate tenants before.

'If this house is not complete and ready for my family to move into by the end of the week, I can promise you that it will be the last job you ever do for the Hudson's Bay Company.' Louis's eyebrows shot up in surprise. 'I'll be mailing a letter on Friday, informing Head Office that the house is fine *or* I'll explain the reasons for the delay. If it's not finished, I will also recommend that you get no further employment from the Bay.' I knew that there were several building projects due to be assigned the following summer and Louis Mercier knew it too. He hemmed and hawed and blustered explanations. Exasperated, I finally said, 'If you need a beer so badly, bring a case to work with you. But I don't want to see you in the pub during working hours.' Subdued, Louis assured me the house would be ready in a week.

It was and we moved into a beautiful home, completely furnished down to the last dishtowel and teaspoon. Louis Mercier may have had a fault, but his workmanship was superb.

During the weekend we had a chance to look over the town. Waterways was built on six blocks located on the west bank of the Clearwater River and nestled up against the hillside. The main street ran parallel to the railway station and was built up on one side only. The centre block started with the hotel, then Bill Mitchell's cafe and poolroom, Sutherland's drugstore, a log cottage, and ended with the Hudson's Bay Company store. The cottage had been owned by the Mackenzie River Transport but had been acquired for temporary use as a post manager's dwelling. Leo Pachinsky's bakeshop was adjacent to our store and the aroma of freshly baked bread greeted us each morning as we opened up for business. Naturally enough, we sold Leo's bread and cakes in the store.

On the next block was a large wooden building which was used for everything -- dancehall, theatre or badminton court -- depending on the season. The rest of the block was occupied by a string of homes.

The corner lot on the other side of the hotel was vacant. Then came Johnnie's barbershop, the local post office operated by Mr and Mrs A.T. Penhorwood, Mr Berubé's general store and, tucked in behind, was Charlie Eymundsen's house. Charlie owned the

local telephone system which connected up the business
establishments in both Waterways and Fort McMurray. It was an
old-fashioned method of communication using dry-cell batteries:
he changed them regularly when he collected his rental fee from
his customers. Each phone had its own call -- a combination of
long and short rings made by cranking a handle on the instrument
so that whenever the phone rang, you had to listen carefully and
count the rings. It was one massive party line.

Beyond was Bob Labarge's establishment where he kept his
horse and wagon and all the necessary adjuncts of a dray business.
He hauled everybody's freight from the station, supplied cordwood
in the winter and moved almost everything that was moveable.

On the street behind the main block stood the 'Coffee Pot'
owned by Dolly and Lil Burge, and a few houses on one side.
Across from them were the Roman Catholic Church and the local
skating rink. The Anglican Church, a simple frame building with
a steeple, was on the next block along. Beside it was a private home
and then the Company's new house, right next door to the local
school and its large playground.

Between the railroad track and the river was the reason for
Waterway's existence. The river bank was lined with docks which
were used by a number of transport businesses: British American
Oil operated by Syd Hawkins, a retired Royal Canadian Mounted
Policeman; McInnes Fisheries, a commercial fishing business on
Lake Athabasca; the Mackenzie River Transport, owned by the
Hudson's Bay Company, with its warehouse, office, dining hall,
stores department, staff rooms and the manager's house; the
Northern Transportation Company's warehouse; and the Imperial
Oil depot, operated by Jack Fairbairn who also had a wholesale
flour agency. Jack's wife had the only private automobile in town.
It was a little two-seater coupe and she tootled around in it even if
she only had to drive a quarter of a block from home for a loaf of
bread. The street running back from the hotel held a Hayward
Lumber Company hardware and lumber supply outlet managed by
W. Bromley; a taxi service run by Louis and Bessie Demers; and
Gus Hawker, a free trader. Gus later moved north to Uranium City

where he prospered by outfitting uranium prospectors. I think he even ended up as Mayor of the town.

A salt plant, owned and operated by the Dominion Tar and Chemical Company was on the outskirts of town on the road running from Waterways to Fort McMurray. It produced the 'McMurray' brand of salt. There was a tremendously rich body of salt underground and it was mined by pumping down hot water, drawing the brine to the surface and evaporating it. Bert Ayres was the plant manager. By providing year-round employment to a number of citizens, Dominion Tar and Chemical Company was a stabilizing influence on the economy of Waterways.

Beyond the salt plant, the Saline Creek ran in a series of pools and rapids through a fold in the hillside to join the Clearwater River. The creek was famous for its grayling fishing and during the following years, we spent many happy hours fishing its waters -- usually wetfly with a 'Black Doctor' for the best results. Next to smallmouth bass, grayling is my favourite eating fish but it must go straight from the water to the frypan. Even an hour's delay will allow the flesh to turn soft and flabby, so a frypan was always part of our lunch equipment. Beside the creek, a road ran up the hill behind Waterways roughly three miles to the airfield. Quite a few residences were scattered along the hillside, most of them occupied by Transport employees.

The road from Waterways to Fort McMurray was about three miles long and about halfway along it was the settlement of The Prairie where the shipyards of both the Mackenzie River Transport and the Northern Transportation Company were situated. Here all the repairs to the boats and barges were completed and here they were drawn up out of the water each fall and stored over the winter. There were a few homes in The Prairie, a small dairy farm which supplied fresh milk, and a diesel plant which generated electricity for both towns.

Fort McMurray was a quiet little town on the bank of the Athabasca River near where it was joined by the Clearwater River. On the main street were a bank, post office, a couple of trading stores, Angus Sutherland's main drugstore where he supplied a very potent and oft-requested 'tonic', Mrs O'Coffey's Hotel, a doctor's office and the long-established Hudson's Bay Company trading post of Fort McMurray. The manager was Jimmie Boyd, whom I had last met at Grassy Narrows in 1935.

Between the main street and the hillside, stood a few homes and the Roman Catholic Mission and hospital, a high school, the Royal Canadian Mounted Police detachment consisting of Corporal 'Tommy' Thompson and one constable, and a Royal Canadian Corps of Signals unit which handled all telegraphic communications to and from the North.

An expanse of good gardening land between the village and the Athabasca River was known as the Hudson's Bay Reserve. The twenty-seven acres was, I believe, originally part of the North West Company's post on that site, and came to the Hudson's Bay Company with the amalgamation of the two companies in 1821.

A backwater called the Snye joined the Athabasca and Clearwater rivers and was the headquarters of several small floatplane companies providing air service to Lake Athabasca and other northern points. It was from this spot that Punch Dickens, pilot of Western Canada Airways flew the first passenger service down the Mackenzie River in 1929.

In my travels, I discovered that the best way to find out about the people in a new place is in the barbershop, the pub or the local store, so I made it my business to have a weekly trim at Johnnie's barbershop, stopped at the pub for a pint occasionally and personally greeted customers in the store. I heard all the local gossip, learned who our customers were and let them get a look at me too.

Near Waterways, a side road branched off the McMurray road and ran up into the hills. One day, as I concluded a conversation and escorted a gentleman to the door, one of the locals standing at the counter spoke up. 'You know where he comes from, don't you?'

'No. I just met him this morning. Something special about him?' I asked.

Several people laughed and one said, 'He's one of those crazy scientists up at the Abasand. Do you know what they are trying to do?' By now, everybody was trying to put me in the picture.

'Would you believe that they're trying to get oil out of the tar sands? Did you ever hear anything so nutty?'

'I can't say that I have,' I replied, 'but science is discovering new things all the time. Maybe this will work too.' My answer brought forth hoots of laughter and derision. 'Exactly where are the tar sands?' I asked.

An old-timer took me in hand. 'You go along the west bank of the river from Fort McMurray and it runs about sixty miles north to Fort McKay. But don't you try to go to Abasand though,' he admonished. 'It's all very hush-hush and they don't let nobody in except them that works there.'

They continued to chuckle about the experiments they heard were going on. 'You know what I heard the other day?' Everyone stopped talking to hear the latest rumour making the rounds. 'You won't believe this but I heard that they are even using *electric washing machines* to try to separate the oil from the sand. They're all daft, if you ask me.' As this purveyor of local news walked to the door, he looked back over his shoulder and said, 'Next thing you know, they'll be building rockets to the moon.' And everyone laughed, including me.

How could we visualize that in the next twenty-five to thirty years, the quiet little backwater village of McMurray would be a thriving modern city connected to Edmonton by an all-weather highway with a bridge across the mighty Athabasca River. And that the Athabasca Tar Sands would be a multi-million dollar operation.

The change of management procedure went forward without a hitch and Tom Lindley left for the east by train on the following Friday.

The Waterways store was nothing much to look at and differed greatly from the normal trading post set-up. It was a shoddy one-storey clapboard building which the Company had bought a few years previously from Jean Boisvert, a local trader. It had a false front and a heavy rubberoid roof and was heated by a coal furnace in the basement. There was a small office and marking room at the back and a couple of little warehouses to the rear. I was the third post manager, preceded by Jim Winter and Tom Lindley, who had both gone forward to be district managers.

Within two weeks, the apprentice clerk left and Hugh Fraser, an experienced assistant who knew his job thoroughly, arrived to take his place. Hugh lived in the house with us and, outside of the fact that both of us came running when Bea called 'Hugh', our domestic arrangement went smoothly and he quickly became one of the family. Barbara and Jennifer thought he was wonderful, especially when he made them a plywood dollhouse one Christmas.

Jim Boyd, the Fort McMurray manager, and I didn't hit it off at all. For some reason I could not understand he had a continual chip on his shoulder and kept making sneering remarks about the Waterways store being a 'specialty shop'. He left the Company in 1943 and his replacement, Fred Mitchell, was a welcome relief. He came from Elgin in Scotland where I had gone to school and we got along famously.

Before Christmas, the district manager and the inspector paid a visit to Waterways. District Manager J. Bartleman, was a trim, middle-aged Scotsman with iron grey hair and clipped moustache -- very much a gentleman of the old school. Always immaculately dressed, he was inclined to be a little long-winded and pompous when explaining things, but he was a fair-minded boss. Men who served under him swore that he was the best district manager they ever had.

The inspector, Mr B. Clark, was a New Zealander, tall and slim and although taciturn, there was always a twinkle in his eye. He wasn't afraid to take off his jacket and muck in and was always receptive to any suggestions about the running of the store.

I hadn't liked the store layout and I'd made some changes. The centre had been taken up by four large plywood bins crammed with patent medicines, toiletries and cosmetics. I ran this stock down as quickly as possible until the remainder could be put on shelves. Then I threw out the bins and replaced them with display tables for women's and children's wear. Two segments of shelving right at the front of the store were filled up with moccasin rubbers and overshoes and I moved them to the back marking room and substituted hanging racks for women's dresses. Although Mr Clark had approved, Mr Bartleman wasn't too pleased with the changes, especially as they had been done without his knowledge. I was glad therefore when the Mackenzie-Athabasca District was split up in the summer of 1942. Mr Bartleman retained charge of the Mackenzie River and Bruce Clark became District Manager of Athabasca District in which Waterways was situated.

Business at the post progressed steadily but I found it boring. There was no rush to outfit trappers in the fall, as was the case at my previous posts. Every Friday I ran off a number of stencilled handbills offering grocery specials for the following day and had them distributed by Peter Bromley. There were no great shortages despite the war, although things like salmon, sardines and various brands of canned vegetables and fruits were in short supply. Butter, sugar, tea and coffee were rationed. The most serious shortage we had was nylon stockings. Instead of the usual gross that was ordered, we got a token shipment of two or three dozen. So I took the problem to Bea.

'Hmm...we have to make sure there isn't any favouritism,' she said with a grin, 'and that includes me. So I think the best thing to do is get the names of all the ladies in town, put them on strips of paper and toss them in a hat.'

'That's fine, but how do we let the women know who's won?'

'There won't be any losers or winners, honey.' She got up and walked around the room as she worked out the plan. 'We'll take all the names to the next meeting of the Women's Institute and get someone to draw the names at random and I'll make up a list.'

'Then I can post it in a prominent place in the store so that everyone can see it,' I suggested.

'Right. That's a good idea. And when the nylons come in, the first names on the list get their choice. We better limit it to two pairs though. That way everyone will eventually be able to buy some.'

And that's the way we did it. As the precious shipments of nylon stockings were received, each lady, in strict order, was

Bill Gourlay, manager of the Temagami store, 1942. Mr Gourlay drowned accidentally the following summer in Lake Temagami.

allowed to purchase her two pairs. The system worked well for the duration of the shortage and there were no complaints.

Shortly after New Year's, I returned to Temagami to pack up our personal belongings. W.B. 'Bill' Gourley, my successor as post manager, was the most unorthodox individual I have ever met. Born at Ferry-Port-On-Craig, Scotland in 1904, he had come to Canada as a young man to make his fortune. He worked at many jobs around the country, including spending some time in labour camps in the 'dirty thirties' where men worked for their board and tobacco. Heading west, he worked for a while for a free trader, went on to jobs with the Can-Alaska Trading Company, and the Northern Traders who operated down the Mackenzie River. When Northern Traders was taken over by the Hudson's Bay Company, he joined up with the Bay in 1938, spending some time in the Peace River District until he was promoted to manager at Temagami, Ontario.

Bill's passion was letter writing. He wrote to anybody and everybody, and had files of letters from all over the world. Among his correspondents were film stars, convicts in Sing Sing prison and half-breeds in the Peace River District. During one of our conversations, I mentioned that my wife was expecting a baby and

*Jennifer and Barbara (right) enjoy the doll house
built for them by apprentice clerk Hugh Fraser*

since we already had two young children, I planned to hire someone
to help her in the house. He jumped up and went to his files.

'I know just the woman for you. She's a half-breed at Fort
Vermilion and they don't come any finer than Celina Norris. I'll
write a letter tonight and tell her to get in touch with you.'

Thus we contacted and hired Celina who lived with us and
assisted my wife in looking after the children during the years we
were at Waterways. Bill was right. Celina Norris was a gem. I'll
never forget Bill Gourley. His roving career was unfortunately cut
short when he was accidentally drowned in Lake Temagami on
August 27, 1943. Hundreds of people around the world would miss
his letters.

Our new house at Waterways, designated as style 9D, was one
of Mr Watson's designs, so I presumed he was still experimenting.
It was a storey and a half and extremely comfortable inside, with
two bedrooms up and two down. The outside, however, looked
quite severe. All trim was cut to a minimum. Exterior walls were
of waterproof plywood and the eaves had no overhang to keep out
the sun. All this was done to cut the weight of the building, for the
cost of shipping materials for a complete house from Edmonton to
Aklavik or the Western Arctic was very expensive.

Shortly after I returned from Temagami, we ran into trouble with the sewage disposal system which consisted of a two-chamber tank buried in the ground close to the bathroom. All household wastes flowed into the first tank where they liquified, then went into the second tank where they collected until the tank was full. A bell siphon allowed the contents to flow out into the dispersal field buried about a yard deep under our backyard. The effluent was distributed by perforated pipes in a herringbone pattern from the main pipe over the entire field, where it was supposed to slowly sink into the ground before the next emission, which took place about three times a day. Unfortunately the frost had sunk deeper into the earth than the pipes and the whole system was gradually freezing up.

It was a dirty job! We lit a huge bonfire to thaw out the ground and then dug a hole at the end of the main pipe which we thawed out by boiling water and, using a garden hose, injecting the steam. For the first time, my thoughts of an outside biffy were favourable.

In the spring we had the whole thing re-dug increasing the depth of the pipes by another two feet, with a foot of sand and gravel placed underneath each pipe. Every autumn, the entire system was covered with horse manure a foot deep. It stunk for a while but it did the trick!

Later on, when the snow began to melt from the roof, we ran into another problem. As I walked into the house after closing the store, Bea and Celina were busy with mops and pails, cleaning up water that was trickling down the living room walls. The furniture was all in the centre of the room, curtains were down and the kids were having a great time.

I reported the matter and Mr Watson came up immediately to see what had gone wrong with his experimental house. He soon located the trouble. The house was supposed to have a continuous vapour barrier running up the studs and right around and over the roof. It hadn't been installed properly and Mr Watson was very upset with the builder. To make it easier to work on, someone had cut the vapour barrier at the eaves and as a result, our living room walls were, as Barbara said, 'crying'. The plan was sound but the workmanship wasn't. Louis Mercier spent a few weeks at our house making the repairs.

Two years later, we noticed that the exterior plywood was checking and the resin bonding was bubbling out. After another call to Winnipeg, they advised that the whole outside of the house be covered with 8" cedar siding. We painted it white, installed dark blue shutters at the front windows and the house looked a lot more cosy. Thank goodness we had no more building woes!

The ground was very fertile and I was able to grow excellent vegetables and flowers. I put in a lawn in front and then one summer an expert from the Morden Experimental Station in Manitoba passed through Waterways. He was most interested in my horticultural pursuits and sent me some elm trees and a few mixed fruit trees to see how they would fare so far north. I planted them around the edges of the property. One day, an old man who lived up the street and worked as a night watchman at the salt plant stopped to admire them. 'My, those are grand trees! It's the first time I've seen an elm tree growing since I left Ontario fifty years ago.'

With the coming of spring, the riverfront sprang alive. The Mackenzie River Transport office staff arrived from Edmonton and took up quarters. They were headed by H.N. 'Dad' Petty, agent in charge; Jack Barker, marine superintendent; Ernie Berg, chief steward; and H.T. 'Happy' Hamilton and Basil Walker, head billers. The married men brought their families and moved into houses provided by the Mackenzie River Transport. The single men and girls lived in separate bunkhouses.

Over at The Prairie shipyards the gang of carpenters, painters and blacksmiths were busy at work fixing and caulking the freight barges and boats. As soon as the ice went out of the river, the craft were all launched and brought up to the Waterways riverfront for loading. The Clearwater River usually broke up ahead of the Athabasca River so it was necessary to have barges loaded and ready to go down north immediately the ice flowed free from the Athabasca.

H.N. 'Dad' Petty, agent in charge of the Mackenzie River Transport office, Waterways, in front of the office and warehouse, 1940. Mackenzie River Transport was part of the Hudson's Bay Company's operations.

Trainloads of freight came in and were spotted in front of the warehouses where they were unloaded by gangs of Indians under the supervision of Hank McCormick, the local warehouse foreman. The freight was stacked in the warehouse in separate compartments under post headings. Freight marked 'Double Diamond' was stowed by itself. The 'Double Diamond' mark denoted goods urgently required and destined to go downriver on the first shipment. The freight was taken on two chutes down the riverbank to the dock. These chutes were fitted with an ingenious endless belt arrangement which hooked onto the handtrucks and enabled the freight loader to sit on the handles of the truck, both going down and coming back up.

About sixty Indians were employed, half Chipewyan and half Cree. The Cree came from around Portage la Loche and the Chipewyan from various settlements along the railroad. There was always great competition to see who could handle the most freight. The Cree considered themselves superior and looked down on the

Chipewyan. I once heard a Cree say contemptuously to a drunken Chipewyan, 'Taissez-vous, maudit sauvage.'

As usual, the Indians wanted to be paid at the end of each working day and Hank McCormick and I worked out an arrangement suitable to all. When each man completed his work, he was handed a chit for the hours worked which I paid in the store at the standard rate per hour. At the end of the week, Hank brought me his complete timesheet which I charged to District Office. I sold the Indians any merchandise they required and turned over all remaining cash due to them at the weekend. This worked very well for everybody and I got added sales in the store.

Dave Hutchison, general manager of the Mackenzie River Transport, eventually arrived to take charge of operations. A rather pompous individual, full of the importance of his own area of the Hudson's Bay Company and completely dedicated to its interests, he firmly believed that the Fur Trade Department revolved around the Mackenzie River Transport and existed only because of the Mackenzie River Transport. As for post managers, he had no use for them. Consequently, I saw very little of him.

The staff of the Northern Transportation Company had already taken up residence and were busy getting their craft ready. As the Mackenzie River Transport gave the Hudson's Bay Company freight first priority, the Northern Transportation Company handled most of the freight for free traders down the river. One of their contracts was to handle high-grade ore from the uranium mines on Great Bear Lake; this was shipped out in sacks for refining. When uranium ore was discovered on the northeast shore of Lake Athabasca and Uranium City sprang up, the Northern Transportation Company was taken over and became a Crown Corporation. They were then equipped with beautiful steel diesel tugs. No more getting hung up on sandbars for them. As Julian 'Hoolie' Mills, their senior captain said, 'You just reverse engines, give 'er the gun and blow the sandbar out from under you.'

And then we were invaded by the United States Army!

The great Canol project had begun. Its objective was to develop the oil wells at Norman Wells in the Northwest Territories and pipe it approximately six hundred miles northwest through the mountain passes to a refinery at Whitehorse on the Alaskan Highway, for use in the Alaskan theatre of war.

One fine morning in the spring of 1942, a freight train pulled into Waterways carrying the advance party -- an American battalion of engineers with a full complement of jeeps, trucks, bulldozers, and building materials -- to build a camp at The Prairie. Within a week, two more battalions of engineers -- one black and one white -- arrived and the advance guard carried on down the river to erect similar camps at Fort Smith for handling freight across the portage and at Norman Wells, their final destination.

Apparently the Hudson's Bay Company had been asked by the Americans to help in handling the vast cargoes that were going down north. Mr R.H. Chesshire arrived from Winnipeg with his secretary, Evelyn Little, to supervise operations. Normally one vessel, the *Northland Echo*, was sufficient to handle the northbound freight. Now a second vessel, the *Athabasca River* which had been up on the stocks at The Prairie 'in mothballs' was hurriedly commissioned and put into service. John Sutherland, a retired HBC marine engineer who lived in Waterways came into the store one morning, a big smile on his face and with a new spring in his step, to arrange credit for his daughter Barbara. He informed me that he had been re-engaged as second engineer on the *Athabasca River* and was proud as punch to be going back to work.

The *Athabasca River* and *Northland Echo* were stern- wheeled, wood-burning boats, looking for all the world like the Mississippi River showboats one sees in the films. They were shallow draught but could handle a tremendous tonnage. Depending on the time of the year and the depth of the water, they could handle up to seven barges at a time. The barges weren't towed but were hooked up in front of, and on either side of the vessel and pushed down the river. At intervals downstream, woodcutters under contract by Mackenzie River Transport had produced many hundreds of cords of wood and piled them on the riverbank where the vessels could pull in and renew their fuel supply to feed the ever-hungry boilers.

Soon freight trains began arriving day and night bringing more bulldozers and heavy equipment, and car after car loaded with pipe for the pipeline. The pipe was piled up on every vacant space along the riverbank, ready to be loaded on barges. Six hundred miles is a lot of pipe!

Sometime later, the army had steel tugs and steel barges brought in from the States. They were cut in half with acetylene torches and loaded onto flatcars, then welded together again at Waterways. Civilian workmen, mostly American, came to do the work and handle the boats. They worked in shifts around the clock. At the Waterways Hotel, poor Happy Cave -- he was tiredly happy and far from poor -- had the concession in the dining room and was worked off his feet. He had contracted to feed the civilian workers and soon his kitchen was going twenty-four hours a day with lines of men standing around the block shuffling forward slowly to get in and eat.

We were extremely busy in the store. I hired another two girls -- Jacquie Woods and Sandra Sandulac -- but I was still forced to appeal to District Office for further help and Terry Hebert and Grace Rhyason were transferred from Cold Lake. These girls were tremendous. Jacquie lived at home but Kay, Terry, Grace and Sandra moved into the log cottage beside the store which I converted to a staff house. They worked together in perfect harmony and knew their jobs backwards. For the next three years, they were lifesavers. According to an article in the September 1943 edition of *The Beaver*, the American army shipped a total of 29,400 tons of freight out of Waterways during that hectic 1942 shipping season. Of that total, the Army itself handled 9,135 tons and other carriers 5,265 tons. The balance of 15,000 tons (50 percent of the total) was handled by the Mackenzie River Transport, in addition to carrying troops and civilian personnel. All this was on top of their regular freight deliveries to Hudson's Bay Company posts on Lake Athabasca and the Mackenzie River, and in the Western Arctic. It was a tremendous feat of logistics and hard work.

The S.S. 'Mackenzie River' heading for Norman Wells pushing a total of five Hudson's Bay Company and Canol barges, 1942.

For the first week or so after the arrival of the U.S. Army, everything was pandemonium. Corporal Thompson, the Royal Canadian Mounted Police officer in charge of Fort McMurray looked the situation over and decided that he would need reinforcements. He got reinforcements and we now had two policemen stationed at Waterways and two at McMurray. The Colonel in charge of the Americans decided that troops who were off duty would go week-about -- whites to Waterways and blacks to McMurray.

Most of the black troops were from the northern states and most of the white soldiers, from the south, so there was some fear of racial clashes. On the whole, the military police did an excellent job. I can recall only one incident that happened early on. A couple of white soldiers came in to Bill Mitchell's cafe which was crowded and imperiously ordered a black soldier to give up his seat. There was a flash of a razor as the black turned and the white found his tie neatly cut off at the neck. For a long time, that tie was pinned up on the wall behind Bill's counter as a sign that there was to be no racism in his cafe.

The local beer parlour was packed to the rafters from opening to closing. It was impossible to go in and sit down to enjoy a quiet glass of beer and, unless you ordered a tray of beer, the waiters ignored you. The tray held twenty glasses of beer at 10 cents a glass for which the Americans would grandly slap down three $1.00 bills. Those who couldn't get a seat in the pub bought beer by the case and sat outside on the sidewalk. The Mounties soon put a halt to that.

During those days, to obtain liquor in Alberta you had to have a permit which you mailed to the government liquor store in Edmonton along with a money order covering your requisition. The following week, your order came up by train and was unloaded into the express shed at the station. Pretty soon the express shed was bulging every week with liquor orders. I swear that every man, woman and child in Waterways and McMurray had a liquor permit and ordered their full quota each week. You had to fight your way through a crowd of American soldiers and civilians, all waving greenbacks in your face and offering any amount in return for your order of liquor. It was only a matter of time until the bootleggers moved in and the taxi drivers were doing a roaring business.

We were getting used to the ever-increasing numbers of uniformed men in the community and business in Waterways was booming. Shopkeepers walked around town with an almost permanent smile on their faces, as their store doors swung open and shut all day long.

But the biggest money maker in town was old Maggie Tyndall. She arrived with a bevy of good-looking, half-breed girls from one of the local settlements along the railroad. They set up an establishment of tents on the river on the outskirts of town and were open for business. As it was daylight for almost twenty-four hours a day and there were only scrub trees growing by the riverside, we couldn't help but notice the steady stream of uniforms coming and going along the riverbank.

HBCA Photograph Collection 1987/363-C-7/12B

Activity at The Prairie, where civilian workmen, mostly American, set up prefabricated barges for shipping pipe and equipment north for the Canol Project.

An army truck pulled up in front of my store one day and proceeded to erect a large tent on the waste ground across the street. We were all very curious. What were the Americans up to now? Then the tent was up, counters taken inside and most of the workmen left, except for two who placed a very large sign in front. One of the clerks came to my office and said, 'Mr Ross, what's a pro...prolix...I don't know how to say it. Maybe you should come and look at the sign in front of the tent.' And there, in big, bright, bold letters, the sign proclaimed to all the world that this was the *Prophylaxis Tent.* Right in front of my store!

Not waiting to explain its meaning, I dashed over to The Prairie to have a word with the Colonel. The tent was removed to another location that afternoon. And obviously someone explained the meaning of the sign to the girls but it wasn't me.

Most of the problems we had with the Americans were mundane but others were downright infuriating. As I worked in my office one afternoon, a major arrived to see me. We shook hands, passed the time of day and then I asked him how I could help him.

'May I close the door?' he asked. I nodded and he quickly shut the door, pulled his chair up to my desk and said, 'Mr Ross, you and I are men of the world. We have a small problem that we hope you can help with.'

Thoroughly mystified, I wondered what in the world I could do that the United States Army couldn't. 'Well, I'll certainly do what I can, Major. Just what is it you want?'

He glanced at the closed door, placed his elbows on the desk and lowering his voice to almost a whisper said, 'It's the officers.'

Completely confused now, I said, 'What about the officers?'

'I guess you've seen Maggie Tyndall's place down by the river.' I admitted that one could hardly fail to notice it. 'Those Indian and half-breed girls are good enough for the men and NCO's but ...' He hesitated.

'Go on, Major.'

'I'm sure you know what I'm getting at, Mr Ross. You have been here in Waterways for awhile and you know the people and we...that is, I was wondering if you knew of any white girls who would be good enough for the officers?'

Slowly I got to my feet. As he saw the expression on my face, he stood up quickly and started to back up towards the closed door. 'Never mind, Mr Ross, I can see that I came to the wrong place.'

'You certainly did, Major. But before you leave, let me answer your question. Frankly, Major, I don't know of one American officer who would be even half good enough for any woman in Waterways.' I opened the door wide. 'Now get the hell out of my office.'

I don't know what happened to that officer but I never saw him again.

Not too long after the sign incident, the girls in the store complained that they were being bothered in the evenings by white soldiers knocking at the staff cottage door. So once again, I went over to see the Colonel. 'I'm sorry about this, Mr Ross. I'm sure they don't mean any harm. It's just that they are so far from home and I guess they miss talking to a pretty girl.'

'You're probably right, Colonel, but the fact remains that your men are annoying my girls and I want it stopped.'

That evening, as the store was closing, a jeep drove up and two huge black M.P.'s stepped out, with .45s as big as cannons strapped to their hips. They took up positions, one at the front door and one at the back door of the cottage. Until it got too cold even for amorous American soldiers, the M.P.'s stood on guard day and night and the girls no longer had any worries.

Everyone seemed to have money to burn and all the soldiers wanted to buy souvenirs. After all, Canada was a foreign country. Any native beaded moccasins or fringed jackets were snapped up immediately. Cowichan sweaters, the badge of bush pilots in the north, were another popular item. Made by Indians from British Columbia from unscoured wool, they were sold out as fast as I got them in. Soon I was writing and wiring to all the nearby posts to replenish my stock.

The soldiers were terribly bothered by mosquitos and we had a great run on mosquito bars, which hung over their beds, and headnets. When I ran out of these and couldn't get any more, I had several women make them out of netting and when that was exhausted, they used curtain scrim. The boys swore that Canadian mosquitos were the most vicious they had ever encountered.

In the midst of all this hubbub, our third daughter, Dorothy Louise, was born at the Roman Catholic Mission Hospital in Fort McMurray on June 20, 1942. There were no complications and both mother and baby were back home within a week. Celina Norris ably took charge of the house and kept everything running smoothly.

By mid-summer 1942, the vanguard of the Canol project reached Norman Wells and established a base camp. From there the six-hundred-mile long pipeline would be built across to Whitehorse. To take care of the needs of the hundreds of civilian workmen and soldiers, the Company decided to establish a commissary at Norman Wells called the Canol Store. My assistant Hugh Fraser was transferred to manage it. We were all sorry to see him go, especially the children. Hugh had been such a capable assistant that I wasn't surprised at his promotion to the charge of his first post. Wendell Peterson, a young, newly hired apprentice, was sent from Winnipeg to replace him but after spending the winter, he left to join the Navy. After that I had no male assistant.

All through the winter of 1942-43, supplies for Canol continued to arrive at Waterways. More pipe arrived weekly as well as heavy machinery of every description. By mid-winter there were almost three hundred bulldozers, and other machines, parked in the railway yards at Waterways with their engines running. The exhaust from the vehicles hung in a diaphanous cloud over the area until a cold wind dispersed it. I queried this apparent waste of fuel but was told it was much cheaper to keep the engines running steadily than to run the risk of allowing them to freeze up and become unserviceable over the winter.

The 1943 shipping season was every bit as busy as the previous summer's but was conducted in a much more orderly fashion. The original soldiers had moved on down the river and new troops had taken their place. By the end of '43, the Waterways end of the operation was being run by American civilian companies -- first Bechtel, Price & Callaghan and then by Turnbull, Sverdrup & Purcell. By the end of 1944, the Canol project was over as far as Waterways was concerned. The troops and two civilian companies had all gone downriver and all traces of their camp at The Prairie wiped out.

There are many stories told about the Canol project -- some of them true, some of them not so true. I have my own two favourites.

When the troops first arrived in the spring of 1942, they suffered badly from the cold during the spring evenings, as they had no heaters in their huts. An American major asked me if I could immediately secure a quantity of sheet metal heaters complete with radiation chambers and the necessary piping. I wired our Edmonton office and got their reply that the goods would be shipped on the next train. When I asked the Major how payment would be made, he said, 'Send me an invoice and we'll see that you receive a cheque.'

At the end of the month, I forwarded an invoice, in quadruplicate. As was the Company's policy with such accounts,

HBCA Photograph Collection 1987/363-C-7/3B

Road scrapers for the Canol project await shipment north from the railway yards at Waterways, Alberta, 1942

each copy was stamped 'Payment to be made to Edmonton district office' and the account transferred from my books to Edmonton for collection.

Several weeks went by and I received a note from the Major. Four copies of the invoice were not enough. Could I let him have six copies?

Another note arrived. Six copies of the invoice were okay but each copy should have been stamped with the statement that *'Price does not include any Canadian domestic tax.'* Six copies were mailed with the required statement.

Two months went by and a different major came to see me. The battalion that had purchased the stoves was now downriver and his battalion was responsible for all outstanding accounts. Could I make out a new account in six copies, with the necessary statement re taxes but in the name of his battalion? Again, I complied.

Then I had another visitor, a civilian this time. Bechtel, Price & Callaghan were now responsible for all outstanding accounts. Could I make out an invoice in their names?

Still later, a representative of Turnbull, Sverdrup and Purcell called and we went through the whole dreary routine again.

About a year later, cheques began to arrive, addressed to the Hudson's Bay Company in Waterways. In all, I received six separate cheques -- all in payment of the same bill. It was too much for me. I sent them to Edmonton with a covering letter and let them clear up the mess.

My other story took place in Waterways while I was there but I wasn't actually present. Joe and Smitty, our two Royal Canadian Mounted Police constables, paraded the town daily and took turns making a night patrol to make sure all was under control. Smitty, a recent recruit, was reasonably enough built but Joe was a magnificent specimen, well over six feet tall and built like a truck.

On patrol one Friday night, Smitty ran into half a dozen white soldiers who were well boozed up and making a nuisance of themselves at the front door of the dance-hall, whence they had been ejected. Smitty quietly asked them to move on. The GI's took umbrage at this and, forming a circle around him, taunted the young Mountie saying this time the Mountie wouldn't get his man. The taunting turned to shoving and pretty soon to man-handling. Fortunately the arrival of a van manned by Military Police prevented a nasty scene and the offenders were quickly loaded into the vehicle and driven away.

Incensed, Joe went over the next morning to complain to the Colonel who expressed his regrets. He asked Smitty to return that afternoon to identify the culprits. Promptly at two o'clock, the men who had been on pass at Waterways the previous evening were paraded and Smitty picked the six men out of the ranks. The military police corroborated the identification and the Colonel said, 'Thank you, officer. Just leave them to me. I'll see that they are suitably punished.'

'I'm afraid it is not as simple as that Colonel,' replied Joe. 'You are in Canada and these men have committed a civil offence -- obstructing an officer in the course of his duty. I will have to take these men to Fort McMurray to appear before a civil magistrate.'

The Colonel didn't like this at all. 'Is there no other way we can solve this problem?' he asked.

'Well,' said Joe, 'there is one way we can keep it out of the courts.' He slowly unbuttoned his tunic, folded it and handed it and his Stetson to Smitty.

'Just send them up one at a time and then we can consider the incident closed.'

One by one, Joe beat the living daylights out of each soldier in front of his buddies. Then he meticulously adjusted his Stetson, saluted the Colonel, and bade him a formal good day.

There was no trouble for the Mounties after that!

On the whole, the residents of Waterways and Fort McMurray look back on the American invasion with fond memories. There were a few ruckuses at the start but once official authority clamped down, everything went fairly smoothly. Most of the troops were a bunch of homesick boys in a foreign country. Bea and I invited many of them to our home for a meal or a game of bridge. They enjoyed playing with the children, hearing a woman's voice and forgetting, for a brief time, that there was a war on. The Colonels of the various regiments must have been well briefed in diplomatic relations. They listened and took effective steps to iron out any complaints they received from the local civilian population.

With the closing down of Canol in Waterways, Bea and I were able to relax a bit and take time to enjoy our leisure. While Celina looked after the girls, we played tennis on the Mackenzie River Transport courts. Tennis was very popular with the younger people and the courts were crowded every evening.

In the winter, we played badminton two or three nights a week and on the rare occasion, I even won. We also had a regular bridge club. Bea joined the local Women's Institute and on her meeting night, I played billiards at the poolhall with the boys. One table was regulation billiard size and Bill Mitchell kept it in remarkably good shape.

There were fishing trips on Sundays along the Saline Creek and in the summer and fall, blueberry and cranberry picking. Louis Demers drove us a few miles up the airport road and came back later to pick us up. A cookout was part of the trip -- the children loved pork and beans and sausages.

Most Sunday afternoons in the summer, there were softball games between ladies' teams at Waterways and Fort McMurray; in the winter, ice hockey between the men. There was a great sporting rivalry between the two towns. Walter Skinner, now manager of the Hudson's Bay Company store at McMurray, and I organized hockey games between the 'old men' whose skating ability was minimal. They provided a lot of fun and brought out larger crowds than the regular games. A collection was taken at all these contests to augment the fund for buying comforts for the boys overseas.

I'm the world's worst skater and although I spent more time on my knees and backside than on my feet, I took part in those hockey games. I desperately wanted to score a goal. Just one! The girls at the store stood on the sidelines rooting for me whenever we played and I tried very hard to achieve my ambition. When success eluded me and I returned to the store, goal-less once again, they put their heads together and came up with a plan guaranteed to appeal to any stout-hearted and thrifty Scotsman. They promised to present me with a brand new quarter for each goal I scored.

Finally, it happened. I was flat on my stomach. The winger shot the puck in my direction. It hit my outstretched stick. And, almost in slow motion, it trickled into the net. I had scored!

A few days later, Grace Rhyason, Kay Gangstad and Terry Hebert marched into my office and ceremoniously presented me with my quarter. A hole had been bored in the centre through which they passed a long blue ribbon tied in a beautiful bow. After a speech extolling my prowess as a hockey player, they hung my medal around my neck. I was a proud man.

Unfortunately, people I know from that period of my life only remember me as 'the worst hockey player in the world.'

I was in charge of selling war bonds at the store and if we were short of selling our quota, we could always count on Jack Fairbairn. He just pulled out his chequebook and wrote a cheque for the balance. A most generous man!

The Governor of the Hudson's Bay Company and his party rest on the Canol pipeline in Dods Canyon, 1944 (l to r): R.H. Chesshire, Manager, Fur Trade Dept.; Governor Sir Patrick Ashley Cooper; C.S. Riley, Chairman of the Canadian Committee; P.A. Chester, General Manager; D. Hutchison, Manager, Mackenzie River Transport.

In the late summer of 1944, the Governor of the Hudson's Bay Company, Sir Patrick Ashley Cooper made his first visit to Canada since 1939. There were rumours that he would visit Waterways but, as I had no official notification from District Office, I paid no attention to them. Then we heard that he was going to arrive in town by the following Wednesday's train to inspect Mackenzie River Transport. Mr Hutchison, the General Manager, was throwing a big dinner for him the following night. True to form, neither the store manager at Fort McMurray nor I received an invitation. We were both disappointed but knowing Mr Hutchison's aversion to post managers, we weren't surprised.

The Governor arrived in a private car attached to the train which was switched to the siding by the Mackenzie River Transport buildings. As I sat in my office the next afternoon, Mr Petty, the local Mackenzie River Transport agent, bustled in. 'The Governor is here! The Governor is here!' he exclaimed.

'Yes, Mr Petty, I know. He arrived yesterday.'

Almost stammering with excitement, he said, 'You don't understand. He is here in the store. Right now! He wants to meet you.'

With little enthusiasm, Mr Hutchison introduced me to Sir Patrick, a very tall, impressive-looking man. Accompanying him were P.A. Chester, the Company's General Manager in Canada, and C.A. Riley, a member of the Company's Canadian Committee. I showed the party around the store and I was amazed at the pointed questions which the Governor asked in relation to the Company's business. He knew what he was talking about.

When he asked about living conditions in the North, I said, 'Perhaps you would like to see our house. It is one of the new experimental houses being built by the Company. My wife and I are very happy with it.'

Mr Hutchison looked at his watch, fidgeting nervously and muttering something about a timetable. So I added, 'I can guarantee you a good cup of tea!'

The Governor smiled and said, 'Now that I would really appreciate.' As they left, I hurriedly called Bea to warn her of our distinguished, if unexpected visitor.

Bea's mother, Mrs Guy Dingle, was visiting us and it turned out that she and Mr Riley were old acquaintances. While they chatted away, Bea showed the Governor around our home and told him how much she liked it. Once tea had been served I excused myself and left. That evening I learned that they had stayed about two hours. Sir Patrick and my mother-in-law had gotten along famously. He was quite interested in her name. 'Dingle is an uncommon name. I know there is a Dingle Bay in southern Ireland,' he said, 'and yet, this is the third time I have come across it in a very short time. The railroad car we used to travel here was kindly lent to us by the Western Division Superintendent of the Canadian National Railway, Mr Stan Dingle. Any relation?'

'Yes, he is my nephew,' said Mother, proudly.

Sir Patrick went on. 'And recently the daughter of a very close friend of mine in Scotland married a young Canadian doctor who was doing post-graduate work in Edinburgh.'

'That would be Dr Tom, another of my nephews.'

'Congratulations Mrs Dingle, you have quite a remarkable family,' the Governor remarked. And Mother beamed!

The next day I learned that Mr Hutchison had been furious that his afternoon's itinerary had been completely disrupted by me. 'Oh well,' I thought to myself, 'you may have entertained Sir Patrick Ashley Cooper to a transport dinner, Mr Hutchison, but my wife and I entertained him to a proper afternoon tea.'

In the early fall, Bea and I took the girls to Winnipeg for a holiday. In the bottom of our much-travelled and somewhat battered steamer trunk, I stowed away a case of 12-gauge shells which were in very short supply in civilization. Grandpa Dingle was tickled to get them. Now he and his friend, 'Shorty' Kennedy, could go duck hunting that fall.

We were quite worried by the fact that none of our daughters had, as yet, been baptized. We had never been stationed at a post where there was a United Church minister. Grandpa Dingle set it up for us. Dr G.A. Woodside, an old friend of his, agreed to come over to the house and perform the ceremony. And quite naturally, I went out and bought a bottle of Hudson's Bay Best Procurable to celebrate the event.

Grandpa was scandalized! 'Put that bottle away,' he insisted, 'and don't you dare to bring it out when the minister is here.'

The girls were baptized standing in front of the living-room fireplace. They thought it silly having water sprinkled over them and had a hard time controlling their giggles. Afterwards, as we sat over a cup of tea, Grandpa exclaimed to Dr Woodside, 'Do you know what that crazy son-in-law of mine did? He went out and bought a bottle of Scotch.'

The minister laughed. 'And what do you think I've been sitting here for? Bring out that bottle and we'll wet the babies' heads in true Scottish fashion.' Grandpa sipped his dram in a very subdued manner.

After a short stay in Winnipeg, we all went down to Minaki for a couple of weeks. We rented a cottage at Holst Point where Bea and I had first met and for a little while, relived our courtship days.

Bea Ross's kindergarten class. The ladies, seated, (l to r) are Bea Ross, Mrs Jackie Woods and Mrs H. McCormick. Kneeling, Mrs Jack Barker.

Before we left Winnipeg, I went down to Hudson's Bay House and arranged for a kindergarten course to be sent to us at Waterways. It was provided by the Company at no charge to me and was supplied by the Calvert School of Baltimore, Maryland. When we returned to the post, Bea started the two older girls in kindergarten. As a former teacher, she pronounced that it was a very good course and it wasn't long before the word got around. In no time we had six of our neighbour's children taking lessons along with Barbara and Jennifer.

While Waterways, Alberta was a merchandising store as opposed to the fur trade posts to which I had been accustomed in Ontario, we still did a fair amount of fur buying. There were several differences however. No longer did I have to go through the lengthy business of discussing and deciding upon fur trapping debts with the Indians. All our customers were half-breeds who had regular summer jobs and earned good wages with the various river transportation companies. To the Indians, trapping was merely a winter sideline. Most of them seldom went out for longer than three or four weeks and usually bought their trapping supplies and paid for them in cash. They ran regular monthly accounts at the store and I charged any groceries or other requirements needed by their families during their absence. They always paid their accounts promptly.

Instead of meticulously baling our fur collections and forwarding them to our sales department in London, England, we were encouraged to make weekly shipments to Montreal. The British Government had an embargo on furs at this time -- from July, 1940 until November, 1945 -- so sales and shipments were handled differently during these years. At Waterways any fur we bought during the week was stuffed into a gunny sack and, once cleared by the local game warden, expressed to our fur sales department in Montreal. There, the furs were either sold locally by auction or shipped to our outlets in New York, wherever the price was the most advantageous.

In Ontario, squirrels had been looked upon as 'squaw fur.' A squirrel pelt was only worth about 10 cents and they were not trapped specifically. Any that a trapper got in his traps were given to his wife as pin money. But now, squirrels were worth approximately 50 cents each and soon the price went up to $1.00. One of my hunters, a man who cut cordwood downriver for the Mackenzie River Transport, came in at regular intervals with anything up to five hundred squirrels at a time. They were all beautifully stretched, each neatly shot though the head with a .22 and tied in bundles of 25. The first time he came in, I started to open one bundle to examine the individual skins. He was outraged. 'You don't have to look at each bundle, Mr Ross. They are all first-grade. I don't even bother to bring in damaged ones. You ask anyone. My furs are top quality or I don't sell them,' he said indignantly.

As I knew him to be an honest man and a very good customer, I took him at his word and paid him top price for the lot. After he left, I examined his full shipment carefully and sure enough, they were all Number One skins. I never doubted his word again.

Initially, I had only one competitor in town -- Gus Hawker, the local free trader. Gus had married into a half-breed family and got the business of most of his wife's relatives. Unfortunately for him, the price of his merchandise was quite a bit higher than mine. He didn't have the advantage of being able to purchase stocks direct from the manufacturer as the Bay did, but dealt mainly with local wholesalers in Edmonton. So I didn't lose too much fur to him.

Later, another trader set up business in town. He built his store on the vacant lot opposite the hotel and had a very good stock of drygoods, especially men's woollen underwear, socks, workshirts and gloves. He obtained the merchandise from the commissary of the gold mine at Goldfields on the north shore of Lake Athabasca when it closed down.

The only time I had any serious difference with my district manager, Bruce Clark, was over the purchase of this stock of drygoods which was much needed in our business. When we were asked to bid on it, the mine owners had already packed the merchandise in cartons and all we had to bid on were the detailed inventories. My district manager, Bruce Clark, decided that he couldn't take the chance. The Company insisted that before we made an offer on the goods, we should be allowed to open the packed cases and examine the merchandise. When permission was refused, we didn't put in an offer and lost the lot.

The new trader was a quiet Scotsman from Inverness named Alec McIvor. He was difficult to get to know until I discovered that he played bridge and I invited him to the house. He demurred at first but when I said, 'Alec, you know and I know that we will cut each other's throats during business hours but why can't we be friends outside of business hours?' He grinned and accepted my invitation. To our mutual delight, we had many furious bridge battles in the coming months.

There was no open season for beaver then in northern Alberta. Just after open water in the spring of 1944 as I went to open the store one morning, I was surprised to find two game wardens waiting for me at the front door. 'We have a warrant to search your store for illegal beaver,' they informed me and held up the document. There was no use in arguing so I opened up and invited them in. They searched the store thoroughly from cellar to attic, then did the same to the warehouse.

'I'm sorry, Mr Ross, but we'll have to search your home and, of course, the staff house,' the warden said, apologetically.

It took some time and when Bea asked me what they were looking for, I could only shrug my shoulders. Barbara and Jennifer thought it was a great game and Bea and Celina were hard put to keep them out from underfoot. When the wardens had completed their very thorough inspection and, of course, found nothing, I asked them again what was going on. 'We've received information that a large quantity of contraband beaver has been taken from the Northwest Territories to Waterways to be shipped south. We'll find it if we have to take the whole town apart.' As he opened the door to leave, he apologized for the intrusion. 'We know very well that you wouldn't deal in contraband beaver, Mr Ross, but we have to search everyone and to make it look good, we started on the Hudson's Bay Company store first.'

The whole town was buzzing. Later in the day, I learned that there were twelve game wardens and the Royal Canadian Mounted Police in town. They searched every store in Waterways and every building on the waterfront but no beaver turned up, so they held a meeting. The head game warden asked, 'Are you all sure you didn't notice anything unusual? Anything out of the ordinary? Think hard. There has to be something we missed. Let's go over it again. Where did each of you search?' One by one the weary searchers recounted their day's activities.

'Sir, we checked everything. We even moved mattresses off the beds and believe me, that's the first time some of them have been moved in years.'

Another man piped up. 'I was checking outhouses too and we did find a still in the basement of...'

'Never mind that now,' interrupted the harassed warden. 'If the still was working, the beaver weren't there. Anyway, by the time we get over there to close it down, the still will be long gone.' He pointed to a young warden and asked 'How about you, son? What part of town were you searching?'

'The docks, sir. We didn't find a thing. The foreman was very helpful and the place was neat as a pin. Everything was in its place and well...except for the barrel bottoms lying around, there was a place for everything.'

A Mountie stood up. 'What's that about barrel bottoms?' he asked.

'Well, constable, the whole place was real tidy except for the barrel bottoms,' said the embarrassed young man, 'and it just seemed unusu...*unusual! Sir, it was unusual!*' he cried exultantly.

The Police hastily dispatched men to the railroad depot and telegraph wires sang as orders were sent to Edmonton to search the train. Obviously someone had cut the bottoms out of oil barrels, stuffed the skins into them and shipped them south by railroad. But by then it was much too late. The barrels had been removed at a siding before the train reached Edmonton and were now safely over the border into British Columbia when they could be sold legally.

The Snowshoe Rabbit or Varying Hare is the basic food of fur-bearing predators -- foxes, wolves and lynx. Studies show that the rabbit is noticeably cyclical. The numbers increase every year until the tenth or eleventh year when, either through disease or lack of food, they die off. The following year rabbits are very scarce. During the years of plenty, the predators have lots of food and rear large healthy families. Thus they are also cyclical, coinciding roughly with the rabbit.

Since my arrival in 1941, red foxes had gradually become more plentiful and by the winter of 1944-45, there were red foxes everywhere. Trappers who had previously produced a few were now bringing in fifty to a hundred pelts at a time. But still the tariff price increased. I couldn't understand it. Foxes formerly worth $2.50 were now worth anything up to $10.

Instead of taking their furs to each individual buyer for him to bid on, it became the custom for everyone to bring their pelts to Bill Mitchell's pool parlour and then invite Gus Hawker, Alex McIvor and myself to come and bid. The successful bidder had to put cash on the table and tote the furs back to his store. I got more than my fair share. I had one advantage over the others. I could play snooker. One night a week when Bea had her ladies meeting, Syd Hawkins, the British American Oil agent; Bert Viney, the station agent; Vic Tanner, a local painter, and myself met in the poolhall to play billiards. Vic and I usually arrived before the others and he instructed me in the gentle art of playing snooker. Most of the trappers fancied themselves as masters of the game and once I had become proficient, I challenged the trappers. 'If you win, you put your furs up for bids. If I win, you sell them to me.' The trappers thought this was a great laugh and took me on. But I won the right to buy their fur more often than not.

The fox cycle peaked in the spring of 1946 and, as was inevitable, the price dropped. I received the news by telegram one Saturday morning. The value of a fox pelt was down by more than 50 percent. About half an hour after I had decoded the wire from District Office in walked Bill Auger, one of my best trappers. He and his brother had just come back and had about four hundred skins between them. 'How about coming over to the house to look at the furs instead of us bringing them to the store,' Bill asked. 'There's quite a load and they're all prime.'

I was in a quandary. 'Bill, you and your brother have always sold your furs directly to me. I'm going to suggest something strange but I want you to trust me.' The brothers looked at each other in bewilderment. 'Will you put your furs up for bid this time and ask the other two buyers and myself to come over to your house this afternoon?'

'But why, Mr Ross? We've always sold our skins to the Bay. Anyway we have things to do this afternoon. Tomorrow would be better.' I could see that the men were very upset at this turn of events.

'No, Bill,' I said, 'it must be this afternoon. You both know that I've always been honest with you. Trust me again,' I pleaded. They walked away from me and whispered together, then returned and agreed to do as I requested even though they didn't understand.

That afternoon, we all arrived at Bill's house at The Prairie, graded the massive pile of furs and handed Bill our sealed bids. Bill opened the envelopes one by one, looked at me in anger and amazement and announced that Alec McIvor was the high bidder. As we loaded his furs into his car, Alec asked what was going on. 'I've never known Bill Auger to be so surly. What did you bid?' I said we'd talk later and went in to explain the situation to Bill and his brother. Incidentally, my bid was less than half of Alec McIvor's.

As we sat down at the bridge table that evening, Alec said, 'That was a hell of a trick you played on me this morning.'

'No trick, Alec,' I replied. 'I had advance information and, you know what we always say, business is business.'

'Oh well,' he replied ruefully, 'I guess I can't win them all, but I didn't lose all of this one. When I went back to Bill's house, I looked at your bid and knew something funny was up. As soon as I got back to Waterways, I went over to see Gus Hawker and told him it was too bad that he had lost out by such a small amount and offered him a good deal to share the furs. He jumped at it and I sold half of the pelts to Gus.'

In the summer of 1944, I was advised by District Office that Messrs C.H. Harford and G.A. Beare would be making an inspection of my store. Graeme Beare came to Canada with me in 1930 and I hadn't seen him since. He was now a trainee district manager. Clarence Harford had been transferred from the Winnipeg retail store to the Fur Trade Department as an assistant to the General Manager in June, 1943. When they arrived, they were all business. They were going to check my entire stock, they said.

I was very proud of my stock-keeping system. Each post was supplied with a complete set of stock sheets which also showed the mark-up percentage to be applied to each item of merchandise. As the sheets were too bulky to fit into one binder, I divided them up into departments with a looseleaf binder for each. Where required, I added blank sheets and broke men's, women's and children's wear down into size and colour ranges. Tom Lindley was the innovator of this system and I expanded its use. Each of my assistants was placed in charge of two departments, given the stock books and required to do a monthly stock check entered in the appropriate column. A monthly timetable was drawn up and every week I expected two completed stock checks on my desk. From them, I made out requisitions for replacements.

Over and above the percentage markups which the Company deemed advisable there were certain restrictions placed by the Wartime Prices and Trades Board which applied mainly to children's wear and to men's work clothing. As I received bulletins from the Board the amendments to markups were entered in my stockbook and any existing stock in hand adjusted to the new selling price. When Mr Harford announced that they were going to check my stock, department by department, I asked, 'Which department do you wish to start with?'

'Mr Beare will check men's wear,' he replied. I called in Kay Gangstad and asked her to get her stockbook and assist Mr Beare.

'Do you want to check another department, Mr Harford?' I inquired.

'Yes, I'll do women's wear,' he replied. So I called in Terry Hebert, told her to get her book and, as they left, I went about my work in the office.

Two days later the whole stock checking was completed. I asked Mr Harford how it had gone. 'Splendidly, splendidly, we didn't find a single error. You run an excellent post, Mr Ross.'

I thanked him and asked, 'May I ask you a question, Mr Harford?' At his nod of agreement, I said, 'Where do I go from here?'

He looked at me in surprise. 'What do you mean? I don't understand you.' I explained that I felt I could run a much bigger store than Waterways and that I would like to manage a post that had better education facilities for the children. 'Moreover, I'm thirty-two years old now. Once I get to be thirty-five I know the Company won't consider me for any great advance.'

'Oh, I see. You mean you would like to be a district manager.'

'Yes,' I said, 'I'd like to be a district manager. But if not, I know I can run a much larger post than this one.'

'You surprise me, Ross. I didn't think you had any ambitions beyond store management. But I'll bring the matter to the attention of Winnipeg,' he assured me.

Fred Mitchell left Fort McMurray in the fall of 1944 to join the Navy. I was sorry to lose a good friend and a first-rate fur buyer. When the war was over, Fred came back to the Company, transferred to the Raw Furs Department and became one of their top fur buyers. Walter Skinner came from Fort Chipewyan to replace him.

Late in the summer of 1945, I took a week off and with Bea and the three girls, went by steamboat downriver to Fort Smith. The war was finally over although we weren't affected as much as cities further south. I had imagined that travelling on a steamboat would be just like sailing down the Mississippi River on a paddle steamer but nothing could have been further from the truth.

In the spring and early summer when the Athabasca River was in high flood, such might have been the case but in late summer, with the low water levels, vastly different conditions prevailed. Long sandbars stretched out like a herringbone diagonally from either bank. The pilot was kept busy going downriver ahead of us in an outboard motorboat trying to select a channel through the sandbars. Occasionally we ran aground. Then it was 'full steam ahead' to try to power over the bar; or allowing the stern of the ship to swing around easing ourselves off, backing to the other side of the river, swinging down and we were on our way again. Once when we struck hard, we watched as a tow rope was taken ashore, anchored to a deadhead on the bank and we winched off. We reached Lake Athabasca and had a lovely sail across to Fort Chipewyan. After a short stay, we steamed on to Fort Fitzgerald, the last stop, where everything was unloaded for the sixteen-mile trip across the portage to Fort Smith. We were fortunate to hire a taxi and spent a couple of days at Fort Smith looking around the

Waterways Store, Christmas, 1945

settlement and visiting Harry MacDonald, the Company post manager and his wife. We stayed in the Hotel Mackenzie operated by the Mackenzie River Transport with Paul Kaeser as manager. We enjoyed this break from routine and flew back to Waterways by DC3.

Shortly after our return, W.T. Winchester came to serve his repatriation with us. Bill, another recruit from the Old Country in 1930, had joined the Air Force and had been stationed with the Peace River/Yukon Staging Command. He was one of the first to be demobilized and was sent to Waterways for a short term to get back into the swing of things before taking over a post of his own. He lived with us during that time and then left for his posting. After his stint as an officer in the Air Force, I could see that he wasn't too keen on going back to the routine of fur trading and I wasn't surprised to hear that he left the Company and went into business for himself in a small general store in Edmonton.

Ken Retallack, who had joined the Royal Canadian Air Force while still an apprentice, was next to arrive. He brought his wife and small daughter and I got him fixed up in one of the Mackenzie River Transport houses which was vacant for the winter. He was a great help and I was sorry to lose him when he was transferred to Fort Grahame. Eventually Ken was put in charge of one of the major western line posts.

PART II

The Training Period

In March, 1946, I received instructions from District Office to report to Winnipeg on May 1st for further training. We were expecting our fourth child but the baby wasn't due until July so I suggested that Bea and the girls go to Winnipeg a couple of months ahead where she could stay with her parents and look for a house to rent. Bea agreed and the move went smoothly until it was time to say good-bye to Celina Norris who had been an integral part of our lives in Waterways. Bea and the three tearful girls found the parting most difficult.

After seeing the family off with their crammed steamer trunk, I took the time to pack all our personal belongings properly -- thanks to Hank McCormick, the Mackenzie River Transport foreman who provided several sturdy wooden crates.

About a week before I was due to leave, my replacement, Les Martin, arrived from Terrace Bay and I moved into the hotel. I welcomed the good meals for, while I can whip up some delicious offerings over a campfire, a modern kitchen defeats me. The change of management inventory was carried out and the following Friday I caught the train for Edmonton where I stayed overnight and visited the District Office. There I was led to understand that the Company was planning to open a large retail store in Prince George, B.C. and that I was to be given special training in Winnipeg prior to taking charge of this operation. I was delighted. I had already worked in Ontario and Alberta and had visited the Northwest Territories, albeit briefly, and I now looked forward to seeing British Columbia. Bea was still looking for a house and, with this news, I hoped she hadn't found one.

Bea and the girls met me at the train in Winnipeg and I immediately asked the question uppermost in my mind. 'Have you found us a place to live?' She gave me a funny look. 'That means you didn't get my last letter. I posted it a week ago.' When I indicated that I hadn't, she said, with a twinkle in her eye, 'Are you in for a surprise!' Barbara and Jennifer started to shout something but Bea hushed them and whispered that it was to be a surprise.

'You sure are going to be surprised, Daddy,' said Barbara.

Knowing that there was no way I'd get any answers until Bea was ready to tell me, I bustled them all into a cab and Bea spoke quietly to the driver. The taxi went south on Main Street past Hudson's Bay House -- where I ceremoniously lifted my hat and bent my head -- and over the Norwood Bridge, then turned right onto Lyndale Drive. The Red River ran along the right-hand side of the Drive and on the left was a large open playing field. There were few houses around but ahead of us, on the left, was a long, low, white house with a red roof. The cab stopped in front and Bea said, 'This is it. This is home!'

'Good God,' I exclaimed, 'it looks just like a Hudson's Bay dwelling house.'

'Give the man a cigar,' laughed Bea. 'That's exactly what it is. It's the Bay's latest experimental house.' After a rather circumspect inspection of the house, Bea explained how it all came about.

As I mentioned earlier, the Company had been engaged for the past five or six years in a gradual process of replacing dwellings and stores in the north and a Company subsidiary, the Rupertsland Trading Company, was formed to look after it. They tried several different designs of buildings but were still not completely satisfied. In 1945 their architect came up with what he thought was the ideal solution and presented the plans to the Canadian Committee. 'But,' they stated, 'we can't make up our minds from blueprints. Build us a house and let us see your "ideal solution".'

A suitable corner lot was purchased in Norwood and a gang of carpenters hired by Rupertsland Trading Company set to work in the fall of 1945. The house was finished by spring and furnished according to Company specifications. Naturally it was painted in the standard Company colours. The Canadian Committee was pleased with the house and agreed that it was to be the model. They called it the 12 DB.

Housing in Winnipeg after the war was at a premium. Returning servicemen and their wives had bought or rented every available house and the authorities took a dim view of any dwelling lying vacant. The result was that about ten days prior to my arrival,

Bea had received a call from Mr Chesshire. 'Have you found a house yet, Mrs Ross? I understand Hugh will be back from Waterways very shortly.'

'Not yet, Sir. We've looked all over the city...even in the outskirts. I put our names on the housing list, but, of course, the veterans are entitled to first choice. I guess we'll just have to stay with my parents until something comes up,' she said dejectedly.

'Well, I think I have something that you will like. Can you be at 97 Lyndale Drive tomorrow morning at nine o'clock?'

'Yes. Yes. Of course I can. Where is Lyndale Drive? Never mind, I'll find it. I'll be there, Mr Chesshire, and thank you.' And she ran to get a street map.

When Bea arrived at 8:45 a.m., she was met at the door by Jessie Bacon, household furnishings expert for the Fur Trade Department, who ushered her into the house where the coffee pot was bubbling on the kitchen stove. Bea looked hurriedly around. 'I'll take it. Can we move in tomorrow?' She was so excited she didn't even ask what the rent was.

The house was a one-storey ranch-like building with the outside walls and roof covered with cedar shingles. The windows were double glazed. It had a briquette-burning stove in the living room and a wood and coal range in the kitchen -- just the same as it would be in the bush. The inside walls were all panelled with birch plywood. A passageway ran the length of the house. On one side was a very roomy kitchen and living room, and on the other side were four bedrooms and a bathroom. The two end bedrooms were larger and one of these was designated as the master bedroom. The other was intended as a bed-sitting room for the apprentice clerk who, in the bush, would normally be living in the manager's house.

As far as I could see, there was only one drawback to it. It had only one door -- a back door which led through a glazed and screened veranda to the outside. The architect explained that he could see no use for a front door in the bush as everyone used the back door anyway.

The area was called Norwood Flats and was just starting to be developed. There were so few houses nearby we might just as well have been in the country. About four hundred yards away was the Winnipeg Rowing Club on the riverbank and the nine-hole Norwood Golf Course. It would do splendidly until we moved to British Columbia.

My appointment with Mr Harford, now Personnel Manager, was not until 10:00 a.m. but I presented myself at the office first thing. At the head of the stairs leading to the second-floor Fur Trade Department offices, I met J. W. Anderson, District Manager of the Eastern Arctic. I hadn't seen him since I was a very green apprentice clerk at Grassy Narrows in 1930. He shook my hand and gave me a warm welcome. 'Do you remember that day in Grassy Narrows when you were so homesick you wanted to go back to Scotland and I walked you around the island, talked to you like a father and persuaded you to stay with the Company?' he asked. I acknowledged that I did.

'Well,' he said, 'it looks like it was a good thing I did. I hear that you are going to be trained as a district manager.' This was news to me. I thought I was going to Prince George.

The Fur Trade office was a hive of activity with carpenters and workmen everywhere. They had torn down the walls of district managers' offices and were erecting small cubicles for the accommodation of new managers and administrative staff to take care of the expansion period that the Company had started. I greeted a few friends and then wandered into the merchandise depot to talk to Tom Smith, the depot manager.

'Welcome to Winnipeg,' said Tom. 'When are you starting work for us?' I gave him an puzzled look and asked what he was talking about. 'I understand that you are to be trained as manager of one of the departments in our depot. Haven't they told you yet?'

I was really confused, Inside a week, I had been told I was to be trained to take over a new store in British Columbia; that I was going to be a district manager and now, I was going to be a depot department manager.

I knocked on Mr Harford's door for my ten o'clock appointment. The interview was short. After welcoming me to Winnipeg, he gave me a new contract to sign. I was designated as a 'trainee' at $225 per month minus a rental of $45 per month for the experimental house.

'I want you to work with Ernest Spence to develop a new basic stock plan for the stores on the lines of what you had at Waterways. Come along and I'll introduce you, then you take the rest of the day off and report to work tomorrow morning at 8:30.'

Ernie Spence, a most congenial man, had worked for the Wartime Prices and Trade Board. Now, I learned, it was our job to produce a stockbook with standard markups for use at all the posts. It didn't take too long to come up with three stockbooks -- one for competitive line posts, one for inland posts and one for arctic posts. The further inland they were, the higher the markups had to be, due to increased transportation costs and expenses in operating the units.

Next we set up a basic stocklist for a line post doing between $150,000 and $200,000 annual sales. We figured out what lines should be carried in stock and how many items of each line should be forwarded as the initial opening stock. By the end of May we had finished my part of the work. I enjoyed working with Ernie Spence, albeit for such a short period of time.

My next assignment was to work with Tom Scurfield, Manager of Central Line District. Mr Harford advised me to watch, listen and learn and emphasized time and again, that I had no authority and could make no decisions. So now I knew. I wasn't going to run a store in Prince George and I wasn't going to run a department in the merchandise depot. I was a trainee district manager. At last Bea and I would have a permanent home. No more moving from place to place like itinerant tinkers. And perhaps, finally, we could retire our much used and very shabby steamer trunk.

As I left his office, Mr Harford's last words to me were 'Remember Ross, you have no authority to make any decisions.'

He was a strange man -- a supercilious, middle-class Englishman with a condescending attitude. He held a low opinion of the ordinary post managers and it really annoyed me to hear him refer to them continuously as 'those poor sods in the bush.' It wasn't that long since I had been one of those 'poor sods' myself. I found it impossible to establish any sort of rapport with him. My friends at Hudson's Bay House warned me that he was a hard man to get along with and that he took great delight in running roughshod over anyone who was his junior. If you knuckled under to him, they said, he kept on to see how far he could go before you fought back. If you didn't fight back, then you were finished as far as he was concerned.

A bunch of us -- including Mr Harford and H.E. Cooper, the new merchandise manager -- were having a coffee break in the staff lounge one day. Mr Cooper had just returned from an inspection trip of inland fur trading posts and when asked by Mr Harford what he thought of them, he said 'Ah, they're just a bunch of bloody crap cans.' This was too much for me.

'Gentlemen,' I said, 'neither one of you has any fur trade experience. The only thing you are interested in is establishing merchandise stores.' They looked at me in surprise. 'May I remind you gentlemen that until the stores begin to pay their own way, those 'bloody crap cans' run by those 'poor sods in the bush' are paying your salaries.' And I stalked out of the room.

One of Mr Harford's contentions was that he could go out and hire men off the street, give them six months' intensive training and they would do a better job than any store manager who had served the usual five years' apprenticeship. The man was an ass!

Tom Scurfield was completely different. I enjoyed working with him. He was always straight and to the point and answered all my questions. He had served his apprenticeship in the western Arctic, became District Manager of Saskatchewan and then assumed the charge of Central Line District. As part of the job, I accompanied him on trips to Atikokan, Hornepayne and Foleyet where the Company intended to open new stores. Atikokan (the Place of the Caribou) had recently become the scene of an open-pit iron-mining operation at nearby Steep Rock Lake. They drained the lake and found almost pure iron ore, which was scooped up and taken in huge trucks to Atikokan. From there it was shipped by rail to Fort William and then transferred in bulk ore-carriers by water to the smelters. The company that ran the mine was delighted to turn their commissary over to us. We operated from this store until Rupertsland Trading built a retail store on a choice lot in a newly surveyed section in the town of Atikokan.

Hornepayne, a division point of the Canadian National Railway, was strictly a railroading town. Most of the commercial businesses were located in one block right across from the station. When word got around that the Hudson's Bay Company intended to open a store, prices of existing businesses jumped. As Tom and I surveyed the business section, Tom shook his head and said, 'I don't like the look of this. It's a fire trap. If just one of those stores caught fire, the whole block would go up in flames. No, we'll have to look elsewhere.'

There were no suitable vacant lots available. As we walked along the main street, I said to Tom, 'Have you noticed that all the buildings are on one side of the street?' We walked across and looked at the other side which sloped down about ten feet to the level of the Canadian National Railway property. 'Do you suppose we could get permission to build on this side?' I asked. 'Look, the basement of the store would be at railroad level and make it easy to handle incoming merchandise. And the main floor of the store would be at street level -- up here.' Tom looked around, mulling over the possibilities. Then, always a man of action, he shot off a telegram to the Canadian National Railway's main office in Montreal. In a short time, we had a reply. The Canadian National would be pleased to arrange to put enough land at our disposal for the Company's new store.

Having arranged for the site we set out to purchase a home for the post manager. Once the word got around town that we were no longer interested in local business sites, it was astonishing how much the merchants dropped their previous asking prices.

Foleyet, another railroad town east of Hornepayne had a large sawmill and lumbering operation as its main business. The largest general store was built in the centre of town. The adjacent corner lot was cluttered with store litter: empty soft drink cartons and oil barrels. But the owner wasn't interested in selling and adamantly refused to consider any offers. We went down to the local fire ranger's office to examine the plan of the town and, to our surprise, found that while the store operator owned the lot on which his store was built, he had not bothered to purchase the adjoining corner lot. Tom quickly put down a deposit for the property and another lot suitable for a dwelling house as well. Then he wired Winnipeg and informed them of the transactions.

When confirmation of the purchases was received a couple of days later, we went in to see the store owner. 'Mr Berubé, the Hudson's Bay Company now owns the vacant lot next door and we'll be starting to build immediately. We would appreciate it if you would remove anything that belongs to you.' Confronted with these facts, Mr Berubé quickly changed his tune and we were able to complete a deal to purchase his store with the inventory at market value.

Back in Winnipeg, Bea was approaching her time; her doctor advised that she should expect the child about the middle of July. Around the 11th of that month, Mr Harford called me into his office. 'Ross, I have just received a wire from Mr Chesshire. He's on an inspection trip of the Western Arctic and Mackenzie River and he wants you in Yellowknife. The store is in a mess. So get your things and leave immediately.' He sat down at his desk, took up some papers and I was dismissed. He hadn't given me a chance to say a word.

Realizing I was still standing in front of his desk, he looked up. 'Yes...well, what is it? As you can see, I'm very busy,' he said, obviously annoyed that I hadn't run to do his bidding.

'I can't go to Yellowknife right now. My wife is expecting a child momentarily and I can't leave until the baby is born.'

He looked at me in astonishment. 'Not go? Of course you'll go. Mr Chesshire expressly asked for you. Now let's not have any more of this nonsense.' He glared at me and warned, 'You be on your way by tomorrow morning or your future with this Company will end very shortly.'

'I'm sorry, Mr Harford, but I am not leaving Winnipeg until my wife has her baby and that's final. I'm sure Mr Chesshire will understand and I'm willing to take my chances with him.'

And, once again, I stalked out. I never seemed to leave his presence without having to make a point. I suppose the man had his good qualities -- he must have had to hold his position -- but I never saw them.

In any event, our son, Ian Mackay Ross, was born in Grace

Hospital on July 14, 1946. Bea and I were both delighted that, finally, we had a son and heir.

I left the next evening by plane for Yellowknife.

Yellowknife first came into the public eye in the late 1930s when gold-bearing ore was discovered in the vicinity. By 1938, quite a town had sprung up and, realizing the business potential, the Company dispatched Tom Scurfield to look over the situation. He selected the site of the present store and stayed on to supervise its building and later its management. By 1946, the town was booming with two producing gold mines and continuous further exploration of the countryside for minerals.

The store was on a rocky promontory jutting out from the north shore of Great Slave Lake. Pontoon-equipped planes servicing prospectors' camps took off and landed day and night from a deep bay east of the promontory. The waterfront was built on another bay on the western side of the town and here all the freight destined for Yellowknife was brought in by barge from Hay River. The supplies went through Waterways first, then down the Athabasca River and across the Smith Portage, and then down to the town of Hay River on the west side of Great Slave Lake. Tugs owned by Mackenzie River Transport, Northern Transportation Company and the Yellowknife Transportation Company, pushing the barges ahead of them, plied continuously from Hay River to Yellowknife.

I made myself known at the store and Dick Garnett, the assistant manager took me over to the manager's house about a quarter of a mile away. My first look at the house stopped me dead in my tracks. I couldn't believe my eyes! Whoever had designed the building had made a serious mistake -- they forgot about permafrost in this part of the country and had designed the house with a full-sized basement. The heat of the house warmed the basement, then thawed the permafrost and in a very short time, the house canted over about two feet from the perpendicular.

There was a deep crack in the ground all around the outside of the tipsy building about a foot from the walls. I picked up a pole, stuck it into the crack and it went down about four feet. Gingerly, I walked inside. Where the plumbing pipes went through the

The Hudson's Bay Company store at Yellowknife. In 1946 most of the business was done by the back door: deliveries by air to prospecting camps.

plywood walls of the house, long slits about twelve inches long, had been cut to allow for the seasonal fluctuation up and down. The basement was a mass of supporting trusses and logs which were placed there every spring to shore up the building. Thank goodness I wasn't staying long -- I sure wouldn't want to live there with my family.

Next door were the Royal Canadian Mounted Police barracks. They had a bunch of sled dogs tied out for the summer and they nearly drove me mad during the next few weeks. Like clockwork, every four hours day and night, those blasted huskies poked their noses into the air and started to howl. Since Yellowknife enjoyed daylight for almost twenty-four hours in the summertime, getting to sleep was a difficult proposition and it took me a long while before I learned to ignore both the daylight and the huskies.

There were three cafes in the settlement: the 'Busy Bee', 'Wildcat Cafe' and the 'Roving Hornet'. I had no plans to cook anything other than my breakfast so I visited each of them in turn for meals which were both delicious and substantial.

Besides the bank, there was a local weekly newspaper office -- *The Yellowknife Nugget* -- and the Bromley Lumber Store recently opened by Bert Bromley whom I knew at Waterways, and his oldest son who had returned from the Navy. Numerous private homes were scattered haphazardly all over the rock, each with its private biffy standing about twenty-five yards beyond. It was said that the highest honour anyone in Yellowknife could bestow on you was to lend you the key to his biffy.

The Yellowknife Hotel dominated one part of the town. It was owned and operated by Vic Ingram who had been one of the best prospectors in the country. Unfortunately, his hands and feet were severely frostbitten one winter and he prospected no longer. The beer parlour attached to the hotel was open twenty-two hours a day. The other two hours were spent clearing out the drunks and empty bottles and swabbing the floors. Most days, Vic could be found sitting in the rotunda of the hotel playing cribbage with anyone who was foolish enough to challenge him to a $100 game.

Prior to my arrival, I was told that the Manager, A.W. 'Sandy' Scott had gone out on a much-needed, extended furlough and that the store was in the temporary charge of Dick Garnett, his assistant. Other than Mr Chesshire's bald statement that the 'store was in a mess', I hadn't a clue. It didn't take me long to find out just exactly what kind of mess it was. Dick introduced me to all the staff, mainly young apprentice clerks and a few local girls who waited behind counter, and one older man who was the bookkeeper. There were three offices at one side of the store: Dick's, the accountant's and the manager's office. Dick asked me, breezily, why I had come to Yellowknife, so I told him. He laughed in disbelief. 'There's nothing wrong with this store,' he said. 'I'm in charge and things are going great.'

'I'm glad to hear it,' I replied, 'but I'll just look around for myself.' I wandered into the accountant's office and watched him as he busily posted the previous day's sales into the sortergraph units -- the metal boxes that held files of the customers' duplicate sales slips. He sat perched on a piano stool which had casters and moved slowly along, methodically entering the previous day's credit slips under the appropriate customer's name. More than half

HBCA Photograph Collection 1987/363-E-700-G/30

Dick Garnett, assistant to the store manager, Yellowknife, hangs up his washing behind the staff house. 1946

of the customer's slots had little pieces of white paper sticking out. Curious, I looked at one and all it said was 'O.K. RFG'. I asked the accountant about it. 'These customers haven't paid their last month's bill but they have been okayed by Mr Garnett for their credit to be continued.' I checked them all, one after another and sure enough, all were beyond the amount authorized for their monthly credit rating. Digging deeper, I found that most had always paid their accounts promptly and it was only in the last month or so that they had been allowed to get away with it.

I called Dick in from his office. 'What's all this nonsense? All these customers are overdrawn.'

'You don't have to worry about them,' he assured me. 'I know my customers and they are good for it. They'll all pay up.'

'That's fine. Maybe they will, but the fact remains that they are all over their limit and you're still letting them charge up merchandise.' He continued to assure me that everything would be fine. 'That may be your opinion,' I retorted, 'but I'm sure Mr Scott would be very unhappy if he were to return right now and find the books in such a mess.'

'Don't worry about it, Mr Ross.   I'll take care of it before Sandy comes back from his holiday.'

I looked at his cheerful, carefree grin. 'No, you won't. You'll take care of it right now.   You say these people are all good customers. Okay, prove it.   Make a list of each name and the amount they owe and go out and collect these outstanding debts and I don't want to see you back in the store until you've finished.'

Deeply dismayed, Dick insisted that it wasn't necessary but I cut him short. 'Mr Chesshire says this store is in a mess. Your credit control is haywire and I've been sent up here to put things right. You might be interested to know that I have to submit a report on my findings and a second one on you. Unless you collect those accounts immediately, I don't think you'll like the report I'm going to send in.' He sat down dejectedly and started to make up a list.

I felt sorry for the lad. He had a marvellous personality and aspirations of being the next post manager at Yellowknife. As a result, he was too easygoing with his customers and they were taking advantage of his generous nature. It took him two or three days but he finally collected the outstanding balances. 'Now we can remove all the little white okay slips and I don't want to see any more of them,' I said. 'If a customer fails to pay his account by the tenth of the following month, it is to be brought to my attention at once.' I'm afraid Dick wasn't too happy with me.

During the next few days I wandered around the store, into the reserve stockrooms and the warehouses getting an impression of the place. And it wasn't good. In the back room dozens of expediters -- each equipped with a walkie-talkie -- were coming and going. I watched all this activity for a while, walked back into the almost silent store and came to the conclusion that the bulk of our business and almost all of our grocery trade was being done out the back door! The expediters chattered into their walkie-talkies, received lists of groceries and drygoods required at the prospecting camps and turned the lists over to two fellows who were handling this warehouse business. As soon as an order was completed and signed for by the expediter, it was picked up by truck and taken down to the floatplane base and flown out to one of the camps.

Hugh Ross with D.H. Pitts,
at the Yellowknife store, 1946

The two young men in charge of the whole operation were D.H. 'Des' Pitts, recently returned from the Air Force, and his half-breed assistant, Narcisse Bellerose. True, all their orders were in bulk but the fact remained that these boys were handling half the retail sales of our store. With stockbook in hand, I painstakingly checked the quantities of stock on hand, department by department. The post was badly overstocked, particularly in men's, women's and children's wear, most of it left over from the previous winter. I also found that many items which were regular best sellers were in short supply.

I told Dick how I felt about this. 'First thing tomorrow we are going to make out requisitions for the items we need. They'll have to be brought in quickly before freeze-up. After that you and I are going over the stock again and pick out anything that is slow selling.'

'What for?' asked Dick.

'Well, for starters, we'll mark them all down and put on a sale.'

Dick laughed out loud. 'Mr Ross, sales just don't go over in Yellowknife. It's useless to try. Nobody will come.'

'We're having a sale, Dick,' I insisted. 'If we don't try to get rid of this overstock, then we're going to have to write the whole lot off completely.' We went ahead and pulled out all the bad merchandise and marked it down 50 percent. I made up a large, double-page advertisement to be run in the following week's Yellowknife Nugget. Then the mail arrived.

'Dick, check the mail and see if there's anything urgent. I'd like to finish today if we can.' I went on working.

Dick came bursting in, 'Mr Ross, guess what arrived in the mail'. I looked up exasperated and, seeing the look on my face, he hurriedly explained. 'Mr Ross, it's stockings! Silk stockings! A whole gross of them!' We ran back to the office and there were, indeed, a whole gross of stockings.

'Just what we need to make this sale a success,' I chortled. 'Now, where's that ad I was making up?' As he watched over my shoulder, Dick laughed and said, 'That should do it all right.' In large printed letters, I added 'One Free Pair of Silk Stockings to the First 100 Customers'.

'Now, let's keep our fingers crossed.'

The morning of the sale, we had to fight our way through the crowds of people waiting to get in. The sale was an unqualified success and we got rid of about 90 percent of our old stock.

Towards the end of the day, a smiling tobacco salesman arrived, expecting his usual large order for the winter. I beckoned him over. 'Before we talk orders, there's something I want to show you.' In the warehouse, I pointed out the large overstock of his company's brand of Fine Cut tobacco still on hand from the previous year's shipment. 'You must be a fantastic salesman,' I said. 'There's enough tobacco there for a regiment.'

He looked at the large supply, tapped his pencil on his order pad and suggested, 'I don't think you'll need any Fine Cut but we can fill out the order with other brands.'

'And what do you propose that we do with this stuff? It's more than a year old and we certainly can't sell it at the going price.' The salesman looked discomfited but wasn't willing or able to come up with an idea. 'I suggest that you give me full credit for the entire stock and you can take it with you if you like. Otherwise I'm going to pile it up front at the cash desk and clear it out at five cents a package.'

'You can't do that,' shouted the salesman, all signs of geniality gone from his demeanour. 'It's against company policy.'

'It might be against your company's policy but it's not against mine. You talked the manager into buying this lot last winter. We bought and paid for it but it's not selling so I have to clear it out. I don't think your company would like the adverse publicity very much.' I let him think about it for a minute. 'I suggest you give me a credit note for the whole works.'

Saying no more, he reluctantly wrote out a credit memo. 'But now you can't put it on sale. Can you arrange for it to be taken out to the dump and destroyed?' I happily agreed.

Having smoothed things at the store, I turned my attention to the staff house which housed the single staff. Each member had his own bedroom, and shared a large well-furnished living room and a small kitchen which wasn't used much, as they regularly ate their meals at one of the restaurants in town. The house had become a local hangout for all the young fellows around Yellowknife and there were constant drinking parties and poker games. Non-employees had developed the habit of walking in and out of the staff house whether there was staff present or not. The Mounties had mentioned this fact to me and said that they were getting worried about the goings-on.

One morning, I called all the boys into the office and read them the riot act. 'I don't mind the occasional party or poker game but the staff house is not a public recreation hall. I realize there isn't much up here in the way of entertainment but these activities have to stop. The RCMP have talked to me already and I'm sure none of you want Winnipeg office to hear about it.' I looked at each of them in turn as they fidgeted in front of my desk. 'If anyone doesn't like it, speak up. I'll arrange to transfer you to another post immediately.' When no replies were forthcoming, I delegated Des Pitts to be in charge of the staff house and responsible for their behaviour. 'You're all grown men, and I'm not your headmaster so I won't treat you like schoolboys. Your careers in the Company are ahead of you. Don't jeopardize them'. We had no further trouble from then on.

Sandy Scott returned from his holidays at the end of August and I went back to Winnipeg, and reported to Mr Chesshire. He seemed pleased by the results of my tenure and thanked me for my efforts. 'And by the way, Ross, congratulations on the birth of your son. I noticed you used 'Mackay' as his middle name. Family name, is it?'

'My mother's maiden name was Mackay and we hope that when Ian has a son, he'll carry on the tradition,' I explained.

There was no mention of my argument with Mr Harford.

I had been asked to put in a report on Dick Garnett. All in all, it was a good report and stated that once he had matured a bit, he would develop into a good post manager. He had a flair for dealing with people and a sincere interest in his customers. In due course, he was manager of several of the Company's major line stores.

But I also put in a second report. I suggested that Des Pitts had great future potential and should be watched carefully. As the years passed, it gave me great satisfaction to watch his progress from store manager to district manager and ultimately, to General Manager of the Fur Trade Department.

About a week later, Mr Harford called me into his office. Without any preamble, he said, 'Ross, I've decided that you are not suitable district manager material. You are to leave as soon as possible to take charge of Nakina.'

I could see that he was watching me closely to see what effect this announcement would have but I was determined not to give him any satisfaction. 'Fine, Mr Harford, just give me a few days to pack and I'll be on my way.' He looked disappointed at my lack of reaction but perked up when I asked, 'Would you mind telling me just why you've decided I'm not suitable material to be a district manager?'

Almost cheerfully, he replied, 'Yes, I'll tell you. Ross, you can't write a proper letter.'

To say that I was astonished was putting it mildly. I started to laugh. 'Can't write a proper letter? What the hell do you mean? I didn't write any letters at all, other than to acknowledge any incoming mail in Mr Scurfield's absence.'

Mr Harford started to interrupt, but I went on...'If you told me
once, you told me twenty times that I had no authority and I was
not to issue any instructions or make any decisions while I was
working with Tom Scurfield.' I had a full head of steam up now
and my active dislike of the man could no longer be tempered with
caution. 'For your information, I've seen your letters and they
leave much to be desired. Quite frankly, Mr Harford, your excuse
is for the birds!' And, as I'd done so many times before, I stamped
out of his office.

Bea was upset about the move and especially about my
treatment at the hands of Mr Harford. The three girls had just
started school and we both worried about how they would react to
the change. But we packed up and were on our way back to
Ontario.

Nakina is a divisional point on the main Canadian National
Railroad, situated almost due north of Fort William, now Thunder
Bay. Everyone in town ate, slept and talked railroading. The
Hudson's Bay Company had bought out the Nakina Fur and Trading
Company in 1944 as part of its expansion program. The store was
a brick building on the main street directly across from the railway
station and roundhouse. It was an old-fashioned building with the
living quarters above the store and a warehouse behind; it wasn't
in good shape either. Plans were already approved to build a new
manager's house the following summer.

Matt Cook, another of the boys who came out from the Old
Country with me in 1930, was the departing manager. After the
change of management inventory, I got back into a different store
routine. There was almost no Indian trade and very little fur buying
other than the odd Indian who came in once a week on the local
train from Cavell, where our former post had been closed down.
The staff consisted of three local girls and one male clerk who was
soon replaced by Wendell Peterson with whom I had worked at
Waterways.

We settled in and the children started in at the local school but
we soon found that none of us liked Nakina. It was impossible to
keep the store or the living quarters clean and we could not open

The Nakina store: in 1946 an old-fashioned building with living quarters above the store and a warehouse behind. c. 1947

the upstairs living-room windows because smoke and soot from trains shunting in the yards were almost continuous. We did make several friends: Dr McKillop, the local doctor who was also in charge of the railroad hospital; Reverend Neville Clarke, resident Anglican Minister who later became Suffragan Bishop of Moosonee; and a young divinity student who was in charge of the local United Church.

In February, 1947, I received a wire from Mr Chesshire to come into Winnipeg immediately. No reason was given but I set out as ordered, leaving the store in the charge of Wendell Peterson.

I was hardly inside the door of his office before Mr Chesshire roared, 'Ross, what's all this nonsense about your not wanting to be a district manager?' I could see the fine hand of Mr Harford in this. 'We need a district manager to take over Northern Ontario District as soon as possible. Do you want it or not? You have to make up your mind right now.' I started to reply but he cut me off. 'If you accept, you'll be sent to the Fur Training School in Montreal which starts on March 1st. Now, what do you say?'

There was no hesitation in my reply. 'Yes sir, I'll be happy to go to Montreal.'

Having settled the matter, Mr Chesshire invited me to sit down and explained the circumstances. C.H.J.'Jim' Winter had been manager of Northern Ontario for some time and was much respected by his staff. Unfortunately his wife was very ill and her doctor had recommended a warmer climate. Reluctantly, Jim handed in his resignation.

Back in Nakina, I gleefully told Bea what had transpired and we carted out the old steamer trunk again.

'Montreal...it sounds wonderful even if it's only for three months,' said Bea. 'Just imagine, twelve weeks of French cooking, plays, taking walks in Old Montreal. It'll be just like a European vacation except that the Company will be paying the fare. Oh, I can't wait.' She started emptying dresser drawers on the bed. 'What did Mr Harford have to say about all this? I'll bet he wasn't too pleased.'

'You know, Bea, it's a funny thing. I know he was in the office somewhere because I asked. But I walked all over the place and I never saw him once.'

Jack Rogers arrived to take over from me and the transfer of business was soon completed. Poor Jack! He was another trainee who had fallen afoul of Mr Harford.

The Company's Fur Training School was operated by the Montreal Fur Sales Department located at 100 McGill Street. The course was usually of three months' duration with six or eight trainees attending. To accommodate them, the Company had several apartment suites and a house at Crawford Park which we were lucky enough to get. It was located in an English-speaking community on the western outskirts of Montreal, right alongside the St. Lawrence River. When we arrived by taxi, we were greeted by Jack Keats, one of the school instructors who lived right next door with his family.

Across the street was a Protestant school and we quickly enrolled the girls. This was the fourth school for Barbara and Jennifer and the third for Dorothy in four different provinces over a period of two years. In one province, they printed. The next,

their lessons had to be written. Bea's teaching background came
to the fore and she helped the girls through their different
adjustment periods.

A small general store wasn't too far away where, in addition
to groceries, we were able to purchase wine and beer. A most
civilized idea, I thought. Once a week, we took the streetcar at the
end of our street to do our weekly shopping at Steinberg's
supermarket in Verdun. Our purchases were then delivered to the
house.

We loved Montreal. As soon as spring came, we went on long
walks with the children -- with me pushing Ian in his pram -- along
the banks of the river where there were numerous rapids and
stretches of swift water. Bea had relatives in the city who visited
frequently and took us on sightseeing tours around the countryside.
We hired a caleche and leisurely admired the old buildings, quaint
streets and magnificent churches in Old Montreal. Bea was in her
glory.

On the first of March, I left with Jack Keats for the office. It
was easy going into the city as the streetcar started its journey at
the end of our street. Coming back at night, however, was an
entirely different experience. By the time the streetcar got to 100
McGill Street, it was jammed to the doors and we were lucky if we
could jump on and grab the handrails. Chivalry and good manners
went out the window as passengers tried to board the streetcar. It
was every man for himself.

Mr Maurice Jones was in charge of the training school. In
addition to Jack, Mr Jones had two other assistant instructors, Jim
Thom and Ron McIsaac, both former arctic post managers. There
were six of us taking the course: Norm Handford from the Raw Fur
Department; F.R. Donovan, a post manager from the Western
Arctic; Jesse Coffey, not long back from being with the Royal Air
Force 'Pathfinder' squadron, whose job it was to fly ahead of the
night-bombing raids to pin-point and illuminate targets with
incendiary bombs; Jack Morrison; Fred Brewster, and myself.
Morrison and Brewster were both new employees who had been
hired by Mr Harford to prove that he could hire men and train them
in six months to be competent post managers. Jock Holliday, a post

HBCA Photograph Collection 1987/363-F-210

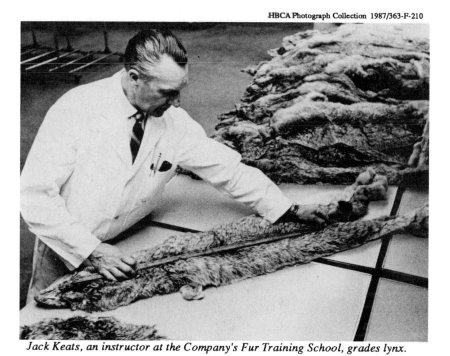

Jack Keats, an instructor at the Company's Fur Training School, grades lynx.

manager of long standing, joined us a week or two later.

If any of us had entertained the idea that the course was a snap, that thought was immediately dispelled. After a short welcoming speech, Mr Jones took us into the grading room -- a long room with tables arranged along the walls in front of large windows. 'This is where you will work,' he said, 'and I do mean work. By the time you are finished this three-month course, you should be able to grade any type of fur from any location in Canada.'

As he spoke, he handed us each a long white coat. 'Wear them at all times, otherwise your clothes will be full of fur grease. And believe me, no amount of dry cleaning will get rid of it. Now, grab an armful of those foxes in the corner and get to work.' We meekly did as we were told and got at it. When we had finished grading our armful of foxes into piles, the instructors thoroughly inspected each pelt. I had been buying fur for more than fifteen years and I thought I was pretty good at it but I soon found out differently. When we finished re-grading them, we grabbed another pile. And

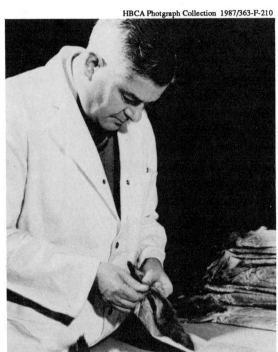

*Maurice Jones, in charge of the Company's
FurTraining School in Montreal, grades mink. c.1949*

so it went on.

Bales and bags of fur arrived daily from posts all over the country which now shipped all their fur to Montreal. Here they were graded and either put up for auction locally or shipped to our auction sales in London, England or New York...depending on the better price.

We were thrown right into the thick of it. Grab a bale and grade it. Then the instructor checked it to see how close we came to his grading and pointed out where we had gone wrong. The prices we arrived at were compared to the price which the post manager had actually paid to the trapper, and which was listed on an invoice enclosed with each bale. Where there was any appreciable difference, an advice was sent to District Office concerned that the manager of the post appeared to be paying too little or, horror of horrors, too much!

Whenever there was a lull in the incoming fur bales, we went back to those foxes in the corner. Those damn foxes --we graded them and graded them until we almost knew each one by sight. They were the holdovers from the 1945-46 buying season when the bottom had dropped out of the fox market. Originally bought at $10 a skin, they were now valued, if one could sell them at all, at around $2.50.

Once the winter fur season closed, we were deluged with muskrat and beaver. Day after day, we measured and graded beaver and sized muskrats until our hands were soft with the animals' grease. I couldn't help but notice that fellow passengers on the streetcar gave me a wide berth. I didn't understand it and when I mentioned it to Bea, she laughed. 'Honey, you stink! No wonder people get out of your way.' I had become so used to the odour that I no longer noticed it.

After a while, we could grade muskrats, tossing them into the various size and grade compartments like playing cards.

All the instructors, including Mr Jones, who sometimes took a turn with us, were first rate but I preferred Jack Keats. Jim Thom and Ron McIsaac could be swayed in their grading, depending on whether they knew the post manager who had shipped in the furs, but Jack Keats had one line and one line only. The pelt either fitted into this grade or it didn't and there was no argument.

I had only one hang-up -- singe. Singe happens to otter and mink when they lie in the warm spring sun. The guard hairs are actually singed by the heat of the sun and hook over, something like a fishhook does. Otter singe I could see immediately, but singe in mink -- especially the fine, dark, eastern mink, I simply could not see. Jack Keats stayed with me, kept showing me and explaining what to look for and how to spot it. Then one day, there it was. I could see it plainly. I wondered how I could have been so stupid as to have missed it for such a long time.

The work was long, smelly and tedious but by the end of the course, I could pick up any skin, from a mink to a lynx, and tell not only its grade but what area of Canada it came from. In some cases, I could even recognize what post sent it in by the particular way the Indians had stretched the skin.

But our time in Montreal was not all work. There were the
Montreal Canadiens. Since coming to Canada in 1930, I had
listened to Foster Hewitt and 'Hockey Night in Canada' on the radio
and had been a Toronto Maple Leaf fan, but I had never actually
seen a hockey game. Once I saw the Canadiens play, I became an
avid Montreal supporter. Of course, we couldn't afford to buy
tickets to see every home game even though I had received a salary
increase of $50.00 a month and on arrival in Montreal was making
a wage of $275.00.

Instead we struggled for standing-room-only tickets. They
were put on sale at a side door half an hour before the game started
and, on game nights, all of us would rush from work to take our
places as near the front of the queue as possible. Having purchased
the coveted ticket, we rushed upstairs and tried to get a front
position on the balcony where you could lean against the railing to
watch the game. Usually we managed to get good viewing
positions. While we waited in the queue, we took turns going to a
nearby cafe to eat while the others held our places until we returned.

Jack Keats and his son both had season tickets and if one of
them couldn't attend, he sold his ticket to me. I had a third means
of seeing the Canadiens play hockey. Next door to Jack lived the
foreman plumber of the Montreal Forum and on very special
occasions, he would smuggle me in as one of his crew. I have
watched hockey games from many strange places in the Forum.

At the end of May our course was completed and Bea and I
reluctantly returned to Winnipeg with the kids and moved back into
the Company's experimental house on Lyndale Drive. During our
stay in Nakina and Montreal, the house had been occupied by
P.A.C. 'Pete' Nichols, who went on to become Divisional Manager
of the Arctic.

When I reported to Mr Chesshire, I found that the Northern Ontario job was off. Jim Winter and his wife had returned from California and he had resumed his old position as district manager. Instead I was appointed to work in Central Line District with Tom Scurfield but this time not as a trainee, but as acting section manager. I don't know where the term 'section' came from but someone in authority somewhere had decided to make a change. Historic names like Saskatchewan District, Manitoba District and Keewatin District disappeared and instead were given numerals so that now you had Section 1, Section 2 and so on. Most of us in the department thought it gave a connotation of a section man working on the railroad so the change wasn't too popular. In any event, the term 'section' didn't last too long and a few years later, all the districts reverted to their former titles. So I shall continue to use the term 'district' throughout.

It was a pleasure to be back working with Tom again, especially as I now had an office of my own. As always, Tom was forthright. 'Hugh, I have a very large district and right now, I'm up to my ears in the western part, especially in the Red Lake area. You knew, of course, that we have opened stores at Cochenour-Willans, Mackenzie Island and Madsen. The gold mines are really flourishing there.' He pointed out the new store locations on a large map pinned up on the wall. 'I'm going to let you look after the posts at the eastern end of the district -- Ombabika, Nakina, Long Lac, Hornepayne, Peterbell and Foleyet. Treat these posts as if they were your own district and if you run into any difficulty, don't be afraid to ask my advice. And for God's sake, don't make any stupid mistakes or you'll hear about it from me.'

It felt good to be back in harness again and out on inspection trips. My first visit to Ombabika was eventful. Jock Mathieson, the manager, was an old-timer who had spent most of his years at remote posts such as Winisk and Severn. It became obvious that he wasn't capable of handling a line store with predominately white trade, especially since a lumber camp had started up about half a mile east of the post. When I arrived, Jock was in great pain from a bad tooth so I suggested that he go into Nakina and see the dentist and I would look after the post while he was gone. The following evening, Mrs Mathieson came into the store after the close of business to tell me that supper was ready. As a matter of course, I put the books and cash into the safe, closed the door and turned the combination lock.

'Oh, my goodness,' wailed Mrs Mathieson, 'you shouldn't have done that. The combination doesn't work. Jock hasn't locked the safe all the time he's been here.' While the combinations for safes at all the posts were relatively the same, it took me almost four hours trying various combinations and a lot of cussing before I finally got the safe opened, reset the combination and oiled the mechanism. On Jock's return, we took an inspection inventory and I found that he was carrying a couple of dozen bottles of 'Florida Water' which contained a certain amount of alcohol and was carried with other medicinal stock. 'What the devil are you carrying this stuff for, Jock?'

'Oh, well...you know...sometimes people ask for it,' he replied in his slow manner.

'That's nonsense. You have Indians trading here and you know very well that Florida Water is on the proscribed list. You can't have this stuff in stock. It's against the Indian Act. We better take the whole lot out and get rid of it right away.' So we took it out behind the post and smashed the bottles on the rocks. There were tears in Jock's eyes. So many cocktails going to waste!

At Nakina, Jack Rogers was much upset because the promised new house had not been built. On account of material shortages following the war, all supplies intended for Nakina had been diverted to building a house at Foleyet. 'I'm sorry Jack, but there's really nothing I can do about it. I know how bad your quarters are. Don't forget I lived in them for a while. But materials are in very short supply and we didn't have a house of any kind at Foleyet. I guess you'll just have to wait your turn.' I could sympathize with him; I well remembered the soot that penetrated every nook and cranny of the place.

At Long Lac, a post originally established in 1814, Mr S.A. 'Sid' Taylor -- an English gentleman of the old school -- was in charge. Always immaculately clad in tweed Norfolk jacket, grey

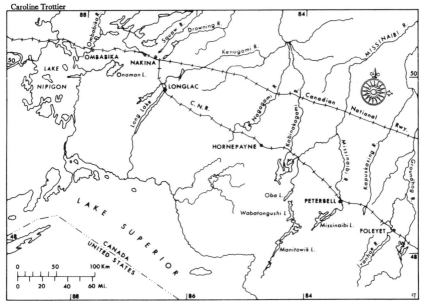

Line posts, eastern end of the Ontario District

flannels and white collar and tie, Sid had been in Long Lac for many years after having served the Company at Lac Seul and White Dog. His wife was one of the Savoyard family of half-breeds from White Dog and I knew her brothers well during the time I was apprenticed at Minaki. Sid Taylor could speak the Ojibway language fluently and was the only post manager I ever met who could read and write in Ojibway syllabics.

We purchased a lot of fur at Long Lac from the natives who lived around the lake but, with a lumber mill to the east and a growing town on the west on the highway from Fort William to Hearst, it looked as if we would have to consider a change of location in the near future. Mr Taylor loved his store which he kept spotlessly clean and, since he was near to retirement, wasn't too keen about changing locations.

Our new store at Hornepayne was going great guns under the capable management of R.S. 'Bob' Cook who went on to be manager of Central Division. Hornepayne was one of the first posts to be equipped with a refrigerated display counter from which we sold an assortment of delicatessen meats and precuts of fresh meat ordered from the packing houses. The time for a fully equipped butcher department with a qualified butcher in charge had not yet arrived.

My next stop, Peterbell, was a small post catering to the needs of a community of Indians and half-breeds working for a local logging company run by the Driftwood Lands and Timber Company. Harry Borbridge, the manager, was without any assistant and working his fool head off to keep his post turning a profit. I took a quick inspection inventory and left for Foleyet.

Hugh Fraser, my assistant at Waterways, was now married and in charge of the post, assisted by a young clerk, Jim Boatman, and two local girls. The old store which Tom Scurfield and I had purchased a year before had been demolished and a fine new store and warehouse were erected on the double corner lot.

Back in Winnipeg, I made my report to Tom. On my recommendation, Jock Mathieson was transferred from Ombabika to Beauval, a small post in northern Saskatchewan which was more within his capabilities. Mac Watson took over from him. Plans were made to move the store building nearer to the sawmill site; the name was changed from Ombabika to Auden. I made several trips in the ensuing months doing the normal routine district manager's chores of inspection inventories and stockbook checks.

On one trip, I arrived at Hornepayne the day after the store had been broken into. The thieves had trundled the safe out of the office and pushed it down the stairs into the basement where it landed upside down. They tried to cut through the bottom of it with axes but, fortunately for us, had been unsuccessful and left empty-handed. Although the attempted theft was immediately reported to the local police, the thieves were never caught. That was the only instance where I was personally involved in a robbery.

I got into a good-natured argument at Foleyet with Hugh Fraser over a marten pelt. I had never purchased a marten skin but I had good grounding at the Fur Training School and when Hugh asked me to value it, I said it was what we called a 'canary', a very light colour with a yellowish tinge on its breast and not worth much. He didn't agree with my evaluation and we spent some time discussing the subject. 'There's only one way to settle the question,' I said.

'Let's ship it in to the Fur School in Montreal by itself and ask for their evaluation.' When I got back to District Office later, I was much relieved to learn that my pronouncement had been correct.

On another inspection trip, I was accompanied by a young Englishman who had just arrived from Britain and was working as an assistant controller in District Office. The trip was designed as an introduction to the workings of our trading stores. We got along well and he asked many intelligent questions. His name was Peter Wood. He later became Treasurer of the Hudson's Bay Company.

A large mining corporation began an open-pit gold mining operation at Snow Lake in northern Manitoba and they asked the Company to provide a store for them as soon as possible, as they were already building homes for their staff. Rupertsland Trading Company designed a pre-fab store which was built in sections in Winnipeg and shipped to Snow Lake where it was quickly assembled. I was given the job of readying the store for opening along with E.R. Lemieux, the store manager, and Bill Kohlmeier who was a grocery display expert. While Mr Lemieux and I filled the dry goods and hardware sections, Bill went ahead with the groceteria. It was a pleasure to watch him at work. He had a designated position for every section -- fruits, vegetables or canned goods and the shelves were filled up quickly. It was my first experience with a store opening and proved to be a great success.

In early January, 1948, I was asked to go to Churchill, Manitoba. Their semi-annual inventory, taken on November 30th, had shown an alarming stock shortage and I had to find out what was wrong. I flew in from Winnipeg and, as a normal procedure, took another inventory immediately. Something was indeed wrong and it meant checking all merchandise invoices since the start of the fiscal year, June 1st.

I went through all the depot invoices covering merchandise shipped from our Winnipeg or Montreal depots first but couldn't find anything amiss. The bulk of the invoices were 'direct order' which the depots rewrote and forwarded to the manufacturers for shipment direct to the post. There were masses of these invoices. I found nothing wrong in extensions or additions so, as a last resort,

I sorted the direct invoices by suppliers and then I found the errors. Somehow many of them had been sent to both our Montreal and Winnipeg depots for payment and had been paid for by each depot. The errors should have been caught by the post's incoming merchandise procedure but obviously they had not. When everything was sorted out and the duplicate payments added up, the total came to about $7,000 -- almost exactly the amount of the shortage shown up by the inventories. I heaved a sigh of relief, packed up the paperwork carefully and took it back to Winnipeg.

I presented my evidence to Ed Leslie, the depot accountant and asked for a credit note but Ed, being another canny Scot, wasn't about to issue a credit note for $7,000 without first checking the whole thing carefully. While we argued about it, in came Cece Stewart, the depot manager and a former post manager, who wanted to know what all the shouting was about. When I explained, he looked at Ed and said, 'Make out a credit note. Whatever fault there is, it's somewhere in our depot system and we'll have to sort it out before it happens again.' Ed looked unhappy and started to argue his case but Cece insisted, 'Ed, you've been a post manager. You know that your stocks must be in balance. This mess isn't Churchill's fault, it's ours. Make out the credit note.'

Everytime I got a call to go Mr Chesshire's office, I wondered where my next port of call would be and in late April, when the summons came, I was off again. 'Ross, I want you to take charge of Saskatchewan District at once. Bill Cobb, the district manager, is required in Edmonton on May 1st and we have no time to lose. Break-up will be starting in the North soon now and you'll just have time for a short introductory trip around your new district with him.' He shook my hand and wished me good luck and I hurried out to make my travel arrangements.

I left with Mr Cobb the following day by train to Prince Albert and from there chartered a small plane from Saskatchewan Government Airways and made the round trip of the thirteen posts comprising my new district. It was a whirlwind trip that took us exactly five days. We only spent a few hours at each post, took a quick walk around the buildings, met the post manager and we were off. By the time the trip was over, my head was in a spin. If someone had asked, I couldn't have told them the location of any of my future charges. I spent most of my time in the air frantically writing notes of names of managers, their wives, and the other details about the staff.

On May 1st, 1948, I signed a new contract as Acting Manager of Saskatchewan District at $325 per month. As always, Mr Chesshire's advice was brief and to the point. 'I want 30 percent gross profit on sales from your district. How you get it is your business. If you have to drop at one post, you must pick it up at another...but at the end of the year, I've got to have 30 percent gross profit.' He looked at me kindly and said, 'You will make mistakes...everybody does but if you are 70 percent correct in your decisions, you'll be doing a good job. The other 30 percent I will certainly tell you about, but wherever I can, I'll back up your decisions. If you run into any serious difficulty, all you have to do is telephone me.' Nothing could have been fairer than that. I quickly signed my new contract and walked out his office, treading on air. I was now a District Manager.

Mr Chesshire was as good as his word. On the few occasions that I had to phone him about a problem, he would generally ask me first what my own solution was and then say, 'All right, let's try it your way.'

Part III

Manager, Saskatchewan District

For the entire month of May, I did nothing but read up on all the files of the district as far back as necessary to get a grip on each subject. I took copious notes, from the names of the firms who handled our freight and when, through conditions of buildings, data on staff, miscellaneous items which had to be checked at the posts regularly each year: from fire equipment, home furnishings and building painting programs to the issue of winter trapping debts.

I went to Birt's Saddlery in Winnipeg and purchased a large leather, accordian-looking carrying bag with four partitions, and carefully packed the tools of my new trade. I carried it with me on every inspection trip. In time, it became known as 'Ross's Travelling District Office'. Although I was kidded unmercifully about it, the bag stood me in good stead over the years. Somewhere in that bag was the answer to every question or problem that arose at a post. It contained the Company's standing rules and regulations, post accounting manual, the latest annual and semi-annual rating reports on post managers and assistant staff, the latest monthly trading results for each post, each post's dwelling standard equipment list, inspection notebook, and various other odds and ends. One important item was a copy of the Company's fur trade code used for telegraphing any change of fur prices and for advising district office of monthly post results.

Another item included was *Slater's codebook*. *Slater's* was like a dictionary -- words listed in alphabetical order -- with an assigned number for each. To send a message, you selected your word with its number, added a prearranged three-digit number and looked up the resulting figure. To decode, the process was reversed. There were two different key numbers; one for messages between district office and the posts and vice-versa; and the other for messages between district office and district managers. With this, I could send any confidential message to district office from any post without the post manager being able to decode it.

From the depot, I ordered two sleeping bags -- a 'Woods Four-star' for winter and a 'Woods Sierra', a lighter bag, for summer use. These were only the beginnings of my shopping list.

Next came a pair of padded windpants; heavy, sheep-lined, air-force-style flying boots; a pair of native moosehide moccasins; thick, wool duffle oversocks and three pairs of heavy wool socks which I stuffed into the bottom of the winter sleeping bag; and a quilted nylon parka complete with fur-lined hood and long enough in the skirt to reach my knees. These completed my winter wardrobe. I wore normal city clothes on my journeys, with a light raincoat in summer and added the windpants, parka and heavy wool gloves in the winter. Since the bulk of my travelling was by air, the sleeping bags were most essential as there was always the danger of a forced landing in the bush. If this happened in winter, it would be impossible to walk for any distance with heavy air-force flying boots; hence the moccasins, duffles and socks.

I set out on a series of inspections designed to cover all the posts in my district in turn. I'm afraid my family saw very little of me until freeze-up. I was away for three weeks at a time and then home for a few days -- just long enough to renew my acquaintance with my kids and have my laundry done. Bea had been a Company wife for some years now and if she wished things were different, she never let on to me.

Usually I left Winnipeg by train in the evening, arrived at Prince Albert by noon the following day where I had made charter arrangements for a Saskatchewan Government Airways Stinson 108 A. The Stinson was a grand little aircraft seating three plus the pilot. It could do 120 miles per hour on skis and 100 miles an hour on pontoons. The charter rate was $60.00 an hour with a minimum guarantee of two flying hours per day.

My first swing was up the east side of the province. Taking off from the river in Prince Albert, we headed directly to Southend Post on Reindeer Lake -- a narrow body of water almost 150 miles in length, running north and south on the border of Saskatchewan and Manitoba. The lake was dotted with islands, several of which had commercial fishing lodges catering to American tourists. There were also a few white commercial fishermen operating mainly in the winter. They shipped their fish by winter road from Co-op Point, halfway up the east side of South Reindeer Lake, to Lynn Lake and thence south by railroad.

Reindeer Lake is drained by the Reindeer River which flows south to join the Churchill River. A few miles below the point where the river flowed from the lake, a dam controlled the flow of water south into the Churchill and then into Island Falls where a large hydro plant serviced Flin Flon. Building the dam meant raising the level of Reindeer Lake a few feet and, from the air, you could spot the damage that had been done to the shoreline.

The Hudson's Bay Company had been in the area since 1795-96 when Fairford House was built on the Reindeer River, and Bedford House about two-thirds the way up the west shore of Reindeer Lake. In 1789-99, the Company located Clapham House on the site of the present post where the river exits from the lake. The post was abandoned and re-opened several times under various names -- Fort Deer Lake, Reindeer Lake, Fort Caribou, until finally it closed down in 1930. When the Company took over Revillon Frères -- a rival trading company -- in 1936, their post at South Reindeer Lake was one of the posts taken over. Though a small operation, it was still making a profit in 1948. Bedford House was moved in 1861 to its present location, a sandy promontory at the northeast end of the lake not far from the mouth of the Cochrane River, and given a new name -- Brochet.

Beside our post, there was a Roman Catholic Mission and a free trader named Steve Russick and we were all surrounded by the Indian reservation.

W.A. 'Bill' Smith, manager of Southend lived there with his wife and one small daughter. His oldest daughter was attending school at St Mary's Academy in Winnipeg. Bill was a shrewd Scot from Aberdeenshire, a good trader and a keen radio operator. He had a 'good fist' on the key and could transmit and receive radio messages quickly. A rather shy man, he was most excitable and I had to watch what I said to him in case he took umbrage and flew off the handle. Fortunately, his wife was the calm, motherly type and kept him on an even keel most of the time.

Bill's daughter Audrey was the reason for the first and only time I acted, quite unwittingly, as Cupid.

The year after she finished school at St Mary's Academy, I dropped in to Southend on a routine visit. Poor Audrey. After spending a year cooped up with only her parents and a younger sister to talk to, she was bored to her boots and completely miserable. She missed the companionship at school and the city amenities and wanted to go 'out' to find work. Only her dad couldn't see her living on her own in town and would not hear of it. I sympathized with Bill up to a point and said, 'Look Bill, I think Audrey should have a holiday. I'm sure Mrs Garbutt at Brochet would be delighted to have her visit. She would enjoy the company.' And Bill reluctantly agreed to try it.

When I got to Brochet, I talked to Bill and Renee Garbutt and they agreed to the plan. After their next radio schedule, Mrs Garbutt issued the invitation and Bill Smith accepted. So, as I was staying at Brochet for a few days and paying for my charter aircraft anyway, I had the pilot make the return trip to fetch Audrey.

To make a long story short, Audrey met a fine young man at Brochet, a soldier attached to the Royal Canadian Corps of Signals weather station. The Smiths were transferred in a year or so to another district, but in due course I received a notice of Audrey's wedding to the young man, a thank-you note and an charming water-colour painted by Audrey 'in appreciation'. It still hangs on my living room wall to remind me of my playing Cupid.

From Southend we flew north to Brochet, where we were met by manager W.R. 'Bill' Garbutt and his wife Renee, both from England. Bill had started his career with the Company down the Mackenzie River and eventually was transferred to Brochet. He was an inland trader and had no desire to be sent anywhere near the 'bright lights' as he described it. Six feet tall, with greying hair, he was a dapper gentleman who looked as if he had his suits tailor-made in Bond Street.

Renee Garbutt was perfectly happy to be anywhere Bill was posted. She was an immaculate housekeeper and a first-class cook and, in addition, she also looked after the regular daily radio schedules. When she first started, she was a bit tentative on the key but Bill Smith from Southend contacted her and coached her along on unofficial schedules until she was most proficient. Her great love was her garden. She and Bill built it from nothing using silt

Mrs Renee Garbutt on the radio at Brochet, c.1954.

brought in from the riverbed several miles away. They had a fine lawn in front with flower borders and a well-stocked vegetable garden at the rear.

Assisting Bill in the store were Frank Henderson, a Scot from Edinburgh and Henry Linklater, a Cree half-breed originally from Pelican Narrows. Bill didn't speak the native tongue so Henry was official interpreter. Frank Henderson came to the Bay from Revillon Frères in 1936 and had been at Brochet ever since. He retired in 1950 and returned to Scotland. Although he had only one leg, he managed to get along very well on his crutches. In the wintertime, he wore one snowshoe and attached a miniature snowshoe to the foot of each crutch and scrambled on, often leaving his companions behind.

Bill had a puckish sense of humour as I soon found out. Sitting in his office one afternoon, he quietly asked, 'Mr Ross, do you remember a letter you sent out about a month ago? It was about the fall hunting debts.' When I acknowledged that I did, he went on. 'And you said that none were to be issued until you came in early September to authorize them?' I nodded in agreement. 'Well, I'm afraid that won't work here,' he announced.

'I don't understand, Bill. Why won't it work here?'

'Well, you see, it's like this. Most of the native hunters are Chipewyan and they don't hang around the settlement. They come in for treaty and leave again right away. Some of them don't even come in for Christmas. These men are good hunters and they stay out on the traplines all winter, returning only at Easter.' He glanced at me, looking very serious and explained, 'They follow the caribou herds, you know, and one or two families have already left for the trapping grounds.'

'I see. What did you do about their debt?' I asked.

'Well,' he replied, poker faced, 'I had no authorization from district office...'

'Oh, good God, Bill,' I interrupted. 'Don't tell me you let them go without giving them any trapping debt?'

There was a moment's silence, then he started to grin, 'No. I didn't do that. I just gave them the same amount as I gave them last year.' He handed me a list. 'Here's my proposed list of debts for the fall.'

'Okay Bill, you win,' I said as I signed my approval. 'Next year, I'll know better and get in touch with you much earlier.' It was a well learned lesson. I couldn't be too quick to take things for granted. Every post had its own individual character and I had to learn them all. Up until now, I had been accustomed to natives hanging around the post until late September or early October before going out for the winter, which left plenty of time to discuss trapping debts with the hunters.

While looking through Bill's stock in the warehouse, I came upon a section of dry goods and yard goods neatly piled up but with no cost-landed mark on them. 'What's the story here, Bill?' I asked.

'Mr Ross, look at them. The natives won't buy these yard goods. They're okay for white trade but they aren't colourful enough for the Indians.' We went through all the goods, which were all in light pastel shades. 'They must have been bought by some of the new-fangled merchandise boys in Head Office. They haven't a clue what sort of things native people prefer,' he added, sarcastically.

He was right. The material was good quality but quality didn't count as much as colour. 'Have you tried putting them on sale?'

'I tried, but the Indians won't look at them at any price.'

I thought about the problem for a minute. 'Tell you what Bill. We can't leave the goods to lie here and rot. Let's make out a detailed list and I'll try to peddle it to other posts in the district when I receive their winter requisitions. Mind you, I can't guarantee their full value but that shouldn't matter too much. You've written them off anyway.' It took me about two years to disperse the dry goods throughout the district.

Most of the Indians were Chipewyan with a small smattering of Cree. They were great hunters and spent most of their time north in the Barren Lands. I was fortunate enough to meet Horace McCallum who came in for his debt prior to leaving the post. Horace was acknowledged as the best trapper in the area and he spent a lot of time apprenticing young men to become proficient in his art. Each winter he took half a dozen young men, trained them in the finer points of hunting and trapping and paid them a regular wage. Of course, all the fur caught belonged to Horace. According to the post records, his catch each winter was at least five hundred mink.

At Horace's request, Bill took me into the hardware warehouse and showed me a beautiful washing machine operated by a gasoline motor -- still in its case. Bill put a little gas into the tank and started it up and Horace proudly gave me a demonstration. 'This is mine,' he declared, rubbing a cloth along the top until I thought the paint would come off. Later that evening Bill told me the story. Horace had been in funds the previous winter and had ordered the machine. It stayed in the warehouse, in its crate and was only operated when Horace brought a number of his admiring friends over to show them the fine machine that he owned. And there the washing machine stayed for several years before Horace decided that everyone for miles around had seen his magnificent purchase and he finally took it home.

He was a grand character, Horace was. His annual great treat for his family and relatives was to charter a Norseman from Lamb Airways in The Pas and fly them all out to the Trappers Festival. One year, Mr Lamb chided Horace. 'Why don't you load up this plane with flour, tea and lard? There's lots of room. The plane can handle it.'

Horace looked at him disdainfully. 'When I want grub or anything else, I go to the Hudson's Bay man at Brochet. He gives me everything I ask for.'

Besides the Hudson's Bay post, Brochet settlement consisted of a Roman Catholic mission, a free trader whom I knew only by the name of 'Old Man Shieff', a Royal Canadian Corps of Signals wireless station, and a local game warden. The RCCS station was staffed by an NCO and three signallers and was responsible for taking and sending out weather data. Jim Cumines, the game warden, was employed by the Saskatchewan Department of Natural Resources but he had the responsibility for the Manitoba side as well.

Bill and Renee Garbutt stayed at Brochet until Bill retired in 1967. They were there for twenty years.

From Brochet, we flew south across the Churchill River to Pelican Narrows. First established to combat the Montreal traders in 1793, it was abandoned in 1799 and then briefly re-opened in 1818-19. The post was permanently established in 1874 at its present site on the north shore of Pelican Lake where the Narrows connected it to Mirond Lake. It was on the old fur trade route running from Cumberland House through Beaver Lake to the old Frog Portage from Wood Lake to the Churchill River.

The manager, Pete Pederson, was baching it and was assisted in the store by a local Indian, Andrew Cussiter. Pete's wife was ill in the Prince Albert Sanatorium. Because he was unable to get out to visit her very often I had great sympathy for him when he said he was looking for another job closer to Prince Albert. He left us the following autumn and went to work as sub-Indian agent at La Ronge. When his wife recovered and was able to leave the sanatorium some years later, Pete quit his job with the Indian Department and bought out a small free trader in the village of La Ronge.

In the fall of 1949, Andy McKinley arrived with his wife Myra and young daughter Pearl from Hay Lakes -- one of our western posts -- to take charge of Pelican Narrows. Yet another Scot, Andy was a good solid native trader and thoroughly conversant in Cree. In fact, he talked the language better than any other man I ever met.

At Pelican Narrows, there was the usual Roman Catholic Mission and an Anglican Church which was only used on occasion by visiting ministers, there being no resident Anglican priest. Shorty Russick, well-known as a dogsled racer in The Pas Derby, ran the opposition store. Shorty's younger brother, Steve, ran the opposition store at Southend. A field officer with the Department of Natural Resources was also stationed here. Later on, the Saskatchewan Government established both a school and a nursing station. I didn't stay long but headed west to Stanley on the Churchill River.

Situated on the eastern shore of Mountain Lake, one of the many extensions of the Churchill River, Stanley was easy to pick out from the air from a long way off. It was dominated by the shining spire of its white Anglican Church -- one of the oldest churches in western Canada. There was no resident minister but regular Sunday services were conducted by the Band Chief, Nehemiah Charles. He was a grand old man who took his twin duties of lay preacher and Band Chief very seriously.

The Stanley Mission Church was erected in 1856 under the direction of the Reverend Robert Hunt and his wife, with the assistance of a Scottish carpenter who taught the Indians how to square logs properly. It is said that the Mission was named for Mrs Hunt's home in England -- Stanley Park. In 1878, the Reverend Samuel Trivett, newly ordained and just married, arrived with his wife, Annie Maria, to take charge of the Mission. The following year in September 1879, Mrs Trivett died in childbirth at the age of 27. Trivett himself conducted the service for his wife and baby daughter. They were buried below the floor of the church at the chancel steps.

The federal and provincial governments jointly took over the Stanley Mission Church a few years ago and declared it an historic site. It is considered the best example of historic architecture west

Roy Simpson

Stanley Mission Church built in 1856. June 1953.

of Winnipeg, but is still available for continued use by the Indians of Stanley Mission with a Cree priest in residence.

The Company post, originally established in 1831, is located across the lake from the church, around which the Indian settlement is built. We were welcomed by R. H. 'Bob' Middleton from Fraserburgh, Scotland and his charming wife Nancy, a daughter of Captain Smellie, a former master of the Company's arctic supply ship *Nascopie*. Bob, another old-time fur trader, could be relied upon to do his job properly. Stanley was, in my opinion, one of the most picturesque of the Hudson's Bay Company's posts. The local natives, all Cree, were great trappers and always paid their debts promptly.

From Stanley, we flew south to our post situated in the settlement of La Ronge. A large lake, La Ronge was noted for its lake trout fishing. As it was connected by road to Prince Albert, approximately 135 miles to the south, it was a newly discovered mecca for American sportsmen. The road was blacktopped as far as the summer resort area of Waskesiu in Prince Albert National

Park with the balance of the road north still gravel. There have been fur trading posts on La Ronge since the late 1700s. A French-Canadian, Jean Etienne Waden, was there in 1776. Peter Pond wintered there in 1780-82, and Simon Fraser in 1795-96. The Hudson's Bay Company entered the scene in 1797 when George Charles established a post. It was abandoned in 1831 because 'the surrounding country had been much impoverished' but was re-opened in the summer of 1894.

As settlements go, this one was quite large, having besides ourselves, a free trader, fishing tackle shop, two restaurants, a garage, a school and nursing station, and several camps and outfitters catering to tourists. It was the main base for Saskatchewan Government Airways whose float planes took off in all directions from here. A landing field for wheeled planes was being built a mile or so south at the mouth of the Montreal River.

La Ronge also had a training school for smoke jumpers -- a bunch of young daredevils who were employed each year by the Provincial Department of Natural Resources and taught to fight forest fires. Whenever a fire was pinpointed, they parachuted at low altitude from an aircraft, equipped with a jumping chute to enable them to clear the pontoons. With the equipment they carried, they were able to control small outbreaks before they reached major proportions.

A local post office, Department of Natural Resource office and a Royal Canadian Mounted Police detachment completed the settlement which was strung out for almost a mile along the western shoreline.

W.A. 'Bill' McKinnie was the manager. Stocky, sandy-haired and, of course, Scottish, he was a first-class trader with a keen sense of humour. His command of the Cree language was second only to that of Andy McKinley at Pelican Narrows. Bill was in the middle of preparing for the summer tourist onslaught, so after examining the buildings and doing the routine checks, I didn't take up too much of his time. With the exception of the warehouse, the other buildings were all of recent construction. The warehouse was very large -- too large for the present needs of the store now that they were serviced by a highway from Prince Albert on an almost daily

HBCA Photograph Collection 1987/363-L-5

Customers examine the merchandise in the Hudson's
Bay Company store at La Ronge. Autumn, 1946.

basis. But it had been built before the road was constructed and was intended to hold a year's supply of trade goods.

I finished my charter flight at La Ronge and Bill and his wife, Irene, drove me south the fifty-odd miles to Montreal Lake Post which was built just off the highway at the south end of Montreal Lake. Historical records are scant but it appears that the post was originally established around 1885 at a point on the lakeshore about one mile east of the Revillon Frères post. When the Company took over Revillon Frères in 1936, they closed their own post and moved over into the Revillon buildings. At one period, freight for northern posts was delivered here by horse-wagons from Prince Albert, then taken by canoe up the lake and down the Montreal River to La Ronge.

With the building of the highway from Prince Albert to La Ronge, following the east side of the lake, many families moved away to the middle and north end of the lake to concentrate on commercial fishing so the store was rebuilt on the highway in the early 1960s. Unfortunately the government decided to re-align the highway, taking the new route much further east which left our post high and dry. It was closed down on 31 July 1973.

The store, warehouse and apprentice clerk's house were built of logs, now old and in a delapidated condition. The dwelling house -- a cottage-type construction -- was one of the most awkward houses I have ever seen. It was tiny and there was no place in the living room where a chesterfield could be fitted, as the room had five doors leading from it. One led to the front veranda, another back to the kitchen, and the other three doors led to small bedrooms. The grounds were low-lying and marshy and the mosquitos were a holy terror.

The local Indians lived in poverty, for there was little fur in the area for them to trap. They did some commercial fishing on Montreal Lake but it was confined to the north end where a small settlement called Molanosa had sprung up. The Indian agent from Prince Albert tried to get them jobs during the summer and fall, mainly working in the wheat or sugar-beet harvest fields in Alberta. Later on, we arranged for them to have a pulpwood cutting contract with a Prince Albert wood contractor, 'Spike' Dawley. After the natives had cut a certain amount of wood, manager W.A. 'Wally' Buhr and later on, Jim Boatman went out each Sunday, scaled the wood and stamped each log with the contractor's brand. Wally paid the natives for each cord and billed Mr Dawley who hauled the cordwood south to the sawmill at Prince Albert.

There had been a succession of managers since 1944 -- mostly young men back from the war who were doing their repatriation before going on to take charge of larger posts. The present manager was a young married man named Jim Trafford. In 1944, post manager Jack Denton retired and opened up a small store on the highway about two miles away from our post. He sold groceries to the locals and served coffee and sandwiches to passing motorists but, in his heart, he was still a Hudson's Bay man. Whenever he came over to the post to get his mail, he would virtually inspect the place and made no bones about what he thought were the present manager's shortcomings. He drove Jim Trafford crazy and although he tried to take all Jack's criticisms in good spirit, he and his wife were glad to be transferred west the following year.

I travelled by regular bus service from Montreal Lake back to Prince Albert and then home, having completed my first inspection of the eastern side of my district.

After spending ten days in Winnipeg with Bea and the family and attending to necessary chores at District Office, I tackled the western half of the district. From La Ronge, I flew a little more than one hundred miles northwest to Patuanak post. It was built on a long, tree-clad bit of land formed by the Churchill River making a U-turn from the north end of Isle a la Crosse. It was given post status in 1921. The Roman Catholic Mission stood next to the post and the settlement buildings were scattered along the lake shore. It was known as Patuanak to the Cree -- named from the rapids on the river as it entered the lake. For some reason, the Company maintained the name 'Pine River' for many years although the original Pine River outpost, which is now closed, had been located on the Churchill River about thirty miles east by canoe.

Jim Kirk, a young married Canadian who had served overseas in the Royal Canadian Air Force was in charge. Although the main revenue came from fur, the local natives also did a bit of commercial fishing and Jim was most confident that this part of the business could be greatly developed. We discussed it at great length and I promised him that I would look further into the matter.

From Patuanak, we flew seventy-five miles northwest to Portage la Loche. Built on the east side of Lac la Loche (or Methye Lake), the start of the mighty Churchill River system, it was only a few miles away from the historic seventeen-mile long Methye Portage, which crossed the height of land from Lac la Loche to the Clearwater River. Every year, the fur trade canoe brigades from Norway House met the brigades from the Athabasca and Mackenzie rivers. Incoming loads of trade goods were transferred one way across the portage and outgoing bales of fur the other way. When the exchange was completed, there was the usual regale and after a week-long celebration, the voyageurs left on their return journey.

HBCA Photograph Collection 1987/363-P-27

The Store Manager's dwelling at Portage la Loche. Under the management of John Blackhall this post was turned around from the 'hell-hole' of the fur trade to a profitable post. c. 1941

Composed mainly of Chipewyan and a few Cree, Portage la Loche had an imposing Roman Catholic mission, a hospital and school which were both operated by the Sisters, and a Department of Natural Resources officer. John Blackhall, the post manager came from Peterhead in Scotland and was within a few years of retirement. Most of his life with the Company had been spent in Ungava in the Fort Chimo area. His post was run by the book and he insisted that everything be shipshape at all times. He was strict with his apprentice clerks but any young man who served under John Blackhall got a first class training. Whether he knew it or not, John was referred to by his clerks as 'Mr H.B.C.'

His wife, Bertha, was part Eskimo, and a member of the Labrador Ford family. She had been parted from her own two daughters while they were still young, as John insisted that they be sent to his relatives in Scotland to be brought up and educated in civilization. Bertha sorely missed her girls and as a result, she tended to mother any apprentice clerks. Sometimes John 'harrumphed', complaining that it was not good for discipline but Bertha calmly went her way claiming that since she was denied the pleasure of rearing her daughters, it was her privilege to treat each

Roy Simpson

The old store at Portage la Loche with the manager's garden in the foreground. By this date, 1955, a new store had been built.

clerk as her son. And the young men loved it. Every clerk who served under John Blackhall has fond memories of Bertha.

Portage la Loche was a poor place -- poverty stricken and disease-ridden. For years the natives suffered every disease from tuberculosis to syphilis -- the inevitable inheritance of the annual regales of the canoe brigades. Only herculean efforts by the federal and provincial governments succeeded in overcoming these diseases and cleaning the place up. As the post never made much profit, it had been bandied back and forth between Athabasca and Saskatchewan districts. Post managers hated it and dreaded being posted there. It was the hell-hole of the fur trade where you were sent to vegetate until retirement.

John Blackhall might have been one of those managers but he refused to accept his fate. The secret of his eventual success was the lowly squirrel. From being 'squaw fur' worth a nickel or a dime, squirrels had increased in value over the past ten years to fifty cents and then to $1 or more per skin. And the spruce-covered country around the post was crawling with squirrels. In spite of the fact that we shipped out anything from 35,000 to 50,000 per year, their numbers never seemed to diminish. John encouraged the natives to go after them and gave them small debts. Gradually, he regenerated their interest in trapping and they stayed away from the village, catching mink and foxes as well and soon Portage la Loche was on its way to becoming one of the most profitable posts in the district.

Instead of using .22 rifles to shoot the squirrels, the Indians used coils of cable steel snare wire -- meant for trapping foxes and wolves. Each coil was made up of 20 or 24 strands of tightly twisted steel wire. They cut the coil into lengths, then painstakingly separated the strands and made them into small individual snares. Four to five snares were attached to poles about five feet long and two or three poles were propped against the bole of a spruce tree. The squirrels scampered up and down the tree trunks, especially on sunny days, and so fell victims to the strategically placed snares.

My next stop was Buffalo Narrows, some sixty miles south, built at the narrows between Peter Pond Lake and Churchill Lake. Our course took us over the La Loche River, which wound like a serpent for miles between Lac la Loche and Peter Pond Lake. Some dilapidated buildings, known as Bulls' House, at the mouth of the river caught my attention. Latterly, oxen had been used instead of manpower to haul freight over the Methye Portage and as there was a plentiful supply of wild marsh hay nearby, the oxen were wintered in the buildings. Hence the name 'Bulls' House'.

Two-thirds down Peter Pond Lake, a narrows was formed by a peninsula jutting out from each side. The western peninsula was know as 'Old Fort Point' possibly because a fur trade post had been located there at one time. To the locals, Peter Pond Lake was known as Big Buffalo Lake and Little Buffalo Lake, while Churchill Lake was called Clear Lake. Buffalo Narrows was of comparatively recent origin and owed its existence to Waite Fisheries Ltd. of Big River, Saskatchewan. They made it the focal point of their commercial fishing operation in northwest Saskatchewan and in 1943 erected a modern fish filleting and freezing plant. Our store was established in 1942 by Tom Scurfield when he was manager of the district because most of the natives at our former post at Clear Lake moved down to Buffalo to take part in the commercial fishing. The Clear Lake post was then closed down. In addition to the native population there was a large contingent of Scandinavian fishermen who sold their catch to Waite Fisheries.

Besides our store there was a hotel run by a Chinese man, Der Tom; a telegraph office; nursing station and a Roman Catholic Mission and school. Our local opposition was an Armenian, Kelly Shattilla who also had the post office. W. D. (Doug) Johnson, our store manager, was a born salesman, keenly interested in merchandising.

'This man is too good to be left at this post for long,' I thought. 'He can handle a much bigger operation than Buffalo Narrows.'

Doug introduced me to all the local people including Bill McLean, the local telegraph operator. Communication on the west side of the province was easy. A provincial government telegraph line ran from Meadow Lake north through Green Lake, Beauval, Isle a la Crosse to Buffalo Narrows, with a fully qualified operator at each point. From Buffalo, a telephone line extended north along the east shore of Big Buffalo Lake and up the La Loche River to Portage la Loche. At Bulls' House at the river mouth, an extension ran south down the west side of Big Buffalo Lake to our post at Dillon, so our post managers at Dillon or Portage la Loche could ring up the operator at Buffalo Narrows and transmit their messages by telegraph -- a far cry from the isolated posts of my days in the 1930s.

Waite Fisheries was an extensive operation. They bought fish winter and summer, processed it at the local plant and shipped most of it as frozen fillets to the United States. During the summer their fishboat went around the fishing grounds on the various lakes and purchased the newly netted fish daily.

In the winter, when the fishermen set their nets under the ice, Bombardier snowmobiles were utilized to pick up the catch. As a by-product of the fishing operation, a most successful mink ranching business sprang up, using the offal from the fish plant as

Nancy Middleton

Buffalo Narrows, showing the nursing station in the foreground, left, and the Roman Catholic Mission and school, right. c. 1950.

mink food. Mr Waite himself had a large mink ranch, as did several of his employees and many of the white fishermen. By 1956, there were thirty-three mink ranches in the area with a combined total of 21,000 mink. Credit for the success of the ranches has to go to Mr Halvor 'Henry' Ausland who owned a large ranch on Deep River, a few miles east of Buffalo Narrows. From the start, he became interested in genetics and did a lot of experimenting to produce new mink strains. He originated the 'palomino' strain -- a light brown or dark orange colour. In fact, he made more money selling breeding trios -- two females and one male -- than he actually made in producing mink pelts. He was more than generous with advice and assistance to other embryo ranchers and was always quick to lend a hand when requested.

    The Company's fur sales department in Montreal took a deep interest in Buffalo Narrows and, once a year, after the season's litters were born, they sent Fred Mehmel of the Winnipeg Raw Fur Department up to do business with the ranchers. Based on pelt production, each rancher was offered an advance payment depending on the state of the current market. In return for a contract, the pelts would be consigned to the Hudson's Bay Company's Montreal auction and when they were sold, a final payment was mailed to the rancher -- less the Company's handling commission. A supply of knockdown cardboard shipping cartons was supplied to the post and once pelting time was finished, the post manager was extremely busy filling out the forms, packing skins and forwarding them by air express to Montreal in time to catch the first sale, when prices were usually at their best.

Inevitably ranch mink escaped from their pens and interbred with wild mink. The result was a nightmare for the post managers. Trappers brought in skins of every hue and naturally expected to be paid at wild mink tariff price. It created a problem for the managers and my answer was to supply them with a ranch mink tariff which was lower than wild mink, with the injunction 'when in doubt, buy them as ranch mink and don't worry if you lose some of the crazier skins. Let the free trader buy those.' Jock Holliday, a fellow student at the Montreal Fur School spent some time one winter at Buffalo Narrows as a relief manager. When I met him, he just shook his head in bewilderment over the odd-coloured pelts. 'I thought I had seen everything,' he exclaimed, 'but those strange mink at Buffalo Narrows just drove me crazy.'

To return to the business of fishing, Doug Johnson didn't miss a trick. He had a scow fixed up as a store and, under the charge of a clerk, had it towed by the fishboat under the command of Big Louis Morin, all around Clear Lake to the various fishing grounds. In this way we were able to supply the natives with their basic supplies on the spot. Special orders for dry goods or hardware were sent by letter to the post and the customer received the merchandise on the next fishboat run. In the winter, the old Clear Lake post was opened as a wintering outpost in charge of a clerk. The same routine applied except that the vehicle was a snowmobile. Since running the outpost was a trial run for clerks prior to being promoted to the charge of a post, I was surprised at the reluctance of promising clerks to accept the wintering assignment. It was only thirty miles away from Buffalo Narrows, was in direct communication by short-wave radio and the clerk could come down most weekends by snowmobile. My surprise ended when I visited the outpost that winter. The old post manager's home was being used as a combined store and dwelling but no maintenance had been done in years. Most of the plaster between the logs was loose or had already fallen out and the place was cold as charity. Whenever a storm blew in -- and that's just what it did -- it blew right into the house! I didn't take my parka off the whole time I was there. The following spring, Rupertsland Trading Company designed and built a prefabricated combination store and house which was heated by an oil heater and from then on, I had no difficulty in getting clerks to accept the Clear Lake winter posting.

Dillon, on the west side of Big Buffalo Lake, was only a fifteen mile hop by plane. Steve Preweda, a Winnipeg boy just back from frigate duty with the Royal Canadian Navy, was manager of his first post. His wife Aggie was the sister of Bill McLean, the telegrapher at Buffalo Narrows. Steve was a good, sound post manager who worked with the local Chipewyans extremely well.

Situated at the mouth of the Dillon River, the post was tiny with only the Company's building and a Roman Catholic mission. Formerly known as Buffalo River, it was operated as a wintering outpost from Isle a la Crosse since around 1888 and was raised to post status in 1916. The natives were predominently fishermen and not very good trappers. Fortunately there were lots of squirrels in the area and we purchased a respectable number each year, although not nearly half as many as at Portage la Loche. Hunters would only go away for two or three days at a time -- what we called 'pot hunters'. The average amount of debt given out at any one time was $3.00 to $5.00; anyone who received $10.00 was a big man. The debt was just enough to give the hunters a couple of boxes of .22 shells, tea and tobacco. They didn't use snares...just shot the squirrels through the head with their .22s. Although I have said that the natives were a shabby lot, to visit Dillon on a midsummer evening, you would think they were the most carefree bunch in the world. Having sold their fresh fish to the daily fishboat and spread out their nets on the grass to dry, they sat around, happy as kings, feasting on canned sardines, tinned peaches and soda crackers.

From Dillon, we flew fifty miles southeast to Isle a la Crosse where I dismissed my chartered aircraft. I wanted to spend some time discussing the local commercial fishing possibilities with the post manager. Isle a la Crosse Lake has two main arms -- one running north and a secondary arm, Aubichon Bay, running northwest. The settlement stood on a large flat promontory where the two arms met. The Hudson's Bay Company was established here in 1799 by William Linklater to combat the activities of the North West Company whose trading post, Fort Black, stood a few miles south where the Beaver River flows into the lake. After the union of the two companies in 1821, Fort Black was abandoned and the main job of Isle a la Crosse was to supply sufficient quantities of buffalo pemmican to feed the annual canoe brigades. Governor George Simpson is on record as having severely admonished the local factor, Mr Clark, for neglecting his main duty and spending too much time in the pursuit of fur buying.

W. T. 'Bill' Watt, the manager and another Aberdonian, was getting close to retirement age. A veteran of World War I, he had spent his earliest years with the Company in Ungava and around James Bay. He was an excellent trader and a good trainer of apprentice clerks. His wife, Bella, a lady with a pawky sense of humour whom Bill met in Scotland, loved gardening and the grounds around the dwelling house were a mass of flowers. She was one of the many Company wives who created a bit of home in the wilderness for their husbands and families. I especially looked forward to visiting their home because although it was the usual cottage-type, similar to that at Montreal Lake, it was much larger and had a brick fireplace in the living room. Almost every home in Scotland had a fireplace -- they didn't have central heating yet -- and Bill, Bella and I spent many a pleasant evening relaxing with our feet up in front of a blazing wood fire and sipping a dram of whisky.

Bill took me along to visit the settlement. The Company owned a large tract of land and we had to walk about half a mile along the shore road before coming to the first buildings strung along the shoreline. They were the Royal Canadian Mounted Police barracks, a sub-Indian agent's building, a Department of

Natural Resources office and telegraph office. Beyond was an hotel and trading store owned by Marcien Marion, the local big shot. A half-breed, Marcien was a member of the Legislative Assembly for Saskatchewan representing the local riding on behalf of the Liberals. He claimed that his forebears had come from the Red River and that Marion Street in St Boniface -- the French-speaking city across the Red River from Winnipeg -- was named after one of his ancestors. Next was a large Roman Catholic mission with several priests and nuns, the school and the hospital. Dr Lavoie was in charge of the hospital and when he retired two or three years later, he was replaced by Dr Hoffman, a German emigrant and his wife. Walking back to the post, I remarked to Bill that our store was a long way from our customers, mainly French-Cree half-breeds whose homes were scattered all around the mission property. Bill agreed. 'We do have one advantage though. We have the post office in our store and since they have to come to us for their mail, most of them do their shopping with us too. In any case, all the other land is owned by the mission or the various government departments so I doubt whether we could obtain a suitable site for a store.' I took note to further check into this at a future date.

Bill and I spent a long time discussing the potential commercial fish buying at both Isle a la Crosse and Patuanak. While it is true there were plenty of whitefish at both places, most of the fishermen's time was spent in hauling their catches by dogsled or horsesled from the fishing camps to the posts. Marcien Marion, our opposition, owned a Bombardier and was able to go around to the individual fish camps and pick up the catch which he sold to a fish buyer from Meadow Lake.

'If we had a Bombardier at Isle a la Crosse and another at Patuanak, we could triple or quadruple our catch,' Bill insisted. 'Not only that, we could tap the three lakes on the Churchill River to the east -- Dipper Lake, Primrose Lake and Knee Lake.' I was most impressed by Bill's arguments and anything that would increase our business I was all for. However, the cost of purchasing two Bombardiers would be a major investment. I told Bill that I had a meeting scheduled with Len Waite at Big River in late

September and would see if we could come to some profitable arrangement.

The Bombardier, built in Quebec, is a wonderful vehicle for the north. It resembles a truck on tracks, very sturdy with the capacity of handling a large load. It is built of strong plywood, fitted with two steel-reinforced rubber tracks, has a pair of skis in front for steering and is equipped with a six-cylinder truck motor. From a distance it looks like a tank from World War I.

The next leg of my journey was roughly thirty miles south, up the Beaver River to Beauval. Bill put the post's sixteen-foot boat and outboard motor at my disposal along with a driver and guide. The Beaver River valley is beautiful and I sat back and relaxed, enjoying the warm and sunny day. There were wild ducks everywhere and as we rounded each bend on the river, large mallards rose enticingly from the reeds. 'Someday,' I promised myself, 'I'm going to make this trip in the fall and bring a shotgun along.'

At Beauval, there was my old friend Jock Mathieson, whom I had last seen at Ombabika in southern Ontario. This post was originally opened in 1933 as an outpost of Isle a la Crosse. It was small and Jock was plugging away doing the best he could. The buildings were on the west bank of the river on an upper slope and commanded a lovely view of the Roman Catholic mission and school across the river where most of the natives had their homes. Beauval was on a gravel highway running north from Green Lake to Fort Black and the river was crossed here by means of a large wooden scow-like ferry running on a steel overhead cable. I didn't stay long and hitched a ride on a southbound truck to my last port of call, Green Lake, seventy miles to the south. Here the post stood, by the side of the road on the north end of the lake of the same name, from which the Green River flows a few miles north to join the Beaver River.

The North West Company was in business at the north end of Green Lake as early as 1782. To meet this competition, William Auld built the Hudson's Bay Company post, Essex House, in 1799 about a quarter of a mile from the 'Canadian Settlement'. There was bad blood between the two rivals from the start. In 1805, the Nor' Westers burned down Essex House while the Hudson's Bay men were away for the summer and, later in the spring of 1817, the Nor' Westers took them prisoner and seized all their property. Both posts were still in existence when Captain John Franklin visited Green Lake in 1820.

After the union in 1821, the Council of the Northern Department decided to close down the operation and in 1822 moved it to Cold Lake. Green Lake was re-established a few years later, however, and has been in continuous operation since 1831. It was raided by the Indians in the Rebellion of 1885.

When freight for the north was delivered by Red River cart after having been hauled across the prairies from Fort Garry, or later by steamer, on the North Saskatchewan River, the post was at the south end of Green Lake. Later it was moved half way up the west side of the lake. In the early 1940s all buildings were hauled by traction engine to the present site, under the direction of Tom Scurfield. In 1948, people were still digging up copper cooking kettles at the old sites. Green Lake post is now at the junction point of two roads -- one from Meadow Lake and the other from Big River -- that join and head north to Fort Black on Isle a la Crosse Lake.

The settlement consisted of the Bay buildings; a post belonging to Karl Fuchs, a free trader; a government overseer; an R.C.M.P. detatchment and a telegraph station. There were no Indians around. All the local people were Métis most of whom had been moved from other locations by the provincial governments in an effort to resettle them as farmers at Green Lake. Their interests were looked after by the overseer who also had an experimental farm to encourage the Métis to plant crops. This was the first time I came into contact with the word 'Métis' in the north. When I had heard it previously, it meant half-breeds around the Red River settlement in Manitoba. Now, the Saskatchewan Government applied it to all half-breeds. In the North, there was nothing derogatory about the word 'half-breed'. Everybody used the term. They were either Scots, French or English half-breeds and they were proud of the fact.

The only other occupation at Green Lake was a timber sawmill operated by Gus Porat. He provided employment for most of the locals, and was a decent fellow, well thought of in the community. Frank Milne, our post manager, was another Aberdonian and an old-timer in the service. He had started as an apprentice clerk in the western Arctic, moved to Fort Chipewyan and now to Green Lake. Inclined to be rather easygoing, he handled his duties capably and was well liked by his customers. When he retired a few years later, he bought a menswear store at Meadow Lake and went into business for himself. Frank was the proud owner of an automobile and was good enough to drive me from Green Lake to Prince Albert where I caught the train back home to Winnipeg.

Now that my post inspection of the district was completed, I realized that I was in charge of a first-class operation, a result of the hard work of the previous District Managers -- Tom Scurfield (1941-46) and Bill Cobb (1946-48). The buildings were practically new at all the posts; they had electric power and, for the most part, were equipped with modern plumbing. I was particularly pleased with the calibre of the post managers. Most of them were seasoned veterans who merited the description 'good traders'. The term is peculiar to the Hudson's Bay Company and difficult to describe in a few words. To be a 'good trader', a man must first know how to grade and buy fur. He must also keep the buildings in good repair, maintain the grounds and keep store interiors immaculate and well stocked with trade goods. The books must always be in balance and show a profit, and the debt issue and collection must be properly controlled. To accomplish this, he must have an empathy with his native customers. A knowledge of the language is a great asset. He must have infinite patience and never lose his temper. He must listen when his customer has a grievance and wants to 'talk' with him, be able to judge when a trapper has a valid reason for not paying his debt in full, and be ready with advice when called upon. His word must always be his bond. In short, he is a guide, philosopher, and friend whom the natives can respect and trust at all times and look upon as a friend as well as a boss. To be a 'good trader' is not an easy task.

The moving of freight to our Saskatchewan posts was mainly done in the wintertime. All requisitions for a year's supply of merchandise had to be in district office by the end of September. There, the grocery orders were collated by our grocery buyer, Al Doer. This gave us a tremendous price leverage, as he could place an order out for bid of anything up to ten carloads of flour; seven or eight carloads of lard and several of sugar. Our local opposition at the various posts could not hope to compete with our costs as they were forced to purchase through local wholesalers.

For several years, freight for Brochet, Southend and Pelican Narrows was handled by Transport Ltd., The Pas who had a large freighting operation all over the north country.

As soon as weather conditions made travelling on the ice possible, they set out by cat-train, usually in early January. Each train was made up of several cat-swings -- a cat-swing consisting of a big caterpiller tractor, several high-bunked sleighs covered by tarpaulins, and a caboose where the men ate and slept. It was a slow, difficult job...and cold! The cat drivers worked in four-hour shifts, day and night. The tractor had no cab to shelter the driver from the weather because, if the cat broke through the ice, he had to be able to jump clear immediately. Each cat-swing carried a number of large timber baulks. Many of the larger lakes, Reindeer Lake especially, were subject to pressure ridges -- long ridges of ice up to three feet high caused by air pressure from below -- forcing itself out. In such cases, the walls of ice had to be chopped down and a bridge laid across the crack with the timber baulks.

The cat-train usually made the trip to Brochet first, later swinging south at Deep Bay to go to Southend. With the Reindeer River flowing from the south end of Reindeer Lake, the resulting current made the ice take a longer time to freeze to sufficient depth. Freight to Pelican Narrows was handled later on; there were quite a few rivers to cross on the way so the ice took longer to freeze to the required depth.

About 1952, Transport Ltd. moved its whole operation to Lynn Lake. They continued to service our stores at Brochet and Southend but put me on to a good man, Johnny Highmoor, a freighter from The Pas who did a great job of handling our Pelican

Freight arrives by cat-train at Stanley. Winter, 1954.

Narrows freight.

When I first visited Brochet, I commented on the beautiful flagpole at the post to Bill Garbutt. 'It really is a lovely thing, isn't it?' he said. I tried to stretch my hands around its girth and couldn't. 'You'll never guess where it came from, Hugh, so I'll tell you. It's the mast from the old schooner *Brochet*. It's been around for a lot of years and I guess she still has a lot of life in her yet.' He gave the flagpole a fond pat.

At one time all freight for Montreal Lake, La Ronge, Stanley, Southend and Brochet was handled out of Prince Albert by a firm called R. D. Brookes. Everything was done by horse-drawn sleigh then. The Brochet freight was warehoused at Southend until summer; then the schooner *Brochet* went south to pick it up and sailed back to the post, supplying several temporary outposts or 'camp trades' as we used to call them, along the way. Of course there was now a good highway running from Prince Albert to La Ronge paved as far as Waskesiu, and the freight to Montreal Lake and La Ronge was trucked in on a weekly basis by Saskatchewan Government Transport which also hauled our Stanley freight as far as La Ronge each fall. From there it was taken by cat-train to Stanley by a local contractor, Henry Heglund, whose wife was the local postmistress.

A shipment of flour is brought into Stanley by cat-train. Winter, 1954.

Up the west side of the province the bulk of our freight, including all the winter annual supplies, was handled by Waite Fisheries Ltd. They employed heavy-duty trucks rather than cat-trains, and travelled a good gravel road right up to Fort Black and then across the ice to Patuanak, Isle a la Crosse, Buffalo Narrows, Dillon and Portage la Loche. The trucks moved in convoy and each truck had a snowplow attached in front to keep a good ice road plowed across the lakes. This was good business for Waite Fisheries; the trucks would be going up to Buffalo Narrows empty anyway to bring back fish. With a good load going both ways, they were able to give us a competitive freight rate.

The truck drivers were a hardy breed. They didn't bother about maximum load weights. Broken rear axles were a common occurrence and each truck carried a couple of spares.

There was also a weekly truck service from Meadow Lake to Isle a la Crosse operated by the Brander Brothers, Hugh and Leigh. They had the contract to carry the mail on a weekly basis and usually brought in loads of bread, fresh fruit and vegetables and fresh meat. In the winter, they drove straight to Isle a la Crosse and Buffalo Narrows but in the summer they stopped at Fort Black and took the mail and freight by boat to these two points. About five years later, the road was extended from just south of Beauval right up to Buffalo Narrows with a ferry to cross the Narrows in summer.

In the Saskatchewan provincial elections of 1944, the Co-operative Commonwealth Federation (CCF) party, under the leadership of T. C. Douglas, swept into power completely ousting the Liberals who had held the reins for a very long time. Many years later, when they became a federal party, the name was changed to the New Democratic Party (NDP). The CCF was completely socialistic and held the view that all natural resources of the province belonged to the people and should be administered by the government for the people. In their view, capitalism was not to be tolerated and therefore, the Hudson's Bay Company was high on their list.

I understand that soon after they came into power, they wrote to the Company in Winnipeg offering to buy out our Saskatchewan stores. The offer was gracefully refused by the Managing Director who said, 'We are quite prepared to take our chances against any competition.' I was not much interested in politics but could see that in their four years of being in power, they had done a great deal of good for the northern part of Saskatchewan, the area that interested me most.

In 1946, they took over bus services in the province, made them into a government corporation, the Saskatchewan Transportation Company, and put Bill Bunn in as manager. They organized the commercial fishermen at Reindeer Lake, Wollaston Lake and Snake Lake -- which they promptly renamed Pinehouse Lake, for obvious reasons -- into co-operatives marketing the fish under the name Saskatchewan Fish Marketing Service.

In the same year the CCF introduced the Saskatchewan Fur Marketing Service and held their own auction sales in Regina. The plan was for the trappers to turn in their fur, on a voluntary basis, to the local field officer of the Department of Natural Resources who gave them an initial payment of 50 per cent of the estimated value, and then forwarded the fur to Regina for sale at auction. Several months later, when the furs were sold and the auction's selling commission was deducted, a final payment cheque, less the initial payment, was mailed to the trapper. Although the service was patronized by farmers and part-time southern trappers and by local fur dealers, the native and half-breed trappers in the north turned it hands down. Dealing day-by-day with the native people, we understood how they felt about tomorrow. It might never come. If they were employed weekly, they were paid by the day. They might be dead tomorrow and money wouldn't be any good to them if they couldn't spend it. So the new CCF Fur Marketing Service was of no use to the northern trappers. They preferred the Company's system of giving them a trapping advance which they paid in full when they traded in their fur. And for the twenty years that the CCF party was in power, the two northern constituancies regularly returned Liberal representatives.

J. L. (Joe) Phelps, Minister of Natural Resources and a rabid socialist simply could not understand their attitude and he regularly criticized what he called 'the Hudson's Bay Company policy of keeping the natives enthralled in debt.' When he lost his seat in the 1948 provincial election, I found his successor J.L. Brockelbank much more understanding and easier to get along with.

In addition to their Fish Marketing Service, the government started up the Saskatchewan Government Trading Company with initial stores at Wollaston Lake and Pinehouse Lake, followed by stores at La Ronge and Stanley. Later on, they went into business on the west side, opening stores at Isle a la Crosse, Buffalo Narrows and Portage la Loche.

The government took over M & C (Mason & Campbell) Aviation Company in 1947. It was a local company providing a flying service to all parts of the north from Prince Albert. Now it was called Saskatchewan Government Airways and they completed a landing strip at La Ronge where they had their main floatbase. An Anson aircraft on wheels flew a regular schedule from Prince Albert to La Ronge, then north to Uranium City. From La Ronge a weekly service operated to Isle a la Crosse, Buffalo Narrows and Portage la Loche. Another weekly schedule went east to Stanley, Pelican Narrows and Flin Flon with a twice a month diversion to Southend and Brochet.

It had been the custom for the district manager of Saskatchewan to make a courtesy trip to Regina once a year to pay his respects to the government, so in mid-September, after I had

taken my holidays, I decided to make the trip. I went via Prince
Albert and Big River to keep an appointment with Len Waite, owner
of Waite Fisheries. In Prince Albert I met Floyd Glass, the northern
administrator. Part of his job was to act as liaison between the
cabinet and, in particular, the Minister of Natural Resources in
Regina and the various operations in the north. I liked him right
from the start. He was a pilot and flew his government aircraft
around the north. In the years ahead, I often hitched a ride with
him.

Mr Glass explained that the weekly load to Isle a la Crosse and
Buffalo Narrows was getting bigger and bigger now that they had
obtained the post office mail contract. He wanted to put in a
landing strip at Buffalo Narrows and Isle a la Crosse so that the trip
could be flown by Anson. Buffalo presented no difficulties but the
only ground he could find at Isle a la Crosse was partly within
Hudson's Bay Company property. Taking out a large-scale map of
the area, he showed me the exact proposed site of the strip. It was
obvious that only a small part of the Company's land was required
but without it, there could be no airstrip.

'Do you think the Company would entertain the idea of selling
us this bit of land,' asked Floyd, 'and if so, how much? I need to
know rather quickly so I can prepare proper estimates and I would
appreciate your assistance very much.'

I studied the map carefully, then said, 'Who owns these vacant
properties alongside the Department of Natural Resources office,
the Indian Department and the Mounted Police? And this piece at
the north end next to the settlement?' Floyd checked it over.

'That's all provincial government land,' he stated
emphatically. 'What's running around in that canny Scot's brain
of yours?'

'Floyd, maybe we can make a deal that won't cost you any
money. We don't have official title to the land at several of our
posts. Now...if you are willing to give the Company official title
to the lands occupied by our stores at Dillon, Patuanak and
Southend, plus this particular lot at Isle a la Crosse, then I think I
can arrange for you to have title to that piece of land for your

airstrip.' And I sat back and watched the wheels turning in Floyd's head as he pondered my proposal.

'It's a deal,' he announced, pumping my hand strenuously. 'I can't believe it. As easy as that. I was afraid you might try to hold me up for an impossible price.'

'You realize that Winnipeg office will have to approve it first, but it's a good deal for both of us and I don't anticipate any difficulty.'

Mr Chesshire agreed and in the spring of 1950, I had the pleasure of flying from La Ronge to Isle a la Crosse in the first Anson flight on wheels with Rene Baudais, pilot, and Lefty MacLeod as co-pilot.

John Ross, the manager of our raw furs department agency in Prince Albert drove me across to Big River, a small town at the end of a branch railway line from Prince Albert and built at the south end of long, narrow Cowan Lake. At one time Big River had been a major timber town but now most of the good timber in the area was cut out and the local sawmill, not very busy. The main industry was commercial fishing dominated by Waite Fisheries who also owned the local electricity generating plant and half the town besides. I found Mr Waite to be a most able businessman -- he had to be to control this empire -- and very easy to get along with. I often wondered why the government hadn't taken over his fishing business as part of their Fish Marketing Service. Either it was too large for them to swallow or Len had a great deal of political clout. I never asked him. It was none of my business.

The first item for discussion was our freight contract for the coming winter season. Naturally, Len wanted an increase in rates and I, just as strongly, wished them to remain the same. Actually the freight deal was of great advantage to him. Without our loads of merchandise going north, his trucks would have run up empty to Buffalo Narrows to collect fish. With our freight, he had a payload both ways all winter. Financially, he also profited. As each post shipped out a load of fish, it was invoiced to him through our Winnipeg district office -- the price actually paid plus our handling commission of 2 cents per pound. Per contra -- his invoices for our freight were credited to his account as they were received. At the end of each year, there was usually a fair debit balance when we would receive a cheque in full before May 31st, the end of our fiscal year. So, Waite Fisheries was getting large quantities of fish bought and paid for by the Hudson's Bay Company without his having to go to the bank to borrow and pay interest. Conversely, it was also a good deal for us. We got our freight taken in at a lower rate than other stores paid and increased business from fish buying. After some discussion on freight rates, Len laughed and said, 'Okay, same as last year', and from my 'travelling district office bag', I pulled out the contract which I had prepared for his signature.

During the following days we had long discussions about fish. When I told him of our expectations for Isle a la Crosse and Patuanak and showed him the figures Bill Watt had prepared, he was quite impressed. 'These,' I emphasised, 'are minimum figures. We believe that we can do much better. There's another lake about thirty miles north of Patuanak called Porter Lake and the natives say that it is full of trout. With a Bombardier, we could develop a nice fresh trout production each spring.'

Len laughed. 'Go on. Tell me where you are going to get a Bombardier.'

'You're catching on, Len...but I want two Bombardiers, not one. We'll need one at Isle a la Crosse and another at Patuanak.' As I outlined the plan Bill Watt and I had come up with, Len shook his head from side to side, smiling all the while. 'Look,' I said, 'we'll purchase the necessary extra tracks and spare parts and supply the driver and gas. All you have to do is to adjust your tariff for the various types of fish and you'll recover the cost of the Bombardiers in a couple of years.'

'You certainly aren't asking for much,' he said. 'Do you know what Bombardiers cost?'

'Len, I know they're expensive but check our figures and you'll find that it will pay you and us in the end.' After talking backwards and forwards for some time, he said, 'It's too late to do anything this year. I've already bought two new machines for my Buffalo Narrows plant.' He glanced down at the sheets again. 'Give me a couple of weeks to check your figures...and if your

Bombardier at the Hudson's Bay Company Store, Isle a la Crosse, 1955.

proposition still looks as good as it does on paper, I'll give you two Bombardiers next year.'

He was as good as his word. In the fall of 1949, new Bombardiers were shipped to Isle a la Crosse and Patuanak and we were into the commercial fishing business in a big way. We hired local drivers who knew the country and the people thoroughly. They had to pass a test for a driver's licence at Isle a la Crosse. One interesting side note is that the RCMP insisted that the Bombardiers must be licensed even though they were driven only on lakes and portages, not on the highway. 'Wherever you drive automatically becomes the 'King's Highway',' Pete Nightingale ruled. Fortunately the fish prices kept up and we both benefited greatly in the years to come. Len drove me back to Prince Albert and from there, I flew down to Regina.

My first visit was to Mr Bill Bunn, general manager of the Saskatchewan Transportation Company. They handled our freight from Prince Albert to Montreal Lake and to La Ronge. Bill was a complete extrovert who always enjoyed the good things of life. He had been a commercial air pilot and was very proud of the low number on his commercial pilot's certificate. Our business didn't take long and our freight contract for the upcoming year was renewed. 'When you have finished your visitations,' he said, 'come back and see me before you leave.'

I had a short interview with the Premier, Tommy Douglas. The conversation was general and we did not touch on politics at all.

Next I went to see Mr Brockelbank, the Minister of Natural Resources. New to this portfolio, he couldn't understand why the northern people were loath to accept his government's fish and fur marketing services and mentioned extending the number of government trading stores. I tried to explain to him the Company's position. Contrary to rumours, we did not overcharge our customers, we kept our prices as reasonable as possible, we welcomed competition which gave the customers a chance to shop and compare prices, and we were quite prepared to meet competition from any stores -- government or otherwise. If we failed then it was our fault and the Company post would deserve to close. Mr Brockelbank listened courteously to me but said he was not completely convinced and would be checking the whole set-up carefully.

I liked him very much. He was a most capable man, easy to get along with and prepared to hear the other side of any argument.

Mr E. 'Ernie' Paynter, the Provincial Game Commissioner, was next on my list of calls. He was easy-going in a general way, but woe betide anyone who dared to break his game laws. I don't think even his own grandmother would have been exempt. Part of his job was to supervise fisheries biologists who regularly tested all lakes being commercially fished. Each year, they set summer and winter quotas for different fish species in each lake. We became good friends and I always found him very fair-minded. He allowed me the privilege of purchasing a residents' fishing and gamebird licence. As he said, 'You spend more damn time in Saskatchewan than you spend in Manitoba' -- a fact occasionally noted by my wife.

On completion of my rounds, I returned to Bill Bunn's home as requested. 'Are you a football fan?' he asked. When I replied in the affirmative, he said, 'Well, next year make sure that your visit to Regina is over Labour Day.' Labour Day in Regina was when and where the annual football game between the Saskatchewan Roughriders and Winnipeg Blue Bombers was

J.P. Kirk

*R.B. Urquhart (right) and
H.M. Ross at Patuanak.
October, 1948.*

played. 'We'll take in the game together and then you will stay with me at my cottage at Last Mountain Lake.' This Labour Day visit to Regina became a tradition.

On my return to Winnipeg, Mr Chesshire called me into his office.

'We are promoting Doug Johnson from Buffalo Narrows to take charge of Churchill,' he announced, 'which leaves me with a problem. All the summer holidays are finished and all planned transfers made so we don't have anyone here to take Johnson's place.' He stopped, rubbed his brow as if he had a headache and continued. 'Actually we do have one man here but he's not capable of handling a post as big as Buffalo Narrows.' As he talked about his predicament, my mind was running over the possibilities so when he said, 'Johnson has to be in Churchill as soon as possible. Have you any suggestions for a replacement?' I was able to give him an answer.

'Bob Middleton from Stanley can handle Buffalo Narrows and I'll promote young Jim Kirk from Patuanak to Stanley. If the man you have available can handle Patuanak which isn't too large a post, then I can get things going at once.' And I hurried back to my office and started sending telegrams in all directions. That afternoon, I met R.B. 'Bob' Urquhart who had been doing relief jobs all summer and now was heading for Patuanak. He had never done any commercial buying of fish and he confided to me that he was a bit worried. I thought about it a minute. 'We can fix that, I think. Young Carl Shappert has been at Isle a la Crosse for the past year and has had a winter's fish buying experience. I'll exchange the clerk at Patuanak and Carl can be your assistant.' That evening Bob Urquhart left Winnipeg for his new posting.

It had been quite apparent to me that Doug Johnson was ready for bigger things but I hadn't imagined that his transfer would take place so soon. In any event, he did a first class job at Churchill and eventually ended up as District Manager in Central Line District.

Next day, Mr Chesshire called me in to his office again. 'Ross, I've just read your annual report and frankly, I don't think very much of it.'

As our year-end was May 31st and I had only been in charge of the district for one month, my annual report had been, of necessity, very sketchy. I started to explain this to Mr Chesshire. 'I understand that,' he interrupted, 'but it is your merchandise that I am worried about. You state here that your stocks in the district are in good condition. Is that true?'

'That is what I was led to believe,' I replied.

'Well, they are not. For the whole district, they work out at 80 percent current stock and 20 percent one year or even older. This just isn't good enough,' he pointed out emphatically. 'In a district like Saskatchewan, I expect the stock to be 90 percent current, just as I expect from a line district.' He looked up at me and said, 'What are you going to do about it?'

'I have already gone over the stocks at each post in the district and, in certain cases, have taken writedowns,' I replied. Then I asked him, 'Have the annual accounts for Saskatchewan for the last year been finally completed yet?'

'No, not yet. Why do you ask?'

'Well, Mr Chesshire, if you think that there is too much old stock on hand at the end of last year, then last year should bear the responsibility. I would like to go over each annual inventory and take the necessary depreciation before the accounts are completed.' I thought this a reasonable request, but nevertheless, I held my breath.

With a glint of a smile in his eyes, he said, 'All right, that sounds reasonable. See the district accountant and arrange it, but do it quickly.' For the rest of the week, I was busy going over inventory sheets with a sharp blue pencil, the results of which met with Mr Chesshire's approval.

Having completed that, I spent some time in checking over the annual requisitions received from the posts for the winter shipments. I remembered Bill Garbutt's complaints about the lack of colour in print goods, checked at other posts and found his opinion confirmed so I went to see Len Coote, manager of the drygoods section in the Winnipeg Depot. He sympathized with my predicament and showed me his stocks on hand. 'See for yourself,' he said. 'These are all ordered by the drygoods buyer and shipped from Montreal. We just don't get any bright printed material anymore.'

'Somebody must make it, Len. Isn't there any place in Winnipeg that we can get it?' I asked.

'Oh, I suppose so but we'll have to get the head buyer's consent first,' he warned.

'You know that old saying about "forewarned is forearmed". Let's just go and have a look first and see what we can find.' We spent the whole afternoon in the Winnipeg wholesale district and eventually found a supplier who had just the type of print we wanted. When we returned to the depot with some samples, the head buyer was not amused. 'Our prints are all ordered from the mills in the east by people who know their business. For your information, pastel colours are the latest thing and that's what the white trade wants and buys.'

'I quite agree with you. The white trade will buy these goods, but you try selling pastel prints to a Chipewyan woman at Brochet or Portage la Loche. And remember, most of our customers are native people.'

'But, if you buy materials locally, they'll cost you two or three cents a yard more,' said the baffled buyer.

'Look, you know your business. The buyers in Montreal know their business. But none of you know our customers. Two or three cents a yard more doesn't interest me too much. All I want to do

Nancy Middleton

Barbara Kirk in charge of household furnishings at the posts, with H.M. Ross and Rene Baudais at Buffalo Narrows. In the background is the Waite Fisheries plant.

is get merchanidise that my customers want and are willing to buy. Whether it comes from Montreal or Winnipeg doesn't matter a damn to the women buying the goods. The design and colours do. Now, do I get my prints?'

Reluctantly, he gave in and allowed me to have Len Coote place all my print orders with the Winnipeg supply house. And the Indian women snapped them up.

In October, I made a quick trip to Stanley, Patuanak and Buffalo Narrows to check that the new managers had settled in. Doug Johnson had already gone to Churchill and Bob Middleton was well established at Buffalo Narrows. Bob Urquhart and Jim Kirk were just completing the change of management inventory at Patuanak and Jim would be leaving for Stanley in a couple of days. The apprentice clerk at Stanley had been left temporarily in charge. On my way south, I took an inspection inventory at Beauval and Green Lake and then went on to Prince Albert.

The Canadian Committee had decreed that District Managers should call and check on the welfare of all pensioners in their districts. There were only two in my area, both residing in Prince

Albert and I had already written them, making appointments.

Mary J. Galbraith, the widow of post manager William Galbraith who died in 1925, was living *en pcnsion* in the McKay Hotel. As this was also my stopping place in town, I had already noticed the tall, dignified old lady on several occasions but didn't know who she was. Very slim and erect with a pile of white hair done in a bygone fashion, she was always dressed in dark, ankle-length dresses and wore a white lace scarf around her shoulders. She received me most graciously, almost regally, and during lunch assured me that she was in good financial circumstances. She asked me to thank the Company for their continuing interest in her well-being. Eventually, she moved to the west coast and died there at the ripe old age of 106.

That evening I called on Mr and Mrs Angus McKay. Angus was the fourth generation McKay to work in the Company's service. The first was John McKay, who came out from Scotland as an apprentice in 1790. For many years he was in charge of Brandon House and died there in 1810.

His son, John Richards McKay, continued the tradition of working for the Company and married Harriet Ballenden, daughter of Chief Factor John Ballenden. Their son, William McKay, was born in 1818, either at Beaver Creek Post or at Brandon House. In 1837 at the age of 19, William entered the Company's ranks as a York boat middleman and later as a cooper in the Swan River district. For a time he was an interpreter (1846-50) at Fort Pelly and from 1850-54 was postmaster there. In the years 1854-58, he was in charge of Egg Lake, Touchwood Hills and Cree Camp; from 1858-79 he was at Fort Ellice where he was appointed Chief Trader in 1865; Fort Pitt in Saskatchewan district from 1873-1883 and in 1882 he took charge of Edmonton district during Chief Factor Richard Hardisty's leave of absence. This was truly a remarkable career for a man who started as a middleman in a York boat. He died in Edmonton on Christmas Day 1883, leaving a wife of 37 years, Mary Cook, eight sons and two daughters.

Angus McKay, the son of William and Mary was born at Fort Pelly in December, 1858. Educated at St John's College, Winnipeg, he joined the Hudson's Bay Company as an apprentice clerk at Fort Carlton in 1877 and remained there until 1882 when he was transferred to Prince Albert. In 1885 he was sent to Fort Pitt to help re-establish it after the post had been plundered by Indians during the North West Rebellion. Promoted to clerk-in-charge, he operated Fort a la Corne, 1889-1899; Green Lake 1899-1907; Isle a la Crosse 1907-1909 and was transferred to La Ronge in 1909. He was given the title 'Post Manager' in 1913 and finally retired from La Ronge in 1921 after 44 years service. During the North West Rebellion, Angus McKay joined the volunteers at Fort Carlton and was sworn in as a scout by Colonel Sprout and conveyed messages from Major Crozier to Colonel Irving. He had many thrilling adventures and stories to tell of his experience.

When I met Angus, he was ninety years of age with a needle-sharp mind. We spent a grand evening discussing the Hudson's Bay Company and its affairs. I was very interested in his past life but he wasn't. 'Forget it, boy. It all happened a long time ago. It's history now. Tell me what's happening at some of my old posts.' He was a proud old man and assured me that he was getting along fine financially but somehow I got the feeling that all was not well. Mrs McKay showed me to the door and I quietly asked her to join me for tea the next morning at the hotel. 'I don't think your husband is telling me the whole truth, Mrs McKay. How do things actually stand with you?' She put down her cup with trembling hands, and started to cry. 'Please understand,' I said, 'the Company wants to help you if it is necessary.'

'Angus will not like my telling you but our savings are practically all gone and I don't know how I'm going to meet next month's bills. We have a little money set aside to cover his funeral expenses but that's all.' She dabbed her eyes with her handkerchief and took a deep breath. 'I'm sorry to break down like this, Mr Ross, but I don't know where to turn.' She twisted her handkerchief in her hands helplessly. 'I just don't know what we are going to do. We may have to use part of the funeral money to pay our bills and then what will I do if Angus dies?' I let her talk until she had calmed down. Then I assured her that I would get in touch with Winnipeg immediately.

Angus McKay in his retirement years at Prince Albert, with John Diefenbaker. October, 1951.

After she left, I telephoned Mort Malcolmson, personnel assistant in Winnipeg and told him the whole story. This all happened on a Tuesday. I subsequently learned that the matter was brought before the Canadian Committee on their regular Thursday morning meeting. A sum of money was wired immediately to Mr McKay's Prince Albert bank and an increase in his monthly pension was authorized. Angus McKay, the 'grand old man of Prince Albert' died in 1952 at the age of 93.

My next call was to Colonel Jones, superintendent of the Carlton Indian Agency. I had been unable to contact him all summer, as he was out travelling with Treaty payment parties. He was responsible for all the Indian reservations in Saskatchewan, north and east of Prince Albert. A former military man, he was sure of his own position and authority but he was also most humane and took a great interest in the welfare of the native bands under his jurisdiction. Fortunately, he was also well disposed towards the Hudson's Bay Company and was always made welcome whenever he called at any of our posts. He gave complete authority to each post manager to supply food or clothing to any genuine request from an indigent Indian. 'Just send the accounts to me and I'll authorize them for payment,' he ordered. This was an almost unprecedented concession and I urged my managers to exercise it very carefully and not take advantage of it in any way.

When monthly family allowance cheques were issued to Indians, they were made out in the mother's name. In Saskatchewan, a previous District Manager had set up a separate credit account system in the name of each mother and she was allowed to charge up any food or clothing required for her family during the month. Her husband was not allowed to use this account at all, nor was she permitted to take up the whole of her cheque in credit. The mother must always have a small cash balance on hand after she had received her monthly cheque and paid off her debt.

Colonel Jones had seen this system in action and thoroughly endorsed it, greatly to the chagrin of the provincial government who said it was another instance of the Company's 'debt policy'. The same system was applied to Indian recipients of the Old Age Pension. Now, instead of being a burden to their families, these old men and women were able to live decently and comfortably.

As December drew to a close it became increasingly evident that the appointment of Bob Urquhart as manager of Patuanak was not a success. Approaching retirement age, his health was deteriorating and Patuanak was not an easy post to run, for the Chipewyans are a difficult people to deal with. Staff transfers and holidays are usually taken care of during the summer months and, in mid-winter, it was almost impossible to find a replacement. Fortunately, just after the New Year, a young man who had been home in Newfoundland on holidays from the western Arctic showed up in Winnipeg with his new bride on his way back to his post at Holman Island. With the General Manager's permission, I grabbed him and that was the beginning of a long friendship with Leonard Coates.

Len was a tall, red-headed Newfoundlander with a strong sense of humour. He had that indefinable quality necessary for our business: he was a 'good trader'. He was quick to gain the confidence of his native customers and soon had no trouble trading with the Chipewyans at Patuanak. By the following winter, when Waite Fisheries sent a Bombardier to Patuanak, Len had a profitable commercial fishing business running smoothly. In fact, he did such a good job that he didn't stay long at Patuanak. In the summer of 1950 he was promoted to the charge of Stanley when Jim Kirk resigned to take over his father's hardware business on the west coast. In 1952 he was further promoted to the charge of La Ronge when Bill McKinnie was transferred west to Fort Nelson Mile 300.

In accordance with Company regulations, each post manager had to take an inventory twice a year -- a semi-annual inventory in November or December, and the year-end inventory on May 31st, the close of the fiscal year. In addition, the district manager took an inspection inventory at each post at least once a year. This meant that I took at least thirteen inventories per year and I usually spread them apart so that on each trip, I would do one at larger posts like La Ronge, Buffalo Narrows or Isle a la Crosse, which might take five days, and two at other smaller posts. The inventoried posts were scheduled at the beginning of a trip in case difficulties were encountered with gross profit percentage. If problems arose, I scrapped my intinerary and the post manager and I worked until the problem was solved.

I had little trouble in this regard during my nine years in Saskatchewan and usually it boiled down to the misfiling of invoices. This sometimes happened with younger post managers who had been promoted from apprentice clerks after only two or three year's experience in post work and consequently had received little training in the making up of trading accounts. I made it a point of pulling my accounting manual from my 'district office bag' and step by step, followed the instructions. Of course, I knew the routine backwards but I did this to impress on the post manager the absolute necessity of following each step carefully to eliminate errors in calculation. There is nothing more harrowing than taking a post inventory at the end of a trip and finding errors. Not only are you tired after having been out for two or three weeks and relishing the thought of returning home, but your supply of fresh shirts and socks has usually run out and you have to buy new ones. Bea tried relentlessly to sneak a cake of soap into the suitcase as a subtle hint, but I always found it and left it at home.

At Brochet, c.1950. From the left: Charlie Klein, clerk at Brochet, Bill Garbutt, H.M. Ross and an unidentified pilot.

Saskatchewan District was laid out in such a way that it was easy to drop in to three or four posts after you had finished inventory at one particular post and spend a day or two at each place doing a few of the other necessary inspection checks or simply talking with the post manager and his staff to ensure that the Company's affairs were running smoothly. In addition to inventory taking, cash books had to be checked and balanced and the actual cash on hand counted.   In season, I checked the amounts of individual advances to trappers or commercial fishermen against the authorized amount to ensure that they had not been exceeded. Fire safety precautions were checked regularly.   A ladder was required at each building to reach from the ground to the eaves and from there, another ladder to the crown of the roof.   Stove pipes were cleaned monthly and marked off on a chart on the office wall. Fire extinguishers were placed at specific locations in each heated building and each one was examined twice a year to be sure it was in proper working order.   An adequate supply of refills for the extinguishers had to be on hand at all times. Fire axes, painted red, hung on the walls of each building in strategic positions.

Once a year, a list of post dwelling equipment was reviewed with the manager's wife and duly entered into both her copy of the household equipment book and mine. It covered everything from forks and knives to carpets, bed and window coverings. A minimum quantity was noted against each item and a furnishings requisition was made out to bring the list up to standard.

In the spring, an operating budget covering next year's operation was prepared for each post, which I made up in conjunction with the post manager. As the Fur Trade Department derived its income from the posts, each post had to carry its share of the operating expenses of both Head Office and District Office. When the figures were provided by the controller, they were allocated to each post on a ratio to sales basis.

An estimate of the quantities of the various furs that would be purchased at each post was supplied by C. G. Wilson, the Company's fur expert. This was based on a record of past performance over the years by each post, taking into account cyclical variations for each variety of fur. Mr Wilson also supplied his projected average price for each type of fur. When extended out, the result was the total cash value of furs to be purchased at each post. It never ceased to amaze me how accurately the projections turned out.

For posts engaged in commercial fishing, I obtained an estimate of the price Waite Fisheries would be paying for each variety of fish. Armed with this figure plus information supplied by each manager on his anticipated volume of sales from Family Allowance and Old Age Pension cheques, and an estimate for cash sales, it was easy to arrive at an estimated total sales volume for the year. Then I went over the rest of the proposed budget with the manager, which mainly included the amounts to be spent on wages, repairs, fuel and light, plus district office administration charges. By deducting the total from anticipated sales, the resulting figure for net profit for the year emerged.

Budgets were discussed in great detail with each post manager before our final anticipated result was arrived at, then were consolidated into a proposed budget for the whole district and forwarded to the General Manager's office. Occasionally, certain unforeseeable circumstances would make the figures vary greatly, such as sudden fluctuations in the fur market, changes in the price of fish, or, as happened one year at La Ronge, an unexpected invasion of prospectors seeking uranium. But usually the budget figures turned out to be very accurate.

The post manager submitted a proposed list of trapping advances to be issued by him in the coming trapping season every summer, and I usually made it a point to discuss the lists personally with each manager before giving them my final approval. The lists were not prepared haphazardly. Posts kept up complete files on individual trappers giving the usual data of marital status and if married, the number of family members, and the total amount of each type of fur he had sold to the Company for the previous ten years, and whether he had paid his annual advance in full each year. Any mitigating circumstances known to the post manager were always considered. Perhaps the trapper had been sick for some time or there had been a death in the family, or perhaps the weather had been bad, making trips out to the trapline difficult. All these things were taken into consideration. Then there were always young fellows starting out on their own. Here again, the post manager's knowledge of the man's character had to be the deciding factor on whether or not he would be given an advance and how much he should get.

Occasionally, there were special subjects that we were asked to discuss. On one occasion, we were instructed to bring up the question of retirement and how well the post manager was prepared for it. I usually pointed out that after working for the Company all their lives with house, furnishings and mess provided, it was quite a traumatic experience to find on retirement that you not only had to find a new home but also had to furnish it from scratch. The Company provided a pension sufficient to live decently, but we urged the post managers to set up some form of savings to meet these immediate expenses. A staff savings account service was available whereby post managers could allot a portion of their monthly salaries and receive a higher interest rate than a commercial bank returned. The message from Headquarters was, if you hadn't already done so, start to set up a reserve immediately to take care of your expenses on retirement.

I was quite satisfied with the response. Most of my managers were canny and were already putting savings by regularly, but a few of the younger ones were inclined to spend all their savings when they went out on furlough every two years. To my surprise, in the whole district, Jock Mathieson at Beauval was the best prepared. He had purchased a small property near Rocky Mountain House in northern Alberta which he was renting out until he retired. I suppose this small farm came as near as anything to Jock's idea of a croft in his native Highlands of Scotland.

Another discussion involved the Company's bonus system. For as long as I knew personally, the Company had always had a bonus system which was paid to post mangers and higher ranks. Apprentice clerks and local staff didn't participate; they were paid overtime. The bonus was rather hit or miss in the days when fur was shipped annually to England. Any profits made on the sale of furs couldn't be pinned down to an individual posts but were credited in a lump sum to each district. Excess profits were then distributed to each post manager in the district without taking into consideration whether he himself had had a profitable operation for the preceding year. With the initiation of selling furs in Montreal and New York, as well as England, and making fur shipments to Montreal weekly rather than once or twice a year, it was now possible to determine accurately just how much money each post made or lost on its fur.

The prime consideration in paying bonuses was making a satisfactory profit. This was what the post manager was paid for. Most of the net profit was returned to the Company's shareholders in the form of a dividend, the exact amount being decided upon by the London Committee. We always referred to this as the 'widows and orphans' portion because, at one time, most shares of the Company were held in England in trust for women and children. Once the profit of each district was established, the dividend was paid and the District Manager, and each post manager was paid a percentage according to the amount of excess profits they produced. The general rule was that the maximum bonus a man could receive was 25 percent of his annual salary and the minimum was 10 percent. The latter was usually given to managers whose results were not up to par through no fault of their own, but rather through unforeseen circumstances.

The men welcomed this new policy as a tangible reward for their hard work and I encouraged them to increase their sales wherever possible and keep their expenses low. In addition, interest on capital had to be kept down. 'Don't hold on to any remittances longer than necessary,' I urged. 'Ship your remittances to District Office by every mail. Send your furs purchased every week, if you can, and keep your stocks as low as consistent with the needs of the trade. Every unnecessary dollar that you have on hand means that the Company has to borrow to cover it and has to pay the high interest charges.'

There were only two negative reactions. Len Coates, now at La Ronge, protested in his usual good-natured fashion. 'But the manager in charge of Portage la Loche or Brochet can make a bigger bonus than I can. He buys a lot more fur and has no opposition to contend with. Here at La Ronge I have two opposition stores and there is less fur available.'

Len had just bought himself a brand new automobile and would occasionally drive down to Waskesiu on a Sunday for a game of golf. 'Well Len, you have a very good point. If you really want to give up your car, your golf and your curling in the winter and go back inland, I can quite easily arrange it. But I don't think you'd really be happy inland again and I'm quite sure your wife wouldn't enjoy it.' Len laughed at the thought of his wife's reaction to such a move. In the end, he did a terrific job at La Ronge and earned himself quite a few good-sized bonuses.

It was a different case with another post manager who shall be nameless. I was at his post for a few days taking inventory and he kept nagging at me all the time, not only about the new bonus system, but about practically every regulation the Company had -- wages, promotion, retirement plans. None of them pleased him. And he went on complaining -- during working hours, in the evenings, even during mealtimes. I did my best to explain the Company's policies but nothing satisfied him. I stood it for a couple of days but his constant barrage tried my patience and when he started ranting on again at dinner that evening, I had had enough. 'If you aren't happy working for the Bay, there is only one solution. You've spent the last several days bitching about everything and quite frankly, it looks to me as if you are in the wrong job. I am quite prepared to accept your resignation from the Hudson's Bay Company right this minute.' And I meant it. He looked at me, stunned.

Both of us were startled when his wife began to laugh. 'You should see your face,' she said to her husband. 'I've listened to you rant and rave everytime a district manager was coming...and then again after he left but Mr Ross has called your bluff. I never thought you would meet a district manager who could best you but he has. What are you going to do about your job now?' He sheepishly agreed that perhaps he had been overdoing it. He stayed on but I was was happy when he was transferred out of the district to Western Division.

On June 1, 1949, I was confirmed as Manager of Saskatchewan District at an annual salary of $4,200. The following year, I received a raise of $300; the next three years, an increase of $500 per year and on January 1, 1953, a final raise to $6,600 per annum, which was the maximum salary range for the Saskatchewan District.

On the surface, post inspection would appear to be a simple routine task. You drop into a post, take an inventory, check the cash, check this, check that, and then get into your little airplane and fly away to the next post to repeat the process.

Not so. Post managers are human beings and, especially if they are young, they are apt to make mistakes. Any idiot can go to a post and find something wrong if he looks hard enough, tear a strip off the poor manager who daren't answer back, and then leave the building thinking, 'By God, I sure told that fellow a thing or two.'

But I found that there was much more to it than that. I tried never to forget that I probably wouldn't see the man again for at least three months and, in the meantime, he was still fully responsible for the Company's vested capital in the post and for carrying out his trading duties to the best of his ability. If I left the post with the manager feeling lower than a snake's belly, he could get very discouraged, and say 'to hell with it'.

I always made it a point to discuss errors as we went along and tell or, in some instances, show the post manager the proper procedure. After all, I had been a post manager myself for many years. Before leaving, I made sure I found something positive to say, even if it was only to compliment him on the condition of the buildings and grounds. A 'well done' and firm handshake was a practice that paid great dividends.

A manager of another district told of how he once arrived at a post which was in a real mess. After spending a week cleaning it up, he used his last morning there calling the post manager down for his failings. But, his scheduled plane didn't arrive due to weather conditions and for the next three days, the post manager barely spoke to him and his wife glared across the table at him during meals. In the evenings, they pretended that he was invisible.

I also believed that if the post manager's wife was happy, then her husband would be content and if the husband was content, he would do a good job. So I always bent over backwards to keep the wives in my district feeling happy. Mostly this boiled down to furnishings and equipment which I made sure were kept up to snuff and replaced promptly when necessary.

Barbara Kirk, who had replaced Jessie Bacon as household furnishings expert, made a trip around the district with me in the summer of 1949. As a result,I was gradually able to replace all iceboxes with Servel kerosene-operated refrigerators.

The biggest complaint from the ladies was that, as the household furnishings were all standard and the interior walls were all painted in neutral tones, they always found the houses much the same no matter where they were transferred. Mrs Watt at Isle a la Crosse solved the problem to her satisfaction by having a set of draperies and sofa covers made up. When she and her husband transferred from one post to another, she folded up the Company's draperies and covers, put them away and used her own instead.

Mrs McKinley at Pelican Narrows complained loud and long about the monotonous colours of the interior walls.

'Mrs McKinley, if you don't like the colours, why don't you order paint in the shades that suit you and charge it up to post expenses?' I suggested.

'Can I?' she asked. 'You mean any colour I want?' When I assured her that I meant just that, she was delighted. On my next trip to Pelican Narrows, I walked into a living room with a black ceiling; a foot-wide strip of white ran round the top of the walls and the rest of the walls were painted pink. It was, quite literally, stunning! But I never batted an eye. Those were the colours she wanted and she was happy with them. If and when they were transferred, it would only cost a few dollars to repaint.

When Ed McLean and his wife came from Cumberland House to Montreal Lake in 1953, I was warned by his former district manager that I would have trouble with Mrs McLean. According to him, she was a bear-cat -- always complaining about something. And sure enough, on my next trip to Montreal Lake, Mrs McLean started in about the bland and uninteresting design of all Company houses -- everywhere.

'Why can't we decorate them the way we want? After all, we are the ones who have to live here. I've lived in Company houses for a long time and I'm sick of the standard colours. It's like living inside a scoop of vanilla ice cream,' she declared. Picking up a newly arrived magazine, she flipped through the pages showing me pictures of beautifully decorated living rooms.

'I realize this kind of thing is impractical but just once, I would like to live in a house that I could think of as mine -- my own colours, with curtains to match.' And she threw the magazine down on the table, disconsolately.

I knew only too well how she felt. Bea had frequently voiced the same feelings and I could sympathize with Mrs McLean. 'May I make a suggestion?' I asked. 'Why don't you and Eddie slip down to Prince Albert some half-day, go to a paint store and choose the colours you want. Look through your magazines again and find a design you like for curtains. Then send me the paint samples and the design and I'll get Miss Kirk to find curtains to match.' Her face brightened up immediately and she jumped up, offering me a cup of tea. 'Mind you, I'll expect you and Eddie to do the painting yourselves,' I added.

As we sipped our tea, she pulled out the magazines again, trying to decide on a colour scheme. The next time I went up to Montreal Lake, the interior was all done up in shades of mauve and yellow. Mrs McLean was chirping like a lark and I never did have any trouble with her.

When I first became a District Manager, I found that one of my annual jobs was to make out a rating report on each manager in my district and discuss it with him personally. I don't know when this all started . In all my years with the Company no one had ever discussed an evaluation report with me. I thought it an excellent idea, however, as a post manager's future depended entirely on the rating he received.

I took great care in making out the reports, writing them out by hand and then handing them personally to each manager. When he'd had a chance to read it and think about it, I asked if he agreed with my remarks or had any points he wished clarified. Occasionally someone would query my comments under the heading of accounting or merchandising or fur buying and we discussed the point fully. If the post manager put up a sound argument, I would amend the remarks; but if I felt certain of my evaluation I would say, 'No, you have a little way to go on that subject. Give it another year and then I'm sure I'll be able to make a more encouraging report.' By doing this, each post manager knew exactly how he stood with the Company and what his chances of promotion were.

As a result, I lost a few good men who were promoted to larger posts in other districts. I always took great pleasure in their promotions and there were always younger clerks coming up ready to take their place.

The arrival of mail was a big day at the posts. There were long-awaited letters from home to be read and enjoyed, and put away to be read again and again. But there were always the half-dozen or so buff envelopes from District Office crammed with circular letters and individual letters to the post manager. The circular letters were the bane of the post manager's life and covered any and all subjects under the sun. After a while, you glanced over them casually, muttering 'more bumff' and tossed them aside to be filed under their proper heading.

In his book *The Men of the Hudson's Bay Company*, District Manager N.M.W.J. MacKenzie (more commonly known as 'Alphabet' MacKenzie) stated that he had composed a complete series of circular letters, numbered 1 to 40, which covered every aspect of the operation of a post. This was during the years 1910-11 when he was in charge of Lake Huron District with the district office in North Bay, Ontario. In 1912, he was stationed at Fort William in charge of Lake Superior District and he noted, 'I have been to every post in the district. To show the interest that many of them took in their work, some managers could repeat all my circulars from memory and give the date and number of any of them without hesitation -- and they received them at every post on an average of once a week.' He later stated, 'The system we inaugurated in Lake Huron District is now installed in every district in the country and has worked out with mathematical accuracy and convenience.' Mr Patterson, manager of Lac Seul Post, on being promoted to charge of Nelson River District, asked if he could take copies of the circulars with him. 'They are just cracker-jacks and as good as a dictionary.'

The original circulars, designated as 'permanent circulars', were to be retained in a separate file for reference at all times. I ran into a set of them at Grassy Narrows post in 1935. They covered everything from a formula for mixing whitewash for the exterior building walls, to the proper method of cleaning stove pipes, to how to take annual inventory. The thought always kept running through my head: 'If these instructions are so good, why do we need an inspector or district manager to visit the post?'

Over the course of time, circular letters (non-permanent) became more and more rambling, covering two or three pages and including every cliche known to man. The usual ending was this: 'This is for your information and guidance. You will please, therefore, govern yourself accordingly.' In time, the district manager became more foxy. At the end of each circular was a tear-strip which had to be dated and signed by the post manager and returned to district office in the next outgoing mail. It read 'I beg to acknowledge receipt of your circular number...., dated....... and its contents have been read and thoroughly understood.'

Being a charitable man, I could understand that, in the old days, travelling by canoe or dogteam when districts contained twenty or more posts plus camp trades and outposts, it was difficult for a district manager to inspect each post more than once a year. When I was in charge of Grassy Narrows (1935-37), my post was inspected once. At Temagami (1937-41) I had two inspections. Hence the necessity for all the circular letters. In later years, when I wasn't quite so charitable in my thinking, I decided that the circulars were the district manager's gift to posterity to show his excellent command of the English language, but I always held the nagging thought that they were an 'out' for the district manager. If a problem arose at a post, he could always point to a circular letter number....dated....in which he had covered the subject thoroughly and, therefore, could not be held responsible for the post manager's wrongdoing.

Individual letters to a post were better but still too long -- usually a page and a half at least. To my mind, one page should be sufficient to instruct a post manager to do this or that. In addition to being too wordy, they invariably concluded with the words 'use your own discretion'. Using his own discretion was what a post manager was paid to do and, in most cases, that was just what he did. So why write a letter telling him to do so?

As a district manager, I cut out a whole lot of the letter writing. One circular letter I sent out annually covered the issue of the fur-buying tariff. When the tariff was given to us by our fur expert, Charles Wilson, he also supplied technical notes explaining any difference in the purchase price for each variety of fur; this information was valuable, not only to me but also to the men on the spot buying the fur.

After informing my post managers that I would be making frequent visits each year, I supplied them with an inspection notebook to remind them of any questions they might wish to bring up. I did the same with my own inspection book which I carried with me at all times. 'But remember,' I told them, 'if you run into any unexpected difficulties or have any problems that you think you can't handle yourself, write me or, if necessary, wire me and I'll be at your post within a week.'

I didn't get too many cries for help.

For the most part, I kept my letters short and to the point. Perhaps unconsciously, I aimed them at Jock Mathieson at Beauval with the underlying thought, 'If Jock can understand this, then everyone can.'

Up until my transfer out west in 1941, any letters I received from District Office had always started out, 'Dear Mr Ross'. At Waterways, however, letters began to arrive headed 'Dear Ross' -- an address that I did not like one little bit. Maybe my Scottishness was showing but to me this was an English affectation along the lines of the English Public School 'old boy' system. After receiving a few from Bruce Clark headed 'Dear Ross', I addressed my reply, 'Dear Clark'. He got the message very quickly and thereafter I was Mr Ross once again.

As a district manager, I followed the same procedure. In public or in front of his staff, I referred to each post manager as Mr....... and received the same courtesy. The post manager was the Company's representative in each settlement and his dignity had to be maintained.

In the beginning, I had powwows with the natives at each post.

They all wanted to meet the new Company 'big boss' and size him up. The meetings were formal, with the Chief and his councillors and an interpreter present. As we began to know each other better, the ceremonial aspects faded away. At Brochet, they discussed Bill Garbutt and the tenor of their talk was always 'he is a very strange man and we don't understand him,' followed quickly by 'but we like him and we don't want you to move him away.' I assured them that Bill could stay at Brochet as long as he wished.

The meeting at Portage la Loche was very different. A bunch of locals, headed by one Robbie Fontaine pushed forward insisting that they wanted a meeting with me immediately. I had known Robbie during my years as manager at Waterways when the Portage la Loche natives came down to work for the Mackenzie River Transport. I didn't think too highly of him.

'You're not the Chief here, are you Robbie?' I asked.

'No,' he replied, 'but we all want to talk to you.' I invited them into the office and when they were seated, I noticed that Mr Blackhall was not present and called him in.

'Oh no,' shouted Robbie. 'We don't want him in here. We just want to talk to you. It's him we have to talk about.'

'Robbie, Mr Blackhall is the post manager here. If you want to talk about him, it's only fair that he be present to hear what you are saying.' He stood up belligerently and started to interrupt but I held up my hand for silence. 'How would you like it if the band held a meeting to discuss you and you were kept out?' They grumbled a bit but Robbie backed down into his seat and I went out and invited the manager in.

Robbie made a long, complaining speech -- in English, on which I had insisted, as he was not the Chief of the band. 'Mr Blackhall is a very hard manager to get along with,' shouted Robbie. 'He doesn't treat us right and won't give us any debt.' He looked around at his friends who urged him on with nods and words of encouragement. 'We demand that you send him away and give us another manager that we can get along with.' With that ultimatum, he plunked himself down in his chair.

While I listened attentively to Robbie's ranting, I looked up his record in the customers' record book, and, placing it squarely on the desk where he couldn't help but see his name, I replied, 'What you are really complaining about, Robbie, is that Mr Blackhall will not give *you* any debt. When I look at the record book, I can understand why. Would you like me to read it out to all your friends here and let them know how often you have been given debt and never paid it?'

The other men leaned forward to get a better look. Carefully avoiding the eyes of his cronies, Robbie blustered that his record was private and wasn't anyone else's business.

'Robbie,' I said, 'you have gone about this thing the wrong way round. If you had told me that Mr Blackhall was a very easy man to get along with and gave you all the debt you wanted, I would move him away tomorrow. Instead, you say that he is a hard man and won't give you any debt. Let me tell you, if I was the post manager here, I would do exactly the same thing. Mr Blackhall will remain at this post as long as he wants.'

It was a rather discomfited bunch that shuffled out of the office.

All of the Saskatchewan Government Airways pilots were great fliers. I know, because I have flown with most of them -- Scotty McLeod who later became operations manager, Lefty McLeod, Don Brownridge, Cliff Labey, Stu Miller -- but there was one who, in my estimation, had that little something extra. Rene Baudais, a former R.C.A.F. pilot, was a lean, dark French-Canadian with a quiet sense of humour which always seemed to be bubbling to the surface. I began to ask for him when I booked a charter flight and it gradually became the accepted thing for Rene to be assigned to my flights. Meticulous in every detail, he checked the aircraft from nose to tail, and his searching eyes missed nothing.

Following takeoff, his procedure was always the same. Once the stabilizer was adjusted for level flight, the trailing aerial was unwound and he contacted the base radio station at La Ronge giving our altitude, direction, weather, destination and estimated arrival time.   Thereafter, he broadcast this information every twenty minutes on the hour. Watching his routine always made me feel safe. If, heaven forbid, we had to make a forced landing, La Ronge always knew our position to within twenty minutes which would help considerably to narrow down the search. Any decision as to whether we should fly or not was left entirely in Rene's hands.

Sitting beside him in the cockpit of a Stinson 108 A and flying at anywhere between 7,000 and 10,000 feet, I looked at the country beneath us, spread out in a maze of lakes and rivers of all shapes and sizes. He gave me his aerial maps to study and to follow our course.   I tried picking out a small, peculiarly shaped lake immediately beneath us and then tried to locate it on the map, but by the time I had done so, the lake was far behind us. Rene watched me go through this routine several times and although he smiled quietly, he offered no advice. I was getting frustrated and started to fold up the chart in disgust.

'Can't figure it out, eh?' He opened the chart again and, pointing to a large lake straight ahead, said, 'Look ahead of you first, pick out the largest lake and then check the map. You'll find it by the time we fly over it.' By following his instructions, I soon got to be fairly good.

'Where are we now?' he would ask, and when I confidently announced that we were coming up on Lake ....., he would ask if I was sure.

'I'm sure,' I replied, and pointed to a spot on the map. 'There it is on the map and just south on the left is Lake....and north on the right is Lake....'

He chuckled and slapped me on the back. 'That's right. I'll make a navigator out of you yet.' In time, I came to know the geography of northern Saskatchewan very thoroughly from the air.

In fine weather, he would occasionally hand the steering controls to me, saying, 'Here, you take her for awhile.' The first time he did this, I was petrified and the only thing I moved were my eyeballs for fear that I would put us in the bush.

'Just relax, Hugh.' Then it was, 'Watch your needle. Keep your eye on the compass. Watch the ball and make sure that you are flying level.' 'Needle and ball' became the watchword. I gripped the controls so tightly that my knuckles were white.

'Take it easy,' he said. 'Don't hold the controls so tight. They won't fall off, you know.' As I eased up a little, he said, 'The plane wants to fly straight and level so let her do so.' That first five-minute flying lesson seemed hours long and there was perspiration on my forehead when he took over again.

After I calmed down, I quizzed him about his experiences at air training school. 'Did they put you through all those manoeuvres?' I asked.

'What manoeuvres?'

'You know -- looping the loop, side-slipping -- all that sort of thing.' We were flying along at about 10,000 feet from Patuanak to Stanley and the weather was clear as a bell.

He looked over at me and, with a wolfish grin, said, 'You mean you've never seen any aerial manoeuvres?'

'Only in the movies,' I replied.

'Then tighten your seatbelt.' Immediately he put the plane through a series of loops and spins, ending up with a 'falling leaf'. It took my stomach a long time to crawl up from my boots.

Another time at La Ronge, I decided to make a short side trip up to Stanley to see how Len Coates was doing at his new post. As we strolled down the dock to our Stinson, I noticed a strange aircraft tied up to a buoy in the bay, and asked Rene about it.

'That's our new Beaver. Now there's an airplane for you. It's going to be *the* plane of the bush! You can land or take off in a puddle of water.' Then he turned to me and asked, 'We could use the Beaver to fly up to Stanley. How about it?'

'I'm game.'

It seemed to me that once the plane was up on the step -- which is bush pilot's lingo, meaning that the engine has been gunned for take-off and the floats are just skimming the surface -- it took off in less than 100 yards. When we reached cruising altitude, Rene handed me the controls. 'Here, you take it to Stanley.' He leaned back in his seat and closed his eyes.

As we approached Stanley, I began to circle around before handing the wheel over. When I jostled him awake, he said, 'Well, are you going to stay up here all day? Why don't you land the

Carl Christenson

*Rene Baudais gassing
up at Amisk Lake, 1948*

thing?' And land it I did. The Beaver was a joy to handle. I must be one of the few men who have flown and landed an airplane but have never taken one off the ground.

On another occasion, we were at Pelican Narrows rather late in December. By the 20th I had finished taking the inventory and the weather closed in. The storm continued for the next two days so...no flying. On the morning of the 23rd, Rene said, 'I don't know about you but I want to be home for Christmas so I'm leaving in an hour.' The weather was still thick and I wasn't too keen about going, even though I was anxious to be with Bea and the kids for the holidays.

'Are you sure we can make it, Rene? We won't be able to see the ground from the air. How will we know where we are?'

'I think we'll be okay. I've flown in worse conditions. According to the radio, the weather is lifting a little at Prince Albert. Once we get into the air, we'll fly the Saskatoon navigation beam southwest,' he explained. 'We'll be flying into a right-angle triangle with Prince Albert at the apex. From there the highway runs north to La Ronge and the railway runs east to Nipawin. We should hit one or the other.'

The weather might have worried me but I had complete confidence in Rene and agreed to go. Conditions were rotten at first but the farther south we flew, the more it cleared. Rene had calculated the elapsed flying time and when this was about up, he said, 'Let's get downstairs a bit and see where we are.' Sure enough, there beneath us was a railway track and a huge grain elevator with the name of the station painted in large letters on the side. In a few minutes we landed safely at Prince Albert and I was on my way home in time to spend Christmas with Bea and the children.

George Greening was a legendary figure in northwest Saskatchewan. As pilot for Waite Fisheries, he had a reputation as a daredevil flyer who was prone to take chances. Quite frankly, his reputation scared me and, although he was a very likeable character, I turned down his many requests to fly me around. One day at Big River, Len Waite asked me why I never used George as a pilot, and pointed out how convenient it would be for me to make short hops from Buffalo Narrows -- George's base -- to Isle a la Crosse, Patuanak, Dillon or Portage la Loche. I told him straight that I didn't want to risk my neck. 'You just leave it to me,' said Len. 'I'll have a little talk with George.'

So shortly thereafter, I hired him to fly me from Buffalo Narrows to Patuanak and then to Big River. He treated me as if I was a newborn babe. I couldn't have asked for more consideration. Len must, indeed, have spoken to him. I used him several times after that, when it fitted my itinerary.

One cold winter's afternoon, we landed at Patuanak to find the post manager worried sick about his clerk; he had gone out in the Bombardier that morning to visit a fish camp about twenty miles east of the post and still hadn't returned.

'Leave it to me,' said George. 'I'll find him.' He was back in an hour or so with a very cold and very scared clerk. The Bombardier had conked out on the return trip about ten miles from the post. He tried in vain to restart it, then set out to walk back to the post. The young man was wearing heavy flying boots and when George spotted him, he was making slow progress.

'Why didn't you use the duffle socks and moccasins in the survival kit on the Bombardier?' the manager asked. 'You would have made much better progress.'

'I've never had to use the survival equipment and I didn't think they were necessary so I left them behind,' answered the young clerk, sheepishly. I'm afraid I gave both the post manager and the clerk a rough time of it for disobeying the Company's strict instructions about always carrying the survival equipment.

'Believe me, Mr Ross,' said the clerk, 'I'll never leave the post without that equipment again.'

The weather continued to be extremely cold and when George flew me down to Big River next day in a small Cessna 120, the in-cabin heater wasn't functioning and by the time we reached our destination, we were both frozen stiff and could hardly climb out of the plane. As quickly as my icy limbs allowed, I made my way to the hotel bar and had a good stiff snort of Scotch to thaw me out.

I was only involved in an emergency landing once. Don Brownridge and I were flying from Portage la Loche to Buffalo Narrows on another very cold winter morning. About halfway across the twenty-mile strip of land separating Methye Lake from Big Buffalo Lake, Don put the nose of the plane down sharply and headed for a small lake. Unaware that anything was wrong, I jokingly said, 'What's the matter, Don? Sudden nature call?'

It was a grim-faced pilot who turned to me and said, 'No, but my oil pressure gauge suddenly registered zero so I picked the first landing spot I could see in case the motor packed up in mid-air.' He got us down on the lake quickly and, while I stayed inside the still warm cabin, he lifted the cowling and fiddled around in the engine. God, it was cold outside! I felt sorry for Don but I knew I would be utterly useless as a mechanic's helper. Neither one of us looked forward to spending hours in the bush if the plane was unserviceable, although we had survival equipment and the radio was working. Eventually he climbed back into the cockpit with a broad smile on his face.

'Everything's okay,' he said, trying to rub some feeling back into his frozen hands. 'There's lots of oil in the sump. It looks as if one of the pipes leading to the pressure gauge has frozen.' Greatly relieved, we took off again and arrived safely at Buffalo Narrows. He was right. It was a frozen pipe and Don and George Greening spent that afternoon at Buffalo Narrows making repairs.

Coming off a trip up the west side of the province in early December on my way to La Ronge, I decided on the spur of the moment to have Rene drop me at Beauval to look in on Jock Mathieson. Although it was a casual visit, Jock seemed apprehensive and kept up a nervous chatter as we walked around the store, checking merchandise here and there. Jock just didn't chatter as a rule. He wasn't his usual phlegmatic self and I came to the conclusion that something was amiss, but went about my business until finally, Jock couldn't stand the suspense any longer.

'You're not going to take an inventory, are you? I just did the semi-annual inventory two weeks ago.'

So that was it. Something was wrong with the inventory. 'I might as well do an inventory as long as I'm here,' I replied. I told Rene to carry on to La Ronge and I'd wire him in a few days to come and pick me up. It was a very worried Jock Mathieson who followed me closely all around the warehouse, assuring me at each department that everything checked out -- until I happened to look up. When I queried Jock about a bunch of fishnets hanging from the rafters, he broke down. 'Almost every post has a good commercial fishing business and their profits are much higher than mine, so I gave the nets to the natives on credit.' He was very distraught. 'It could have worked too, Mr Ross, but the fishermen didn't pay for them so I took the nets back.' He pulled the used fishing nets down and lamented, 'They're useless now. They're used and no one will buy them. What's going to happen now?'

I couldn't help it, but I started to laugh. 'Jock, I can't say I blame you for trying. But you should have known better. The natives here don't have many furs and trying to collect extra debt from them would try the patience of Job.' He was visibly relieved at my reaction to his earnest though unauthorized attempts to make a profit. 'Tell you what. We can't take these nets on inventory, so we'll have to write them off. You send them up to Isle a la Crosse on the next truck and I'll write Bill Watt to sell them for you there or at Patuanak. They should get enough to at least cover your costs.' And so it was done. Jock got credit for the nets in a couple of months' time and his percentage profit returned to normal.

When I wired La Ronge for a plane to pick me up, most of the regular planes were busy and they advised me to expect a plane from Prince Albert. The pilot was a complete stranger. He was a pilot-instructor from Prince Albert but he assured me that he was familiar with northern flying. All the bush pilots were masters of their craft and I assumed we would have our normal flight. How wrong I was! When we took off, I automatically looked at my watch, expecting the pilot to check in by radio. When a few minutes passed and he didn't, I said, 'Aren't you going to contact La Ronge and advise them that we are on our way?'

'Oh, right.' And he called. The weather was bad, snowing quite heavily and the visibility was gradually diminishing. The pilot climbed up through the muck until we came out in clear sunshine. We kept flying on and on. I attempted to make conversation but was met with monosyllabic answers so gave up. And we kept flying on until I got restless and looked at my watch again.

'We should be at La Ronge by now,' I remarked. 'Don't you think you should call them again?' I was so used to Rene calling in every twenty minutes I was getting a bit worried about this man.

'Oh. Right!' He raised La Ronge again. When the transmission was completed he turned to me and said, 'I think we have overflown La Ronge. They sounded fainter than the last time I called. With a worried frown, he pulled out the aerial maps, checked his compass and said, 'My God, we must be up over the Churchill River!'

'Well, you better get down and find out where we are.'

Down we went through the snow which got thicker the lower we got. 'I can't go any lower. Look at the altimeter. If I get any lower, we might crash. I can't see the ground,' he cried in a panicky voice.

I grabbed the aerial maps. 'Well, we can't stay up here all day.

You'd better ease down so we can find a place to land. Once we get over the Cambrian Shield there are damned few lakes to land on in a hurry.'

Very diffidently, the pilot eased the plane down and we came out just above the treetops, much too close for comfort. 'Look, there ahead of us...a lake.' He pointed excitedly. It looked familiar. It was shaped like a clam with an island in the centre.

'I know where we are,' I said. 'We're south of La Ronge, I'm sure.' I examined it closely. 'That looks like Meeyomoot Lake, east of Montreal Lake.'

'It can't be,' said the pilot. 'That's impossible. My compass can't be out that much.'

'Impossible or not, this is not Shield country. If I'm right, there's a small river flowing out of the north arm of this lake which goes north to La Ronge. Just follow the shoreline and see.' Sure enough, there was the river. I heaved a sigh of relief and blessed Rene Baudais for teaching me to read maps.

'Now, keep low and follow that river until we hit Lac la Ronge. Then just follow the shoreline west until we come to the settlement,' I said. And so we did. My knees were trembling so much I could scarcely walk when I got out of the aircraft. I tersely told the pilot I was through with him and walked away. Thank God we had flown south where the ground was flat, instead of north. We wouldn't have had a chance among the high granite cliffs of the Shield.

I raised hell at the Airways office in Prince Albert and vowed never again to take a chance with an unknown pilot.

Bush pilots are a breed apart and I salute them all. Day in and day out they fly the North over rugged Pre-Cambrian Shield terrain, often in areas not always accurately mapped. In the winter their job is particularly arduous. Not only is the weather bitterly cold but fierce winds and snowstorms are encountered frequently.

There are no airplane hangars in the bush. When the plane has landed for the night, it is run up on four or five long poles -- always provided by our post managers -- to ensure that the aluminum skis do not freeze to the snow or slush overnight. Then the engine oil

Rene Baudais (right) with Engineer John Sinclair at Beaver Lake, 1948. Canvas covers on the propeller and motors are lashed down for an overnight stop in winter weather.

is drained into a pot and the battery disconnected and both are carried inside to the warmth of the post. Afterwards, a canvas tent-type canopy is placed over the propeller and engine cowling and lashed down.

Prior to takeoff, the procedure is reversed. The pot of oil is placed at the back of the stove to warm up and the pilot bundles himself up warmly and trudges down to his plane. Unlashing the canvas canopy, he crawls underneath it with a blowpot -- something between a blowtorch and a bunsen burner -- and lighting it, stays inside the canopy aiming a stream of hot air directly up against the engine until it is thawed out. The whole operation can take up to two hours. Then it's back to the house for the now-hot oil and the starting battery. The canopy is removed, the battery installed and the hot oil poured into the engine sump. Then, with eyes lifted heavenward, he prays that the motor will start the first crack. If it does, the motor is run until the inside of the cabin is warm.

Meanwhile, the passenger has breakfasted comfortably in the warm house, while the pilot has laboured in sub-zero weather. Once passenger and freight are aboard, the pilot guns the motor, wrenching the skis loose from their supporting poles and away they go over the snow to the next post.

After I had gotten over my initial apprehension of flying in a small plane, I came to love bush flying, especially when I had learned something of the topography of the North. Every season was different -- from the delicate light green of poplars bursting into leaf in the spring, to the yellows and browns and reds of the autumn, with always the dark blue-green of spruce and pine, and the whole scene reflected gloriously in the hundreds of lakes.

In the winter, elk and deer and the occasional moose were easy to spot through the bare trees or silhouetted against the white snow. Every year thousands of caribou passed Brochet. One year the edge of the herd went right around the post buildings. Their southernmost reach was halfway down Reindeer Lake where they crowded in bays along the west side of the lake until instinct told them it was time to return to the Barren Lands. Occasionally 'sportsmen' flew up to bag a good rack of horns. Some sport! It was like shooting fish in a barrel.

I only saw caribou in other parts of Saskatchewan twice. Once they came to Porter Lake about thirty miles north of Patuanak and another time, close to the settlement of Portage la Loche. I was told they were part of the Fond du Lac herd and usually didn't venture south of Cree Lake. Caribou steaks are excellent -- much better than deer or moose meat. At least that was my impression when I first tasted them at Brochet. Or perhaps it was just Mrs Garbutt's excellent cooking. I also had my first taste of another northern delicacy at Brochet -- smoked caribou tongue or, as it was always referred to locally, Fond du Lac bananas.

Spring 1950 will long be remembered in Winnipeg as the year of the Red River Flood. Lyndale Drive, on which our house stood, was particularly vulnerable as it followed a large bend of the river. The City of St Boniface, using all the equipment at its disposal, built a huge earthen dyke which ran behind the houses across the drive from us. The waters of the Red River kept rising and we had to build a wall of sandbags on top of the dyke. Quantities of sandbags were flown in from all parts of Canada and rows of trucks dumped loads of sand at every street corner.

Everyone pitched in, either filling and tying sandbags or tossing the filled bags along a human chain to the top of the dyke. As the water crept up steadily, it was feared that the weight of the combined sandbags and earthen dyke would collapse the bank of the river, so a secondary dyke was built right on top of Lyndale Drive itself. The earth was excavated from a large vacant piece of land just to the right of our house. After the danger had passed, there was a huge area of seven or eight acres dug down to the depth of ten feet. Instead of filling it in, the City fathers sodded it over and turned it into a playing field which is still known as the Norwood Flood Bowl.

The safety of the whole city of Winnipeg was in jeopardy and regular work was at a standstill. Hudson's Bay House was closed down to all intents and purposes. It was surrounded by piles of sandbags to keep the water out and all depot stocks of ammunition and other merchandise had to be moved up from the basement to the third floor. Along with everyone else in the neighbourhood, I was busy working on the dyke. One day I got a call from Mr Chesshire.

'Are you all right, Ross?' he asked. 'How about your family? Have you moved them out yet?' When I told him that the family was still with me, he roared, 'Don't be a damn fool, man. Get them out of the city at once. The Company will go good for all expenses and if any of your personal belongings are damaged, we'll replace them.'

I immediately wired my old friends, Sid Turner and his wife at Minaki who had a cottage down by the lakeshore which they rented out for the summer. Their reply came right back.

HBCA Photograph Collection 1987/363-W-210

The dyke behind Hudson's Bay House built for protection from the flood waters. Winnipeg, 19 May 1950.

SEND FAMILY DOWN BY TRAIN. STOP. WE'LL MEET THEM. STOP. DON'T WORRY.

We packed their bags that evening and tried to get aboard one of the last buses crossing the Norwood Bridge but the driver wouldn't let us on with our dog, so I flagged down a passing truck. We climbed into the back of it and spent that night at the home of Bea's brother, Bob, on Dorchester Avenue. Next day, I put them all on the train for Minaki, and breathed a sigh of relief. At least Bea and the children were safe. Whether they would have a home to return to, was debatable.

Through the good offices of Peter Wood, then assistant controller with the Company who was attached to the military in charge of flood operations, I was given the job of going around to all the canteens which had been set up in schools and community clubs in St Boniface to feed the workers on the dykes, and to check

Sand bags inside Hudson's Bay House during the Winnipeg Flood, May, 1950.

and re-order supplies. I had a Navy amphibious vehicle with a driver and we careened to and from various sections of Winnipeg picking up and distributing chicken, pie, baked beans, hamburgers, doughnuts and even the local Ukrainian delicacy -- perogies.

Everybody worked like Trojans. The people of Winnipeg pulled together, working side by side until the danger was past. I know of at least one couple who met while piling sandbags and who recently celebrated their 35th wedding anniversary.

After the waters of the Red River receded, I was able to go down to Minaki for a weekend to see the family who were having a wonderful time. The three girls were enrolled in the local one-teacher school and enjoying it, so Bea decided to stay there until the end of the school year. In July, I took my month's holidays and spent the time at Minaki with them. The kids were brown as berries, loved the lake and all four of them learned to swim. I even got in a few good rounds of golf on the Minaki Lodge course through the courtesy of the pro, Jack Milligan. When we returned to Winnipeg, most of the mess had been cleaned up and our house was still intact with not a drop of water in the basement.

That fall, on a trip to Portage la Loche, I ran into an infuriated and highly upset John Blackhall. Now sixty-five, he was retiring from the Company's service and had written the Personnel Department to find out what his pension would be. He was incensed at the reply. 'Just look at what they're going to give me to live on,' he raved. 'It's not a pension...it's an insult. After all my years working for the Company, if this is all they can give me, they can keep it. I won't even call in at Hudson's Bay House on my way home to Scotland.'

It took quite a while and a lot of talking but I finally got him calmed down. When the new contributory pension scheme was started, old-timers in the Company's services were given the option of staying on the old plan. Being a faithful servant and fully confident that the Company would always look after him, John had elected to stay on the old pension scheme.

'Aren't you a commissioned officer in the Company, John?' I queried.

'Yes, I am. I'm a commissioned trader and still have my letter to prove it,' he growled. 'A fat lot of good that is.'

'I think your being a trader should have some effect on your pension. I have a suggestion. Wait until you're not so upset, then write a letter -- a reasonable letter, John -- to the Personnel Manager and tell him that you aren't satisfied with the amount of your pension.' I had his attention now and he listened closely. 'Stress that you are a commissioned officer and ask that your pension be re-examined. Don't get mad and write anything in the letter that you might regret', I warned. 'When I get back to Winnipeg, I'll follow it up for you.'

Originally, the Hudson's Bay Company was run along semi-military lines. There were officers and servants. For the most part, the servants were tradesmen, carpenters, blacksmiths or boatmen who were hired at a specific wage for a set period of time.

The commissioned gentlemen, on the other hand, looked after the trading business. Starting out as apprentice clerks, they were then promoted to clerk, junior chief trader, chief trader, factor, chief factor and ultimately, Inspecting Chief Factor. Although their annual salaries were small, they were entitled to a percentage of the Company's shares and to the dividends resulting therefrom. After 1871, the holding of shares by commissioned officers was done away with, much to the displeasure of the officers concerned. They were no longer entitled to share benefits but it still made a difference when they retired on pension. Very slowly, the system was reduced until the titles were merely honorary and, in the end, these titles were done away with altogether. John Blackhall was one of the few Company employees who still held commissioned rank.

I took the matter up with Dick Phillips who had been personnel manager for about a year, replacing Clifford Harford who was now in Edmonton as manager of Western Post Division. Dick Phillips was a strange individual, very quiet and uncommunicative. He had no previous fur trade experience and no empathy for post managers or their mode of life in the bush. He was adamant that he had made his calculations and that they were correct. Just as adamantly, I insisted that he consult with the Canadian Committee Office before he replied to Mr Blackhall.

The Canadian Committee granted John Blackhall a pension that was sufficient to ensure that he and his wife lived comfortably in their retirement. I was sorry, however, that the whole affair had happened, leaving a bad taste in John's mouth after 45 years of faithful service.

One result of this unfortunate episode was that I took a dislike to Dick Phillips because of what I saw as his rigid attitude, and from then on, I conducted most of my business with his department through his very able assistant, Don Ferguson.

I promoted Steve Preweda to replace John Blackhall and Carl Shappert was made manager at Dillon. Carl had the makings of an excellent post manager but his great interest was in radio and television. When he left the Company to take over a business of this nature in his hometown in Saskatchewan, I was sorry to see him go. John Marshall was transferred from James Bay District to replace him. John, the son of a local missionary, was brought up around Moose Factory and Dillon was his first posting.

Steve Preweda and the local officer of the Department of Northern Affairs at Portage la Loche got their heads together. Both were married and each had a young child. Neither of them liked the idea of being cut off from the rest of the world during freeze-up and break-up period and they decided to do something about it.

Scouting the countryside, they found a long gravel ridge with a few trees and a lot of scrub just south of the post. They worked in their spare time with a borrowed mission tractor and converted the ridge into a landing strip big enough to accommodate a twin-engine Anson plane. When it was completed to their satisfaction, they advised Saskatchewan Government Airways. On the next scheduled flight, Stu Miller flew into Portage la Loche, looked over the strip carefully and decided that it was fit for landing. Thus, the weekly scheduled flight from La Ronge was extended from Isle a la Crosse and Buffalo Narrows to Portage la Loche.

The Federal Government established a post office in the Company store. When the local Chipewyans received their first Eaton's mail-order catalogues, they were delighted. Order after order was filled out and sent to Winnipeg for Eaton's to supply 'Cash on Delivery'. To their great disappointment, they found out that they had to produce cash to obtain the merchandise. They approached Steve and asked him to advance them credit to pay for the goods they were buying from Eaton's. They were flabbergasted when he said 'No'.

The post office would only hold the parcels for ten days after which the goods were returned to Winnipeg. For the first few months, the weekly plane was loaded both ways with C.O.D. packages going to La Loche and being returned as 'not paid'. Eventually, Eaton's mail order department got wise to the situation and the names of those ordering merchandise which they could not pick up were put on the proscribed list. The C.O.D. parcels from Eaton's dwindled to a trickle. But the catalogues were still looked forward to, read and used in the biffy.

When Len Coates was transferred from Patuanak to Stanley in

Don Wilderspin and Hugh Ross on an inspection trip of Saskatchewan District, Montreal Lake, 1950.

the summer of 1950, Stan Woodard, a young clerk from Gilbert Plains, Manitoba was promoted as manager in his stead. Stan had been well trained by Bill Watt at Isle a la Crosse and I had no fears that he would do well. He celebrated his promotion by marrying Beatrice Smetka, a nurse in the local mission hospital. That same summer, I lost Bill Smith who was transferred from Southend to my old post of Grassy Narrows in northern Ontario. Jim Boatman, formerly a clerk at Foleyet, arrived with his wife Polly to take Bill's place.

In the early fall, I had the pleasure of taking Don Wilderspin around the district on an inspection trip. He had come out with me from the Old Country as an apprentice in 1930 and I hadn't seen him since. Part of his time was spent in Ungava and latterly in the Mackenzie River District in charge of Fort Simpson; now he was being groomed as a district manager. He asked me all kinds of questions and, from the lofty heights of my two year's experience, I tried to answer him truthfully. One of his worries was 'How do you get along with experienced post managers -- men who are older than you?'

'Don't worry about the older men, Don,' I assured him. 'They know their jobs and will be of great help to you. At least I have always found that to be the case.'

'Yes, but suppose they don't do what I want. Then what?'

'As a last resort, you can use your authority as district manager and order them, but I hope for your sake it never comes to that.'

Don Wilderspin went on to be Manager of the James Bay District where he was well liked and respected by the men at his posts.

In the winter of 1950-51, I got permission from Head Office to move the Isle a la Crosse store up to the lot in the village and contracted the same Meadow Lake firm who had moved our Green Lake post to do the job. The store basement was dug and concrete walls built. Then our large warehouse was moved over by tractor and placed on the foundations. Bill Watt and his staff packed all the store stock into fish boxes and moved them over to the warehouse on the new location which was then used as a temporary store.

The store itself was a little more difficult, as it was of wing type construction. Shaped like the letter T, the main store took up the centre with a wing on one side as office and post office and a wing on the other side for heated grocery storage. The two wings were carefully detached from the main building and the whole moved over in three sections and fitted on the new basement. The move took about three weeks to complete and because of its new location in the village, sales increased greatly.

About a year previously, Bill Cobb was transferred back to Winnipeg from Edmonton and appointed Manager of Central Post Division. There had always been a divisional manager for Eastern Post Division stationed in Montreal and one for Western Post Division stationed in Edmonton, but having a divisional manager in Central Division was something new. Up until now, we had always run our districts, making our decisions as we went along and, if we had any knotty problems to discuss, we went straight to the General Manager.

Now everything had to go through the divisional manager and things were different. There is no doubt that Bill Cobb had the qualifications and the experience essential for his job but he was a complete autocrat. Nothing, but nothing could be done in his division without his say-so. I found him impossible to work with and difficult to work for. Fortunately, Saskatchewan District sales and profits kept increasing so he had little to criticize.

In 1952, there were the usual changes of post managers. Bob Middleton went from Buffalo Narrows to Port Simpson, B.C. and I moved Steve Preweda down from Portage la Loche to replace him. It was almost a chess game. Each move demanded another, so Stan Woodard went from Patuanak to Portage la Loche and Jim Watson, a young clerk from Aberdeen, Scotland was promoted from Isle a la Crosse to Patuanak. Jim had the makings of a good post manager but he couldn't keep his hands off anything mechanical. He longed to be a mechanic. He took his typewriter apart and when he tried to put it back together, he had several pieces left over. The same thing happened to his single side-band radio by which he communicated with Isle a la Crosse. His electric light plant, outboard motor and even his Bombardier went the same way. He was costing us a small fortune in replacement engines, radio sets and other mechanical items. Finally I had to warn him to leave things alone, otherwise he could not stay in charge of a post.

Wally Buhr departed from Montreal Lake to Moose Factory and later became manager of Manitoba District. I moved Jim Boatman from Southend to take his place and put a clerk from Pelican Narrows in charge. Tommy Cockburn had been a model apprentice and his manager at Pelican Narrows, Andy McKinley, had a high opinion of him and was sure Tommy would make a good post manager. Alas, this was not the case.

I visited Southend several times and, on the surface, Tommy appeared to be doing all right. But when his apprentice clerk was moved for the summer months, Tommy fell apart and when I dropped into Southend in the fall, the place was in a terrible mess. When he brought cases of merchandise from the warehouse into the store, the empty cardboard cartons were left lying on the floor and the post was ankle-deep in garbage. Strolling down to the lakeshore, I found the post canoe with the engine still on the stern

*Agnes Preweda at Buffalo Narrows,
Spring, 1955.*

loosely tied up and bumping badly against the rocks. He had gone up the lake to visit fishermen at Co-op Point and, on returning the previous night, had failed to tie up the canoe properly. The canoe pounded against the rocks all night and now had two holes in the bow.

It was enough for me. I suspended him on the spot and sent him back to Winnipeg by the outgoing mail plane. I wired District Office with my report and asked for a replacement immediately, as I was remaining at the post to clean it up. What a mess it was! Even the bedrooms were filthy. It took me an entire week to get the place shipshape, just in time for Roy Simpson and his wife to take over. Roy was a farm boy from Saskatchewan and proved to be one of the best managers I ever had. After we had taken a change of management inventory and checked the annual requisitions, which were woefully inadequate, we made out the supplementary requisitions for the following year's supplies and I left, knowing that the post was once again in good hands.

On a subsequent visit, I learned that all the white fishermen on Reindeer Lake were aware of Tommy's behaviour but none of them said a word to me until after he had gone. He started visiting up the lake, staying overnight at first and then lengthening his trips to two and three days. In mid-August, when the Roman Catholic Bishop visited Southend, Tommy wasn't there and the post remained closed for a week. The fishermen ran a sweepstake on how long it would be before I found out.

Len Coates moved down from Stanley, replacing Bill McKinnie at La Ronge. To take his place at Stanley, I got Victor MacKay, another Scottish clerk who had served his apprenticeship in Saskatchewan District before being moved east to the charge of Nipigon House.

On November 23, 1952, a wire arrived at District Office from Buffalo Narrows.

JOHN MARSHALL, MANAGER DILLON, MISSING AND BELIEVED DROWNED. STOP. COME IMMEDIATELY.

I flew out from Winnipeg that evening, arriving in Buffalo Narrows by noon the following day. I talked to Steve Preweda, our store manager, and the local Royal Canadian Mounted Police. The story they told me was later confirmed.

John Marshall had decided to make one last trip to Buffalo Narrows for the mail before freeze-up. Accompanied by an Indian, he set out by boat but found that the Narrows at Old Fort Point were frozen right across so they turned back to the post. Thwarted in his first attempt to make a final boat trip, John decided to take his clerk, Ron Still, and a native straight across the lake to a small bay on the far side and land them there. He told them to pick up the telephone line trail which ran south from Portage la Loche and travel along it to Buffalo Narrows. They were to overnight there, pick up the mail the following morning and return to the bay where John would be waiting to pick them up.

Ronnie telephoned John at Dillon the next morning confirming the time of their meeting and set out with his Indian companion. The night had been extremely cold and they arrived at the bay to find it frozen over for some distance out from shore. Beyond the ice, a thick steamy fog was rising from the freezing water.

The smooth unbroken shore ice showed that John Marshall had not yet arrived.

'John should be here by now,' said Ron, checking his watch. 'Can you hear anything? This fog is so thick I can't see anything.'

'Listen! I can hear the motor. He's coming,' said the Indian. The sound of the motor came nearer and nearer but still they couldn't see the boat.

'Fire your rifle in the air. He'll hear it and get his direction,' said Ronnie. Both men fired several rounds and then listened intently. The motor stopped. Then started up again.

'He's circling.'

As the sound of the engine faded in the distance, Ron started calling John's name. 'It's no use calling. He can't hear you over the sound of the engine. Wait until he circles around and we'll fire our guns again,' advised the Indian.

Although the two young men could hear the boat circling around several times, the noise grew fainter and fainter and then died away in the distance. They stayed in place for some time, firing their rifles at intervals, but on hearing nothing, decided to walk back to Buffalo Narrows. They tried to raise Dillon on the telephone but there was no answer. John Marshall had not returned to the post. They reported immediately to the Mounted Police and search parties were sent out along the eastern shore of Big Buffalo Lake. They met with no success.

Ronnie Still and his Indian companion managed to cross the thickening ice at the Old Fort Narrows and walked along the shore to Dillon. There was no sign of John and the natives there advised them that he had not returned the previous day.

I talked to Ron Still by telephone and asked him if he could look after the post until I had time to get another manager. If not, I emphasized, I would get the services of a helicopter and come over myself. But Ronnie was made of stern stuff. He had only a few months of experience with the Company but he assured me that he could look after the business affairs satisfactorily until we got a new manager. He ran the post alone for two weeks until the ice became thick enough for Mike Ferguson, a senior clerk, to cross by Bombardier to take charge.

Several weeks later, the prow of John Marshall's boat was found showing just above the ice. When it was chopped out there were two large gashes almost four feet long running along each side of the boat at the waterline. It seemed evident that John Marshall had lost his sense of direction in the fog and kept on trying to run through the skim ice until the cedar wood was worn right through and the boat filled with water and sank. Although dragging operations were begun immediately in the surrounding area of the lake, the body was not found until open water the following spring when it finally came to the surface.

In the years after the 1914-18 war, and during the Depression of the 'dirty thirties' there was an influx of white trappers into the North. These men, generally, were only interested in making a stake for themselves; they trapped out an area and then moved on to find new grounds.

The beaver is an easy animal to trap and the white men killed them methodically, going so far as destroying their dams and breaking down lodges, which was strictly against the law.

Indians, on the other hand, are natural conservationists. When they go out to their traplines, they know how much debt they owe the Company and approximately how many skins it will take to pay this debt. After they have taken a sufficient quantity of fur to pay off their debt and purchase fresh supplies, they ease up on the trapping. They know that it is in their own interest to leave enough stock for breeding purposes so that their particular trapping grounds will continue to produce in years to come.

In those depression years, however, incensed by the white man's depletion of the beaver stock, they too continued to take beaver. Year by year, the beaver declined until the species was in danger of extinction. Then, most of the provinces, including Saskatchewan passed regulations forbidding the taking of beaver. By 1952, this far-sighted action was beginning to bear fruit. Natives reported more and more beaver colonies in their trapping grounds. There was even talk of over-population in some areas. The Department of Natural Resources, with the assistance of local natives, made a detailed survey of the North by dogteam and by airplane, marking on large-scale maps the exact location of each beaver lodge. In the spring of 1952, a limited open season was declared on beaver with each native being given a quota of skins, depending on the number of lodges in his trapping grounds.

It was a hectic spring for me. Half of my post managers had never even seen a beaver, never mind buying one. So right after open water I was busy going from one post to another giving instructions. I asked each manager to produce the beaver he had bought to date and to grade them for me.

'You don't have to go through all that,' one bright fellow said. 'I can easily tell you how much I paid for them by checking the books.'

'Never mind the books. Just grade the beaver. Take all the time you need and give me a call when you're ready.' I went over each pile with the manager and either told him they were properly graded or showed him where he had made a mistake. Many of the skins were of first grade and I passed them easily. Most errors were in the sizing of the pelts. A well-stretched skin is practically oval and is measured by adding the length to the width to get the size according to the tariff. But if the pelt is not properly stretched, several inches have to be deducted to compensate. I showed them how to look for hidden damage on the inside of the skin: telltale marks which would indicate that the beaver had been scratched or bitten in a fight. On the whole, the men did a fair job and all the beaver sold at a good profit to the Company.

When I visited Stanley before break-up, Len Coates told me that the old chief, Nehemiah Charles, wanted to see me, and why. The Anglican Bishop from Prince Albert was due to visit Stanley that summer and the Chief was worried because the church was badly in need of painting. The old man spoke good English and I tried to put him at his ease. 'I understand that the Bishop will be visiting Stanley this summer,' I said. He nodded. 'And you are worried about your church?'

'Yes,' he replied, and went on with a long story about how much it would cost for the paint and how he didn't think he would be able to raise the money from the local band in time to get the

HBCA Photograph Collection 1987/363-S-46

Chief Nehemiah Charles at the Hudson's Bay Company store at Stanley, 1955.

paint job finished before the Bishop arrived.

'If you got the paint, Chief, would you be able to get enough men to do the work?' I asked.

'Oh yes, the men are willing to do the work but we don't have enough money for the paint,' said the Chief anxiously. Nehemiah Charles was not only chief of his band but also a lay preacher and a visit from the Anglican Bishop was an important occasion to him.

'Chief, Mr Coates has very kindly suggested that the Company provide the paint. Would you like that?' The old man was overjoyed and Len looked at me in surprise. He had suggested no such thing. The three of us discussed the quantity needed and I wired for it to be sent in by the first plane. That spring, even though there was a Saskatchewan Government trading store in opposition to us at Stanley, we bought more than 90 percent of the beaver turned in.

Being the farthest north, Southend and Brochet were the last posts to be visited. Although the main lake was still icebound, there was enough open water at each end where rivers flowed in and out to allow the plane to land on floats in front of the post. We were just finishing dinner at Brochet when there was a knock at the door. It was the non-commissioned officer from the Signals Station.

'Sorry to interrupt your dinner but the control station at La Ronge wants to talk rather urgently to your pilot.' Rene Baudais left and we had finished our meal by the time he returned.

'We have a problem. La Ronge reports they have a very sick fisherman at Wollaston Lake and they want to know if I can evacuate him.'

'That's no problem, Rene. What is it -- about sixty miles northwest of here? We can leave now and pick him up.'

'The difficulty is that there's only a small piece of open water about a mile from the fish plant and they aren't sure that it's large enough for a plane to land and take off.'

'Oh, I see,' I said. 'And it's getting dark already.'

Rene looked out of the window. 'It's too late to go tonight. I wouldn't be able to check the landing conditions.' He sat down again and sipped his coffee thoughtfully. 'Here's what I'd like to do, Hugh. We'll take out all our baggage and I'll leave you here. I'll take just enough gas on board to fly to Wollaston Lake and back. Then I'll pick you up, fill the tanks and we'll fly direct to La Ronge.' He grabbed a pencil and paper and did some figuring. 'They've promised to have the man over the ice to the open water at first light. I'll have a good look when I get there and then decide whether I can set the plane down or not.'

And that's how it was done. On our way to La Ronge, I asked Rene how it had gone. 'Well, coming in wasn't too bad but taking off was a bit dicey. There wasn't too much room so I just gunned the motor and prayed!'

When our plane landed at the float-plane base at La Ronge, Mrs Spooner, the local nurse, was waiting and diagnosed acute appendicitis. The scheduled Anson which I was taking was due in from Uranium City so we loaded the patient in a van and, very carefully, drove out to the airport. The patient and I were the only passengers in the Anson and en route south, I checked on him periodically. With no one to talk to, I started to doze. The change of pitch in the engines woke me. I glanced over at the sick man and jumped up. He was turning blue and his breathing was difficult.

'Lack of oxygen,' exclaimed the pilot, Stu Miller. We descended quickly and hedge-hopped the rest of the way to Prince Albert where an ambulance was waiting. I heard later that the fisherman's appendix had ruptured. But being a hardy northerner, he survived the operation and in time, returned to Wollaston Lake. I never saw him again nor do I know his name but somewhere in northern Saskatchewan there is a fisherman who owes his life to the skill and bravery of Rene Baudais.

The work of a district manager was arduous and constant. As I flew over the broad expanses of the northern lakes or along the Churchill River, I envied the district managers of old who visited each post once a year, either by canoe in the summer or by dogsled, wrapped warmly and seated in a cariole, in the winter. They had two or three day's travel between each post with time to relax. By airplane, an hour or two at the most was all that I had between leaving the problems of one post and encountering new ones at the next.

You have to be hardy to live in the North, but there are compensations. I still have fond memories of evenings spent fishing with Bill Garbutt at Brochet for the red-fleshed trout at the mouth of the Cochrane River; casting off the rocks at Nut Point at Lac la Ronge for trout in the spring with Bill McKinnie; and deep trolling for lake trout at Hunter's Bay in the summer. Pickerel fishing at the mouth of the Dillon River was always excellent.

I had promised myself that one day I would bring a shotgun for hunting in the fall. Bill McKinnie had a tent pitched on a fly-through between the twin Potato Lakes about eight miles south of La Ronge. By arrangement, Rene Baudais would drop me in there on a Saturday evening and pick me up the following morning. Bill had the canoe ready and a spare shotgun for me so that I could enjoy the evening flight of the birds and the morning return flight at the crack of dawn. Boy, could he handle a shotgun! Paddling at the stern of the canoe, he'd drop his paddle, take up his gun and hit a rising mallard before I had time to get my gun lined up.

Fishing with Bill McKinnie (right) at La Ronge, 1952.

I made several enjoyable boat trips from Isle a la Crosse to Beauval in the fall of the year, jump-shooting mallards as they rose from the reeds in the bays of the river. Bob Middleton and I spent many evenings duck shooting in the bays of Big Buffalo Lake.

In the wintertime, there were our music sessions. Rene Baudais was a skilful banjo player and, after a while, took his instrument along with him as a matter of course. At Pelican Narrows, Andy McKinley played the fiddle; his wife Myra played the balalaika; and Father Chouinard, the local Roman Catholic priest, occasionally joined us with his clarinet. And there was Bill McKinnie -- a born musician, in addition to his skills as a hunter and a fisherman. He could play anything from a piano to a zither. His local girl assistant played a mean accordian and Pete Pederson, the sub-Indian agent, joined in on the melodeon, so there were many musical evenings at La Ronge.

Bob Middleton at Buffalo Narrows was an expert violinist and we were often joined by Bill McLean, the telegraph operator, on his fiddle and by a local teacher with her accordion. Bob was very proud of his instrument. I took it out to Winnipeg to be checked over and have a new bridge, sounding post and strings installed.

'Could you have it appraised too, while you're at it?' he asked.

Some weeks later, I brought it back. As he checked it over, he asked what the appraiser had said. 'It's a good violin, Bob, and worth a fair amount of money,' I told him, giving him the evaluation slip. 'But it's the bow that is valuable, not the violin.' With surprise and delight, he read the appraiser's report which stated that his bow was made by one of the famous Hill family of London, England, and was a collector's item.

We had a regular weekly bridge club at Isle a la Crosse which included several of the Fathers from the Roman Catholic Mission. The priests were good bridge players and I enjoyed many bouts at the card table with them. The same situation prevailed at Portage la Loche and several times I was invited over to the Mission to make up a fourth.

With the exception of Montreal Lake, La Ronge and Stanley where the natives were all Anglican, the rest of my posts were predominantly Roman Catholic and I made a point of getting to know the individual priests. I have nothing but the greatest admiration for these men who gave up the comforts of the civilized world and made it their life's work to carry their religion to the natives.

Father Egenolf came from Germany, paddled up to Brochet in 1905 and there he stayed all his active life. He remained in the settlement on his retirement -- a small, grey-haired old man sitting in his rocking chair by the stove. He died in 1957 and is buried there.

Father Darveau, now the priest in charge, first came to Brochet in 1946 and on July 6, 1986 celebrated his 40th year there. A gruff-voiced man with a booming laugh, Father Darveau was a French Canadian who kept himself aloof from the store. I found it difficult to get on friendly terms until the summer he was having difficulty with the mission tractor. The radiator kept leaking and when I sent over a tin of sealant, he thawed out and we became quite friendly.

Father Waddel, in charge of Southend in 1948, was a dear old man. Like most Irishmen, he loved a good story and always had a twinkle in his eye. I visited with him for an evening and it was obvious he was lonely.

'How would you like to visit the Fathers at Brochet?' I asked him one evening.

'Ah, that would be splendid, lad, but you know that I am just a poor priest. I cannot afford a plane trip -- not even to Brochet.'

'Well, Father, if you don't mind flying towards the heavens with a Scottish Presbyterian, you can come along with me to Brochet and I'll bring you back in a couple of days. You be ready tomorrow morning at nine o'clock.' Father Waddel was a big man -- quite stout and it was with the greatest of difficulty that we got him hoisted into the back seat of the plane. He enjoyed his visit and during the next few years, until he retired, I was able to take him up to Brochet several times.

His replacement, Father Turcotte, was a completely different type. Where Father Waddel had been jovial, Father Turcotte was solemn and reticent and kept very much to himself. When I was cleaning up the mess left by Tommy Cockburn, I wanted to hire a local woman to scrub out the store and living quarters and asked the local chief about it. 'Oh, you must go to Father Turcotte about that.'

The priest was abrupt. 'Not one woman. There must be two,' he stated. 'I will send them to you.' No explanation -- just a flat statement.

The next morning two of the local ladies showed up and scrubbed for hours but they were never out of each other's sight. Side by side, on hands and knees, they scrubbed and polished floors, filled identical cartons with rubbish and washed windows. It was obvious that they had been warned by Father Turcotte to stay together at all times. For whose protection, I wondered? They certainly weren't in any danger from me but they had their orders and were obeying them. I chuckled quietly as I watched these two very stout women struggling to get into the two-hole biffy to scrub it out.

Father Fleury and Father Remy were the priests at Isle a la Crosse who loved to play bridge. Both from France, they were jolly and full of fun, except when the bridge game was in progress.

When Father Remy was transferred to another diocese, he spent some time in Winnipeg. He visited our home frequently and kept the kids enthralled with his tales of army life in North Africa where he had served his compulsary military service.

Father Ducharme had been in charge of Portage la Loche for years and he ruled his flock with a rod of iron. Women had to wear long dresses -- usually black or some other sombre colour -- down to their ankles; black headshawls and black worsted stockings. Wearing slacks was absolutely forbidden. It was like stepping back fifty years into the past. I never met him but stories about the man abounded. When he retired about 1950 and Father Bourbonnais from Isle a la Crosse took his place, all the old taboos were swept away. Steve Preweda, then post manager, was kept busy ordering in modern, colourful clothing for which the women clamoured. Although still strict with his parishioners in religious matters, in the words of Steve Preweda, he was 'fair and just; occasionally hard-hearted. During my two years at La Loche I found that he was a true friend. If we had any problems he was only too glad to help us out.'

There was two other priests at La Loche -- Father Broggolio who looked after the operation of the buildings and Father Mathieu who was the missionary and made trips to Turner Lake and all the small settlements in the area.

Father Clement was in charge at Dillon during the summer months along with Brother John. They spent the winters at Buffalo Narrows and I didn't see much of them.

Father Moraud spent most of his priesthood at Patuanak. He was looked upon with awe and respect by the natives because, as a young man, he went alone by canoe from Patuanak to Pine River. It was his first visit there and either through his ignorance of the country or his extreme good fortune, Father Moraud succeeded in running the Drum Rapids on the Churchill River. At certain times of the year not even the most skilled natives would attempt to run the Drum Rapids. They always portaged around them. By my time in the area, the good Father was quite an old man with a long flowing beard but he still went into the bush every day with his axe and bucksaw to cut firewood for the winter. It was also said that he bathed every morning of the year at the bottom of the Patuanak Rapids where the water never froze. A hardy man indeed!

In northern Saskatchewan Nurse Josephine (Josie) Walz was fast becoming a legendary figure. The daughter of a Saskatchewan farmer, she was a trained public health nurse and had dedicated herself to working among the native people of this area. She was not employed by the government but was sponsored by the Association of Commercial Travellers in the continuing fight against tuberculosis. Year in and year out, she travelled the north testing for this disease. Always on the trail, she made her way by plane, boat, truck or dogteam and, when necessary, on snowshoes. She was welcomed wherever she went and especially by the Hudson's Bay Company post managers who were bachelors. She darned and mended for them, cooked special meals and before she left, she always baked up a batch of goodies: cakes, pies and cookies. Always quiet and unassuming, Josie Walz was the first to deny that there was anything spectacular about her work. She was 'just doing a job', she claimed. But she holds a place in many northerners' hearts.

In early January, 1953, I flew by scheduled plane from Prince Albert to La Ronge to pick up a charter flight to Brochet. After lunch, I went over to the store to pick up my sleeping bag which I had parked there after my last trip. The store was closed, as it was their half-holiday, but Len Coates, the manager, unlocked the office door and we chatted for about fifteen minutes. Then I picked up my bag, Len locked the office door and went back to his house, and Rene and I took off in a Stinson to fly the two hundred odd miles to Brochet.

When we landed just before dark, Bill Garbutt handed me a telegram which had just been delivered. I opened the envelope and was aghast to read a wire from Len Coates that the La Ronge store had burned down. I couldn't understand it. I had left La Ronge barely three hours ago.

First thing next morning, back we flew to La Ronge. The wooden store was completely gone; only the cement foundations remained. Fortunately, the dwelling house and nearby warehouse were untouched by the fire which had obviously started at the back end of the store, well away from the furnace. The only thing Len and I could come up with was a short circuit. The cash register which stood on the counter at the rear of the store was plugged into an electric outlet on the floor and we surmised that snow had gotten into the outlet, gradually melted and caused a short circuit. Len advised District Office and I sent them a wire saying I was on the spot and would look after things.

The warehouse was a large, substantial, unheated and uninsulated building and we decided to convert it to a temporary store. We scrounged around and got together sufficient lumber and plywood from a community project -- a curling rink -- on the strict understanding that we would replace anything we used as soon as possible. We hired two local carpenters and set them to work nailing the plywood sheets on the inside of the 2" x 6" studding and filled the space between with dry sawdust from the local sawmill as insulation. Then we erected shelving and counters. While I was supervising this, Len drove into Prince Albert with his stockbook and ordered a complete supply of groceries to be delivered by truck. He brought back an oil space heater and a supply of stovepipes. Within a couple of days, our makeshift store was ready and warm for the arrival of the groceries which came the following day.

I notified District Office by wire of our activities and assured them that everything was under control. In the meantime, they forwarded a complete set of accounting forms, stationery, and counterslip books, a cash register, a safe, and sufficient sortergraf units to handle our credit accounts. More than that, they sent up Alec Anderson, the divisional accountant, to assist us in opening up a new set of books.

Within a week of the fire, our store was open for business, but it had been a hectic week: unpacking, marking and filling up the shelves. Alec Anderson was a great help. After the safe had cooled off enough to be handled, he opened it and found that all the ledgers

W.G. McKinnie

The La Ronge store and manager's dwelling, 1946. The store was burned to the ground, January, 1953.

-- though badly charred -- were still legible and thus we had the December month-end figures to carry forward. But when the cash box was opened, the bills were badly scorched and the change was melted into an almost solid mass. Alec carefully closed the cash box without disturbing anything. 'I'll take this into Winnipeg with me,' he said. 'I feel sure that we will be fully reimbursed by our bank.'

One problem arose with our sortergraf accounting system. Usually credit sales bills were made out in duplicate and the previous balance for each customer brought forward and added to their latest purchase. The original was given to the customer and the duplicate copy filed in the sortergraf under the customer's name. But our sortergraf had been completely burned up and we had no records. We had no difficulty with the native debts; most of them had been paid in full at the end of December and Len knew exactly who had an outstanding balance and the amount.

The white customers' monthly accounts were a different matter. Alec sat Len and his staff down at tables in the hotel and asked them to write down the names of all the customers they could remember and what they thought their outstanding bills were. Amazingly, the four different lists, independently made up, were almost identical. The most gratifying thing that happened was that almost all our customers, on their next trip to the store, brought their latest counterslip copy with them saying, 'I know your books were all destroyed but this figure on the bottom is the amount I owe you.'

Len and I made up orders for dry goods and hardware and sent them to Winnipeg for rush shipment. Within a month of the date of the fire, the store was back in full operation.

Rupertsland Trading Company got on the job right away and by the beginning of the summer tourist season, a newer and bigger store with the latest fixtures was built on the site of the old one.

There was the usual shifting around of staff that summer. Early on, Frank Milne retired to operate his own business at Meadow Lake, and Jim Boatman moved from Montreal Lake to replace him at Green Lake. Jim was, in turn, replaced by Ed MacLean from Cumberland House. Jim Boatman didn't remain at Green Lake for long, as he was promoted to a post in Manitoba District. I was sorry to see him go.

Victor MacKay moved down from Stanley to Green Lake and Roy Simpson was promoted from Southend to Stanley. His place at Southend was taken by a newly promoted clerk, Gordon Brown.

Jim Watson was transferred to another district from Patuanak and was replaced by Gerry Parsons from Manitoba District. Andy McKinley retired from Pelican Narrows and, to my great surprise, instead of returning to Scotland as he had always planned, took over the free trader's store at Pelican Narrows from Shorty Russick. He had married late in life and had a young daughter, Pearl. Mrs McKinley was always worrying about her daughter's education. She wanted to get out to the city where Pearl could go to school with other white children. And now here she was going to the local school at Pelican Narrows. I wasn't too worried about Andy being in opposition to the Bay. He had served the Company for many long years and our method of operation was ingrained in him. Much better to have a former Bay man who would always keep a level head in opposition than some unknown trader who could get up to all kinds of tricks to steal the trade from us. So I remained good friends with both of them and always made a point of walking over to visit them whenever I went to Pelican.

Andy's replacement was Ray Evans, clerk at Stanley, but he didn't stay long. He was transferred to Mackenzie River District and replaced by a young Scotsman, Jim Smith, who had just returned from a trip to Scotland and brought back his young bride. Mrs Smith had left a good job in a factory in Paisley. She was a city girl and didn't take kindly to life in the bush. In a short time Jim Smith quit to take a job with the Department of Indian Affairs. I felt sorry for Mrs Smith. She had always worked and knew little of cooking and housekeeping. Her main culinary achievement was 'mince and tatties' -- hamburger meat and potatoes to the uninitiated. David La Riviere, a French half-breed assistant at our store at Green Lake took over the charge of Pelican Narrows.

I was getting fed up with all this moving around of staff. With the exception of Bill Watt and Bill Garbutt, all my experienced hands had gone. I no sooner got a clerk trained to take over the management of a post than he was transferred to another district. I complained to the Personnel Manager but Dick Phillips loftily told me that all staff transfers were made with the best interests of the Company as a whole at heart and that I must learn to take the 'broad view'. Broad view, my foot. My only interest was in the successful operation of Saskatchewan District and it was galling to see young apprentices, whose training I had watched carefully, and young post managers whose long-term promotion to larger posts in the district I had carefully planned ahead, being whisked away to some other district. No wonder my stomach was in knots.

As part of clerk training, I thought it would be a good idea to designate Beauval as a 'jumping off' place. It was a small post, only thirty miles from Isle a la Crosse and the manager there, Bill Watt, could keep an eye on a young man finding his legs at his first essay in post management. Jock Mathieson, however, was the stumbling block. What to do with him? Transfer him to an inland post? I thought it would be better all round to pension him off. He hadn't many years to go and the Company would benefit in the long run. I submitted this plan to Head Office.

The services of any post manager with more than twenty-five years in the Company could not be dispensed with without approval of the Canadian Committee. My proposal was considered at their next monthly meeting. Back came their reply. They had carefully studied Mr Mathieson's dossier and had concluded that because his son was attending the local school, it would be a hardship for the family to be sent where no school was available. They further concluded that Mr Mathieson's abilities as a competent post manager had always been in doubt, but no action had been taken by the Company. The fault, therefore, was the Company's, and not Mr Mathieson's, and he should remain at Beauval until he reached full retirement.

There goes my training post, I thought ruefully, but in a way I was glad. Despite his faults, I liked old Jock. He was a faithful honest employee and regardless of his limited capabilities, had always done his best for the Company. After my initial disappointment, I had to admit the Canadian Committee's decision was a wise one and it made me feel proud to be a 'Bay man'. I wonder how many companies today would arrive at a similar decision. So Jock remained at Beauval until his son finished school; then, after a short period in charge of Dillon, he retired honourably.

When the La Ronge area experienced a mining stampede in 1954, the post had an extremely busy year. The objective of the stampede wasn't gold, but uranium. Prospectors were all over the place, flying in and out of La Ronge and staking claims in some very unlikely places. Floyd Glass had quit his job as Northern Administrator with the Saskatchewan Government and gone into business for himself at La Ronge, starting up a commercial air company named Athabaska Airways. He purchased four Cessna aircraft and set up a base on the waterfront on a piece of land in front of our store which the Company rented to him. His planes, as well as the Government Airways craft, were kept busy all day flying out prospectors to unknown locations. No one would talk

HBCA Photograph Collection 1987/363--L-5

The Hudson's Bay Company store at La Ronge, 1954

about where they were going or what they had found.

For days on end, aircraft owned by mining and prospecting companies carefully flew grid patterns over extensive pieces of territory north and east of La Ronge. Towed by cable behind each aircraft was a large torpedo-shaped object which picked up any anomalies in the ground below. These were recorded by delicate instruments located in the body of the plane. Later, the locations were plotted on maps and checked by ground parties of prospectors. It was all very hush-hush.

Naturally enough, this activity brought in a lot of extra business and Len Coates made a name for himself when one day he forgot to include the fresh meat order being flown out to Hunter Bay. On discovering his mistake he immediately chartered one of Floyd's light aircraft and sent it out with the fresh meat. It cost the Company about $100 to charter the plane but it was the best advertising money ever spent. The word quickly got around that the Hudson's Bay Company always delivered. As a result, most of the prospecting business came our way, leaving the government trading store out in the cold. The rush continued for about a year until it became evident that, while there were traces of uranium in the area, there were no profitable deposits and interest shifted away from La Ronge and back again to Uranium City on the east shore of Lake Athabasca. Only one mine was actually opened and worked -- La Ronge Uranium Ltd. -- about eight miles east of Stanley and near Nistowiak Falls. When this mine closed down, the boom was over.

During the summer, I lost the services of clerk Ron Still who had conducted himself so well at Dillon. In my semi-annual report on him, I stated that he was now ready for a post of his own and he was promoted and transferred to take charge of Shamattawa in the Nelson River District.

January 2, 1955 was a black day for me. I received a wire from Buffalo Narrows notifying me that Stan Woodard and his wife and family had been killed in an air crash. I flew up immediately.

Stan had decided to take his vacation during the winter and boarded the scheduled aircraft, a twin-engined Anson, at Portage la Loche with his wife and two small children. The only other passengers were three Indian children going down to Isle a la Crosse. The pilot was Stu Miller. Coming in for a landing at Buffalo Narrows, the plane suddenly lost altitude and crashed, killing everyone on board. The North lost a good pilot in Stu Miller.

The bodies of the Indian children were flown to Portage la Loche for burial.

It was my sad duty to identify the bodies of Stan and his family. Later I attended the funeral at Prince Albert and expressed my deep regret to the parents of both Stan and his wife, Beatrice. They were a lovely couple. He was a first-class post manager and would have gone far.

After the funeral, I flew back to Portage la Loche and carefully inventoried all their personal possessions, including a host of new toys which the children had received as Christmas gifts. In conformance with the grandparents' wishes, everything was handed over to the local mission to be given to Indian children.

I moved Roy Simpson over from Stanley to take charge of La Loche. I had no immediate replacement for Roy but District Office sent up Bert Swaffield as an interim manager. He was an experienced arctic post manager whose father had been in the

Company's service before him; he was then in Winnipeg attached
to the Arctic Division office. He held the fort at Stanley for a few
months and was replaced by Jock Holliday, another relief man.

In the spring of 1956, Gordon Brown was appointed to Stanley
and his place at Southend taken by Horace Flett, a seasoned trader
from the Nelson River District. Bill Watt was transferred from Isle
a la Crosse to Winnipeg District Office where he did relief post
management work until his retirement in 1958. When I replaced
him with Gerry Parsons from Patuanak, I moved Sangster Jessiman
in his stead. Gerry didn't last long at Isle a la Crosse. The post
was too big for him to handle and eventually he quit and went to
work for the Saskatchewan Government Trading Company.
Leonard Budgell, a Newfoundlander, came from Pikangikum in
northern Manitoba to take over. He was a sound, solid trader and I
was happy that Isle a la Crosse was in good hands.

But the loss of Stan Woodard and John Marshall had been hard
to take and my health suffered.

The winter of 1955-56 was extremely mild, with lots of snow
in the northeast side of the province. Winter freight to Brochet and
Southend was very late in being delivered. The ice was totally
unpredictable that year; an aircraft owned by Hank Parsons of
Parsons Airways in the Pas flew into Pelican Narrows and the pilot
parked his plane in front of the store overnight. When he went out
next morning, it was gone. It had sunk through the ice. Mechanics
flew in, raised it and, after overhauling the motor, flew it out again.

The ice at the south end of Reindeer Lake takes a long time to
freeze over solidly enough to carry catswings, as the whole lake
narrows to flow out to the Reindeer River and there is always a
strong current. Flying down from Brochet which had finally
received its annual supplies, I noticed that there were no catswing
tracks leading to Southend. The post was running short of several
basic food lines. I wired La Ronge to fly in several Norseman loads
of lard, tea and other supplies to tide Southend over until their
annual catswing arrived a couple of weeks later.

Pelican Narrows had a different problem. There were several
swift-flowing rivers between the post and The Pas and Johnny

Highmoor, our freighter, could not get through. He tried breaking new roads to the north of the regular route but always ran up against an insurmountable obstacle -- open water. In the end, he gave up completely and I couldn't blame him. Fortunately, Pelican Narrows was well stocked and didn't run short of any vital supplies.

As soon as open water came, I chartered a Canso aircraft from Lamb Airways in The Pas to fly in our freight. The pilot of the Canso wasn't too pleased. It was a short hop of one hundred miles or so from The Pas to Pelican Narrows and he complained that no sooner had he taken off and gained altitude than it was time to land again. He much preferred his regular run of long distance trips with supplies to points on the DEW line.

We got all our supplies in eventually. As soon as the aircraft beached on the sandy bay in front of the store, a crowd of natives were waiting to unload and carry the freight up to the warehouse. Even kerosene and gasoline were brought in the outer wing tanks of the plane and transferred by pump to empty barrels at the post.

The fly-in operation was very expensive, but in conformance with Company policy, the increased costs were not passed on to the customers. Goods were priced at the basic winter freight rate and the excess air freight costs were charged against the post's operating expenses for the year.

I spent the whole time at Pelican Narrows supervising the operation. I thought it would be too much for David La Riviere to handle alone. David was having a difficult time of it as a post manager. He had the feeling that, because he was a half-breed, he was not fully accepted by the white population -- the school teachers, nurses, the DNR officer and the sub-Indian agent. He believed that even his native customers were unwilling to accept his position as a store manager. On top of that he was having trouble with his books and couldn't get them to balance. It took me several days to check them all over for the previous two months and rectify the errors. All in all, David felt that he was not able to handle the management of a post and asked if I would transfer him back to being an assistant at Green Lake. I agreed and within a month he was replaced by Bev Lacelle, a young manager from another district.

HBCA Photograph 1987/363-B-46/19

*Bill Cobb with
Store Manager Bill
Garbutt. Photograph
Rosemary Gilliat.*

In December 1955, Mr Ritchie Calder, C.B.E., a well-known
Scottish author made a trip through our posts in Saskatchewan
before going to Arctic Canada, gathering material for a book. His
previous books included *Men Against the Desert* and *Men Against
the Jungle* and his forthcoming book was to be entitled *Men Against
the Frozen North.* The arrangements for his trip had been made
through the Winnipeg office.

When I met him at La Ronge he was accompanied by Bill Cobb
and Rosemary Gilliat, a photographer from Ottawa. Cliff Labey
piloted the Saskatchewan Government Airways Beaver.

Going up the west side of the province first, we ran into foul
weather and were delayed by snowstorms for three days at Portage
la Loche. I felt sorry for Mrs Roy Simpson. She was stuck with
preparing food for five more people, in addition to her husband and
a clerk, for three days but she responded magnificently.

When we got down to Buffalo Narrows I had a raging fever
and flu and Mrs Preweda promptly got me bedded down and called
in the local nurse. Between the nurse shooting me full of antibiotics
and Mrs Preweda's ministrations, I recovered after six days. The
rest of the party had gone on with their trip which I really didn't

mind. I found Mr Calder boring and rather full of his own self-importance.

The Fur Trade Department was divided into four different types of posts: the arctic posts, catering to the Eskimo; the inland posts with exclusively Indian trade; the semi-line posts which were a mixture of both native and white trade; and the line posts -- so called because they were on the railway line and catered almost exclusively to white trade.

But there was an additional division called, at various times, Small Stores, Interior Stores and, finally, Bay Stores. Since World War II, the Bay Stores Division had been expanding rapidly due to the Company's policy of opening stores in mining and lumbering towns and taking over stores from the Abitibi Timber Company and the Manitoba Hydro Company. So the Bay Stores Division was demanding more and more attention.

Finally, in January 1953, Hugh W. Sutherland was appointed Assistant General Manager, Fur Trade Department and from then on, to all intents and purposes, he was in charge of the Fur Trade while Mr Chesshire devoted his attention to the Bay Stores.

Hugh Sutherland had joined the Company as a trainee accountant in the Canadian Committee office in January 1940; later that year he joined the Royal Canadian Air Force.

In January 1946, he returned from the service with the rank of Wing Commander and rejoined the Company as an accountant with the Fur Trade Department. In November 1947, he was appointed Controller. From 1954 to 1956, he was in Montreal in charge of the Department's eastern operation. Returning to Winnipeg in 1956, he was later appointed General Manager, Fur Trade Department in 1958. Mr Chesshire became General Manager, Bay Stores Department.

Hugh Sutherland made a point of inspecting all fur trade districts and in the early spring of 1957, accompanied by Charles Wilson and myself, made a trip through Saskatchewan District in the Company's Beaver, piloted by Art Atkinson. We flew via The Pas to Brochet and worked our way west from there. Everything went well until we got to the west side. The winter there had been mild and freight was late being delivered. At Patuanak, the freight

H.W. Sutherland with P.A.C. Nichols, Manager Eastern Arctic District, at Povungnetuk 1962. Photograph R. Phillips

had just arrived and was all piled neatly in the warehouse waiting for the dry goods and hardware to be opened and marked. When we got to Dillon, the store was in a shambles. Sangster Jessiman, the manager, and his clerk were busy opening hardware cartons and the floor was littered with excelsior, metal strapping and empty cartons, and the counters were piled with pots, pans, and kettles waiting to be marked.

'My God,' exclaimed Mr Sutherland. 'I've never seen a mess like this in all my life.' The manager hastened to explain that his winter freight had just arrived and he was in the last stages of unpacking and marking his new supplies.

'Let me see your warehouse,' growled Mr Sutherland. So we all trooped out to the warehouse with me bringing up the rear, hoping for the best but fearing the worst. Lo and behold! The warehouse was as neat and tidy as a new penny. All the flour, sugar and cases of groceries were piled high in neat rows with each case neatly marked with the outfit (year), cost in code and the selling price.

Mr Sutherland started to grin. 'You can thank your lucky stars, Sangster,' he said. 'If this warehouse had been in as bad shape as your store, I would have kicked you right up the backside. Now, if you could only get us a cup of coffee, we'll be on our way and leave you to get on with your work.' With that, he congratulated the post manager and slapped him on the back.

At Isle a la Crosse, the last post to be visited in the district, Mr Sutherland took me to one side. 'We are flying straight from here to Winnipeg,' he said, 'but I think you had better go up to Patuanak and spend a few days helping out the post manager with his stock marking.' Then he added, 'By the way, as soon as you return to Winnipeg, I want to see you in my office.'

'Now, what does that mean?' I wondered. But I waved goodbye and went on up to Patuanak by Bombardier, although I knew that everything would have already been made shipshape there and my services not needed.

It was with some trepidation that I went into Mr Sutherland's office for my appointment when I returned to Winnipeg. 'I have now inspected every district in the fur trade department. Your district was the last one.' He paused and I waited. 'I must say, Hugh, that never in any district have I found staff morale as high as in Saskatchewan. To show my appreciation, I have a small cheque for you.' He handed me a cheque for $500.

I've often wondered if he knew just how high a compliment he was paying me and I thought to myself, 'Boy, if you make the same impression on all the other post managers and their wives as you did in Saskatchewan, you will have the fur trade department eating out of your hand.'

Hugh Sutherland went on to higher things. He became President of the Rupertsland Trading Company in 1963, and in October 1964 was promoted to Deputy Managing Director, Hudson's Bay Company. He also held the positions of Director of the Company; Chairman of the Board, Hudson's Bay and Annings Fur Sales, London, England; and Chairman of the Board, Hudson's Bay Wine and Spirits Company. He retired on February 1, 1976.

For the past year or so, I had been having medical troubles and regularly consulted the Company's doctor, Ian MacLean. In spite of all the pills I was given -- pills designed to calm me down or to pep me up -- I was feeling no better. I'm afraid I snapped at Bea and the kids at home and was not the most pleasant man to live with. Finally, Dr MacLean said, 'Hugh, you are either going to have ulcers or a nervous breakdown if you don't change your job.' I was shocked. I knew that having the responsibility of staff and their families in my district was a great strain sometimes and that I was guilty of taking my worries home with me, but it never occurred to me to give up my position as District Manager.

'Let me go home and talk it over with my wife and I'll get back to you.' That night, after the kids were in bed, Bea and I discussed the situation. 'I can't give up my job,' I said. 'It will probably mean going back to manage one of the bigger line posts. That's the most I can hope for. After all these years, it will be a step backwards.'

'Hugh, you don't realize what the children and I have been putting up with for the past two years,' said Bea. 'It's like living with a wounded bear. You're hardly ever home. The kids don't see you enough and neither do I. And when you are home, you're worrying about the posts. The only time I get out of the house is to go to Girl Guide meetings. We have no social life and quite frankly, I think you should do what the doctor says.' She sat down and started to cry.

Next day, I asked Dr MacLean to give me the necessary certificate and I wrote a letter to the General Manager. It had to go through the usual channels, which meant via the divisional manager and the personnel manager, requesting a change of job. Days and weeks went by and I had no reply. I was getting frustrated. Finally Bea suggested I go directly to Mr Sutherland and talk to him about it. I made an appointment and explained my predicament to the boss. He listened intently and when I'd finished, he said, 'I haven't seen your letter, Hugh. Let me check on it and I'll call you.' I felt much better now that Mr Sutherland had all the details. Later, he called me in and my letter was lying in front of him.

'First, let me assure you that I have not seen this letter until today.' He was most sympathetic. He mentioned the burning of the La Ronge store, the loss of John Marshall, and later of the Woodard family.

'I have no thought of sending you back to a post,' he said. 'You can do better than that. But you do realize that I just can't pick a job for you out of thin air. It will take a little time. Do you think you can hang on a bit longer until I see what turns up?'

Now that I knew something would be done, I told him I could wait for as long as it took.

It was late in July before he called me. 'I've been giving your request some serious thought,' he said, 'and I have an idea. Our general office is in bad shape. It's dreary and very out of date. Miss Boyle, the office supervisor is retiring on September 15th and I would like to replace her with an office manager. Do you think you can handle the job?'

'I certainly do.' This was great. Now I could be home every night and enjoy my family again.

I made my last trip around the Saskatchewan District at the end of July, 1957, accompanied by Jim Glass, formerly manager of Manitoba District who was taking over from me. During the nine plus years I had been in charge, the overall sales in Saskatchewan District had increased every year and, at the same time, the 30 percent overall gross profit required by Mr Chesshire had been maintained. It was a gratifying performance, entirely due to the hard work of my post managers. They were a grand bunch of men. Of course, they benefited by receiving well-earned bonuses but I also benefited. The first two years, I received 10 percent of my gross annual salary; the next year -- 12 1/2 percent; the third year -- 15 percent; the following two years -- 20 percent and the final two years -- 25 percent...the largest bonus amounting to $1,600. The only year no bonus was paid was that in which we bought beaver for the first time in years.

The Company's policy required that a substantial depreciation be taken on all furs on hand at the end of each fiscal year. This was to guard against any future drops in the fur market before the pelts were actually sold. In that particular year, we had bought so many beaver during the last month that the required depreciation practically offset any profit I had gained on the furs already sold. This was a wise regulation, as the fur market fluctuates rapidly and can drop drastically within a few months.

The family and I took a well-earned motoring holiday and I reported for work as office manager on 17 September, 1957.

PART IV

Hudson's Bay House

Hudson's Bay House on Main Street was the corporate headquarters of all the Company's operations in Canada. The main floor was largely taken up by the Canadian Committee Office where the members met in the boardroom once a week to decide the destiny of the Company. The balance of the main floor was occupied by the Land Department which was getting smaller and smaller as the western prairie lands which the Company obtained at the Deed of Surrender were gradually sold off. There also, were the offices of Rupertsland Trading Company, a subsidiary company which looked after all the Company's buildings in Canada.

The offices of the Northern Stores Department occupied most of the second floor along with the offices of the Bay Stores department. The rest was used by the Winnipeg Depot staff who also used the basement and part of the third floor. The remaining space on the third floor held the staff cafeteria and a large lounge, where we bought excellent meals and morning and afternoon coffee at reasonable prices.

The general office of the Fur Trade Department was large. At one end was the Central Post Division accounts, supervised by Alec Anderson and an assistant, plus half a dozen girls who operated the posting machines. In another corner, the controller Norman Simpson had his office with his assistant next door.

The Head Office accounts girls who looked after accounts for the Controller were ably supervised by Jewel O'Sullivan. One of her interesting jobs was to look after the personal savings of the post staff who were encouraged to make monthly deposits for which the Company paid them a very satisfactory rate of interest. Every month, Miss O, as she was called, posted the monthly deposit to each individual account, calculated the interest and mailed a complete statement to the employee.

Iris Harris, the cashier, was next to Miss O, with a safe and filing cabinet beside her. She was responsible for all incoming and outgoing cash; made all executive travel reservations and kept up-to-date pictorial records of every post, complete with a picture of each individual building in the whole of the fur trade.

The inside walls were honeycombed with the cell-like offices of the district managers and in the last corner were three offices: one occupied by D.E. Denmark, Fur Trade Buildings and Lands; the second by Art Lorains, Chief Engineer for the Company's Transport Department; and the third was shared by Art Atkinson, Chief Pilot and head of the Company's Air Transport Division out at Stevenson Field, and S.G.L. (George) Horner, radio technician who had his laboratory originally at the foot of Brandon Avenue.

Next came the filing department presided over by Ethel Grant and two assistants. Around their desks were groups of filing cabinets which held files for the Central Division accounts; Head Office accounts; Transport Division; Buildings and Lands; Raw Fur Department; plus a complete set for each district, broken down under various headings.

I shuddered at the thought of having to learn them all but Ethel Grant was an amazing file clerk. She had an uncanny memory and kept everything firmly under control. You could go to her with a vague description of a letter you had written several years ago, and after a few minute's thought, Ethel would unhesitatingly come up with it.

Between the files and the Controllers's Office stood my little, newly built office with walls of clear glass, furnished with a desk, filing cabinet, safe and telephone. I could finally retire my old 'travelling district office' bag.

Across the corridor was another row of offices -- the 'Holy of Holies'. The General Manager's office was in the corner, carpetless but with a large map on the wall behind the desk, which Mr Chesshire could light up, district by district at the push of a button. Transport Manager, W.E. 'Buster' Brown's office came next. Buster, a former officer with the Royal Canadian Mounted Police and later Manager of Nelson River District, was now in complete charge of all the Company's transport operations including the Mackenzie River Transport, Western Arctic Transport, James Bay Transport operating out of Moosonee, and the Air Transport.

Next came Charles Wilson, the Fur Tariff expert; then Jim Stewart, Manager of the Raw Fur Department; Bill Cobb, the Central Division Manager; and P.A.C. Nichols, Manager of the

Arctic Division.

The senior secretaries had their desks in front of the filing department -- Evelyn Little, secretary to the General Manager; Sarah Goorvich, secretary to the Controller and Marion Wallace, to the Transport Manager. Next was Dorothy Soutter, Arctic Division, and Jean Stark who looked after the accounts of the Transport Department. In the centre were eight or ten stenographers who looked after the district managers -- each girl assigned to two men.

As I sat at my desk and looked out at the forty girls in front of me, I had my misgivings. What had I let myself in for? Could I really administer this area of the Company's business or had I merely exchanged one set of problems for another? I knew all the women through doing business at the office for more than ten years but to be in charge was a different matter.

My fears proved to be groundless. In fact they were just as scared of me as I was of them. I talked to them individually over the next few days, explained that my first job was to modernize the office, and asked for their suggestions. I also made it clear that my office door was always open and if they had any complaints, I wanted them to feel free to come in and talk to me. Slowly we worked up a good rapport. The whole place was unbelievably dreary and I was determined to create better working conditions -- subject to the approval of the boss, of course.

Dick Phillips, the Personnel Manager, had his own little set-up on another part of the floor, with his assistant Don Ferguson, two stenographers -- Natia Barker and Irene Hubble -- and a file girl. From the start he made it clear to me that he was in charge of his own empire and that I was to have nothing to do with it. Happily, I took him at his word. During the following years he needed additional help, especially when preparing the staff magazine, *Moccasin Telegraph.* When he reluctantly requested my assistance, I told him that, while I appreciated his difficulty, I had no staff to spare.

Making up the payrolls was a major chore. The office girls were paid twice a month -- in cash. This meant calculating the net wage due and then figuring how many bills of different denominations were required as well as quarters, dimes, nickels and even pennies. I gave this information to Iris Harris who made out a cheque request to the Bank of Montreal and the next day a bank messenger brought the money over to Hudson's Bay House. Each girl's wages was counted out separately, placed in an envelope bearing her name and the whole placed in my safe overnight to be handed out on payday, next morning. It was most time-consuming.

I did the confidential payroll too. Made out once a month, it covered all executives up to the district manager and equivalent level in Winnipeg, Montreal and Edmonton, including officers at merchandise depots, on transport ships, and pilots. Once the salaries were calculated, the totals were written on small slips of paper bearing the name and bank account number of each payee and forwarded to the main branch of the Bank of Montreal, Winnipeg; they then redistributed the salaries to the individual's own bank. Both payrolls were summarized and a journal voucher made out charging each department with its proportionate share of the total.

The whole procedure was a monotonous boring job and a hundred years behind the times. After a few months of this, I consulted with various office equipment firms and with the Controller's permission, came up with a one-write system whereby everyone was paid by cheque direct to their own bank.

February, each year, was bonus time. I prepared salary lists by departments of all included in my confidential payroll for the controller. When the lists were returned, the amount of each bonus was written in after the recipient's name. I deducted the required income tax, made out the cheques and returned them to the General Manager. He forwarded them to the head of each department to be handed out personally.

Everyone knew when it was bonus time and I had to parry questions left and right. I had many visitors in my office at this time, all apparently innocent and just passing the time of day. But they always worked the conversation around to bonuses. When I denied any knowledge and suggested they speak to the heads of their department, I wasn't too popular. But the payroll was confidential and it would have been as much as my job was worth to let slip any advance information, no matter how vague. Until the bonus cheques were distributed, any papers on my desk were endlessly shuffled back and forth to the safe as each new visitor approached.

For some time I had been checking around the general office and questioning the girls about their office equipment. Then I went to Mr Sutherland with my list of improvements. 'How much is it going to cost?' he asked.

'About $10,000,' I replied.

'Good God, that's a fortune. What are we going to get for the $10,000?'

'For a start, the ceiling and walls require repainting. I've spoken to a lot of people and have decided to have the walls done in different light pastel colours.' I paused but Mr Sutherland indicated I should go on. 'You've seen the floors. I don't know how many years that linoleum has been there, but the it is worn bare in many places. Not only is it ugly, but it could be dangerous if someone trips and falls.'

The boss maintained his silence so I continued. 'I'd like to give each steno and secretary a new IBM electric typewriter with a wide carriage.' Before Mr Sutherland could interrupt, I hurriedly added, 'You know how you always want your monthly and annual statements promptly. Most of them are on wide paper and there is only one wide-carriage typewriter in the office. The girls have to queue up to take their turn at it. And...'

'There's more?'

There was lots more. The list went on and one. The office furniture was in terrible shape. The girls' chairs were worn and had been repaired many times. The wooden desks were so battered that the legs were covered in adhesive tape to prevent stocking snags. The accounts girls were all using hand-cranked comptometers and I thought they should be replaced with modern electric calculators. We ended up by making a tour of the general office where I pointed out all the things I felt should be remedied, and I satisfied Mr Sutherland that my requests were necessary.

The linoleum and painting didn't pose any problems. The Rupertsland Trading Company were our landlords and we were

HBCA Photograph 1987/363-H-101

Cafeteria, Hudson's Bay House. Evelyn Munz, in charge of the cafeteria, Hugh Sutherland and D.H. Pitts. November 1958.

paying them a square-foot rental. Bill Thorogood, the property manager, was a hard man to squeeze money out of but we got the paint job completed and the floors laid with tile.

There were often bottlenecks in the stenographic department when many of the men were in the office at the same time. With one steno looking after two district managers who invariably wanted to give dictation at the same time, it presented quite a problem. Some were efficient, read their mail and prepared their replies before calling in the steno. Others dithered around, then summoned the girl who had to sit, notebook in hand, while he read each letter and thought up a reply. But all of them wanted their correspondence typed and ready for signature to go out in the same day's mail. I asked for and received permission to install dictaphones. It was a struggle to get some of the men to use them but they did and the steno's time was used more efficiently. By the time I had purchased new typewriters and dictating equipment for all the office staff, Jim Grant, the local IBM representative, was almost fawning over me. Not often did he earn so much commission so easily.

Mr Chesshire called me into his office one day in 1951 and said, 'Ross, you have been living in the Company's experimental house for five years now, paying rent. As far as the Company is concerned, the house has served its purpose. Why don't you buy the house and take it off our hands? The $45.00 monthly rent you're paying can be paid instead as monthly installments on the mortgage. All you'd have to do is give us a down payment of $1,000. What do you say? Are you interested?'

'Very interested, if the price is right. The only problem is, I don't have $1,000, Mr Chesshire.'

'I thought you might say that. I guess we can arrange a staff loan for you. As for the price, see Mr Thorogood.' He was the manager of city properties for Rupertsland Trading. 'I'm sure you can arrive at a mutually satisfactory figure,' added Mr Chesshire. 'Let me know how you make out.'

Bill Thorogood was a friend of mine but he was also a keen businessman. He figured that since the house had cost $12,000 to build, it was still worth that amount complete with all the furniture and furnishings. I didn't, so I called in an independent real estate appraiser who pointed out that, regardless of the actual building costs, the house was of an unusual design, having only one door, and he doubted he could get a buyer in the city to pay more than $8,000 for it. In the end, Mr Chesshire agreed to the $8,000 plus $1,000 for the furnishings. I signed on the dotted line and with the aid of bonus cheques, paid off the staff loan in less than two years.

Bea was overjoyed that we now had a house of our own. 'Now that we own it,' she said, 'the first thing we should do is repaint it. All our married life, we have been living in a white house with a red roof. I would sure like something different.' So I painted the roof and the door midnight blue and the outside walls primrose yellow with white window and door trim. Our neighbors were somewhat taken aback and teased us good naturedly, but I noticed that pretty soon, they too began to paint their homes in pastel colours.

Bit by bit, we replaced the oil heater in the living room with an oil-burning furnace in the basement, put a fence around the property and finally built an 8'x 12' front entranceway and porch.

When we first came into the city, I had three ambitions. One was to buy Bea a fur coat; the second was to get a good violin and the third was to own a Jaguar. The coat, I bought in 1949 with a bonus cheque. It was always to be Bea's choice and she chose a fine Hudson Seal muskrat coat.

Next, through James Croft and Son, Winnipeg, I obtained from Hill & Sons, London, England, a beautiful old English fiddle made in 1751 by John Norburn. Its tone was so good it made even my feeble efforts sound professional.

We weren't in any great rush to get a car as I was away so much of the time and Bea didn't drive. Come to think of it, neither did I. Besides it only cost a couple of dollars to take a taxi home when we did our weekly shopping at the Bay downtown. But we took the plunge in 1953. I bought a second-hand Studebaker from Wulf Tolboom who was returning to duty in the Arctic. 'Stella, the Studi' was a grand car and once I had obtained my driving licence, we made good use of it. Every summer we loaded up Stella with two tents, sleeping bags, cooking equipment and the kids and went on a camping holiday. At first we explored Manitoba and western Ontario. Then we extended our trips south to Minneapolis and Brainard before we made our first big trip in 1955 around the Gaspe Peninsula and into the States as far as Gettysburg.

The kids always claimed that they learned more about geography and history on these trips than they did in school. And that was true for me too. Prior to embarking on these sojourns, I spent the winter reading everything I could find about the places we planned to visit. The Gettysburg trip was fascinating as I was already boned up on all the Civil War battles. I continued this practice during the years, studying the Mormon Bible before our trip to Utah and following the Lewis and Clark expeditions.

We became members of the Norwood United Church and Bea was very much involved with the ladies in church work. I eventually became an elder.

After a few years, Bea gave up teaching her kindergarten class. There were too many complications with City Hall over extra bathrooms and the other things required by the regulations. She was only charging $5.00 per pupil per month and the cost of the

extra expenses would have been prohibitive. Instead she got into
Girl Guide work once again. She had been in the organization as
a youngster. In time, Bea became Commissioner for Norwood
District. The girls went through the movement from Brownies to
Guides to Guiders and all three became 'Gold Cord Guides'. Most
of their summer holidays were spent at Caddy Lake, the Girl Guide
camp, first as campers and later as counsellors. Ian started out with
Boy Scouts but later switched to Sea Cadets; his summers were
spent at Camp Stevens on Lake of the Woods.

The kids all did well at school, graduating from Nelson
McIntyre Collegiate, with Jennifer and Ian winning the Governor
General's gold medal. Jen took her B.A. at the University of
Winnipeg and started to work with the Children's Welfare Society.
After a year or so, she returned to university to take her degree of
Bachelor of Social Welfare.

Barbara and Dorothy expressed no desire to go on to university.
Instead they went to commercial college and got good jobs; Barbara
at Boy Scout headquarters and Dorothy at Girl Guide House.

Ian graduated from the University of Manitoba with a Bachelor
of Science and went to work for the T. Eaton Company for whom
he had worked as a councillor during his high school years.

Summer holiday time provided another education for Jen and
Ian. She made frankfurters at Canada Packers and had to join the
Union. Ian was a gas jockey on Main Street, waited on tables at
the Banff Springs Hotel for two summers and learned all about wine
by sampling each bottle purchased. During one vacation, he even
mixed paint for a local paint company in St. Boniface, which we
considered hilarious since the lad is colour-blind.

While the children were going their own way during the
summers, Bea and I started taking motoring trips by ourselves.
With the exception of Rhode Island, we covered every state in the
United States. Why we missed it, I'm not sure. There was one big
difference, however. No more tents and sleeping bags. 'I'm too
old now to have to go out to the bush in the middle of the night,'
said Bea. 'I want the comfort of a motel. Besides, I don't think
they have any loons calling in Arizona.' So motels it was.

In January, 1958, the Company decided to get out of the transportation business on the Mackenzie River. It sold out to Northern Transport Ltd which had been a Crown Corporation since 1941 and was equipped with steel diesel tugs and the latest technical equipment. The Company vessels were old and long past time for renewal which would have been prohibitively expensive. Transportation on the Athabasca and Mackenzie rivers had changed. A road ran from Grimshaw, Alberta to Hay River on the southwest end of Great Slave Lake and all freight for Yellowknife and posts north was being trucked to Hay River. There was talk of extending the road north along the Mackenzie River and running another road north from Buffalo Narrows via Portage la Loche to the south shore of Athabasca Lake, a few miles from Uranium City. Thus Waterways and Fort Smith, our main freight-handling and distribution points, were being by-passed.

Our vessels and freight-storing and freight-handling warehouses at these two points were included in the sale but everything else remained to be disposed of. Jim Woolison, Transport Accountant in Edmonton, had moved into Winnipeg. He was delighted to go to Fort Smith to dispose of the balance of the Company's assets, while Art Lorains, the marine engineer went to look after the Peace River end at Fort Vermilion. For some reason, I was selected to go to Waterways, now a very quiet village.

To get to Mackenzie River Transport property, I had to hire a bulldozer to clear a road in, as the buildings were surrounded by three feet of snow. I posted notices of the sale at both Waterways and Fort McMurray. There really wasn't too much on hand: mostly small tools, crockery, cooking utensils and bedding for the vessels. All had been carefully laid out and inventoried by the port chief stewart, Ernie Berg, before he left the previous fall.

To my surprise, crowds of people came from McMurray and Waterways, all wanting to purchase souvenirs of the Mackenzie River Transport, especially the crockery and cutlery which were emblazoned with the Company's crest. I wish now that I had bought some of them for myself. In two or three days, everything was gone. All that remained were three decrepit old trucks in a garage at The Prairie. Nobody wanted them. I cornered Hank Demers one evening in the Fort McMurray beer parlour. He was now running the local taxi and transfer business. At first, he refused to touch the old trucks at any price. Then I made him an offer he couldn't refuse and he purchased the vehicles for spare parts.

When I wired Winnipeg that I had completed the job and would be returning by the next plane, they instructed me to proceed to Fort Smith to take over from Jim Woolison. Poor Jimmy was a sad sight when I met him in the new hotel at Fort Smith. On his arrival, free of the trammels of the office, he had gone on one tremendous bender. I got him tidied up and loaded him, hangover and all, on the next plane back to Winnipeg.

Fort Smith was a much different proposition than Waterways. I had to sell the contents of a complete hotel -- the Hotel Mackenzie. When the manager heard that his hotel was closing down, he turned off the lights, locked the door and walked away. Everything was left as was: dishes in the kitchen, soiled linen in the rooms and food in the refrigerator.

In addition to the hotel, there were four dwelling houses, one of which was still occupied by the local caretaker, Mr. Piper; a completely equipped garage; and several gasoline storage tanks, with the capacity to hold five or six thousand gallons each. In the letter of instruction which Buster Brown had forwarded for my arrival, I was told that I could not close the sale of any of the houses but must first forward any offers to Winnipeg.

The contents of the hotel gave no problems. Once the notice of sale was posted, the native population thronged in to buy. Clean or not, the question was 'How much will you give me for this?', and in a very short time everything was gone, even the chamber pots under the beds, still half-full and frozen.

Selling the garage was also relatively easy. A young couple, recently arrived, wanted to set up in the garage business on their own. They contacted me and after a bit of dickering back and forth, we arrived at a fair and reasonable price. In compliance with my instructions, I wired the offer to Winnipeg, adding that it was the only offer I expected to get and recommending that it be accepted. Confirmation came by return wire and one hurdle was overcome.

Jesse Coffey, whom I had last seen at the Fur Training school in Montreal in 1947, was now the owner of the Imperial Oil Agency in Fort Smith, having resigned from the Company's service. We met purely by chance and I had dinner with him and his family the next evening. After reminiscing about old times, as fur traders do when they get together, I asked how his new business was going.

'Quite well, really,' he replied, 'but more and more business is opening up farther down the river. In fact, I'm making a trip out shortly to locate a few additional storage tanks for installation at downriver points.'

Seizing my opportunity, I told Jesse about the storage tanks I had for sale. We went down to the shipyard to examine them closely and came to an agreement on price, subject to Winnipeg's okay. But Winnipeg wanted more than was offered and I quickly advised them that Jesse Coffey was the only possible person interested in buying the tanks, and if his offer was not accepted, they would probably have to lie there at the shipyard until they rusted out. I got the okay.

The four houses were the hardest to get rid of. I had offers but, on inquiring at the local bank about the prospective customers, I found that they either didn't have the funds or couldn't qualify for a loan. When I did receive a genuine offer and forwarded it to Head Office, their reply was always the same: NOT ENOUGH. TRY TO GET MORE. Mr Piper, the caretaker who was still living in one house and wanted desperately to purchase it, said, 'Mr Ross, my wife and I have lived in this house for many years. She has created a lovely garden out of nothing and neither of us want to leave at our time of life. I have some money in our savings and I can borrow the rest from the bank but I can't possibly raise my offer.'

I was getting fed up with all this so I sent a wire to the General Manager stating that 'Under the circumstances, I can do no more at Fort Smith. Without a free hand to sell the houses, I feel it best if I return to Winnipeg immediately.' Mr Chesshire gave me full authority to conclude any and all deals forthwith. When I accepted Mr Piper's offer for his little house, his wife wept.

I had to hang around Fort Smith for a few days until the necessary sale documents were ready for signature so I took advantage of the free time to do a little sightseeing. The Chief Warden of Wood Buffalo National Park invited me to accompany him in his Bombardier on an inspection of the herd. What magnificent creatures the buffalo were, with their massive horned heads and shaggy hides. Ten miles out of Fort Smith and we were back a hundred years in time. There were hundreds of them, roaming among the trees and bush in small groups of ten or twenty. In the spring, they would be rounded up and any unfit animals culled and slaughtered. The meat was not wasted. It was dressed, frozen and shipped downriver to the various Indian reservations. I had prime buffalo steak for dinner and found it extremely good.

And then Art Lorains showed up. 'What are you doing here?' I asked.

'Winnipeg said you were having difficulties and ordered me up here when I finished at Fort Vermilion.'

'No difficulties here, Art. Everything is sold,' I assured him and we caught the next plane home.

In 1959, the name 'Fur Trade Department' was done away with and changed to the Northern Stores Department. The reason given was that the Company was extending its facilities to northern communities and offering complete retail services to the mining and lumbering companies which were developing towns in the North. A perfectly logical explanation, as 'fur trade' had a connotation of bartering for furs with the Indians and, in some of these towns, there were no Indians around for miles.But it was, nevertheless, a sad moment for me and no doubt for others. I had joined the Fur Trade Department and, in my own mind, was still a fur trader, but how does one say 'I'm a northern storer?' It just didn't sound the same.

The expansion into northern communities had been going on steadily both in the Fur Trade Department and the Bay stores. We had so many new stores opening up that districts were growing too big and had to be split in two. There was an ever increasing stream of new young faces in the corridors -- trainees or experts in some branch or other -- all properly outfitted in three-piece suits, very serious and intense, and carrying briefcases. The Bay stores had also expanded so much that they had to enlarge their office space with a bunch of buyers and assistants and experts requiring offices.

In the next few years, Canada adopted the Maple Leaf flag and for a time there was great controversy all over the country about the use or misuse of the Red Ensign. Not wanting our use of the Hudson's Bay Company Red Ensign to be interpreted as opposition to the new Canadian Maple Leaf flag, the Company discontinued its use in May, 1964. In its place we flew what was known as the 'Governor's Flag', formerly only flown where and when the Governor of the Company was in residence in Canada. And so today, the white flag bearing the Company's coat of arms flutters above all Company establishments in Canada on 'high days and holidays'. Old 'Blood and Guts' with the letters HBC on the fly is a thing of the past.

At the same time, the old buff mailing envelopes with the Red Ensign on the top left-hand corner were banished and replaced by plain white ones with the Company's name in black letters.

Now the Fur Trade Department was gone completely. The words 'fur trade' became a no-no around Hudson's Bay House and 'merchandising' became the byword. I must confess I was bitterly disappointed at first but on reflection I realized that these intense young men whom I met daily in the corridors were not much different than I had been when, almost twenty years before in 1946, I had come to Head Office from Waterways, full of plans and aspirations. The future success or failure of the Hudson's Bay Company was now in younger hands.

With a trace of sadness, I had to accept the inescapable fact that I was now 'an old-timer'.

D.E. 'Don' Denmark joined the Company in June 1938 as Supervisor of Fur Preserve Developments in connection with beaver and muskrats. A land surveyor by profession, he had previously worked with the Manitoba Government Surveys Branch as a construction engineer and land surveyor. When the Fur Preserve Development work was completed he remained with the Northern Stores Department to look after the leases and land sales covering all the lands owned by the Department around their stores (a post was now called a 'store'). He retired in January 1963 and I was asked to take over his duties.

K.R. 'Ken' Bolt, assistant controller, assumed my old job of office manager with the exception of the confidential payroll which I continued to handle. My salary was now $7,200 per annum. From Don I inherited a cabinet containing a bunch of old maps, a roll of draughtsman's tracing paper; a box of protractors, dividers and other tools, and a few files chock-full of tracings showing our land holdings at various posts together with the positions of the store buildings and any leases or sales already completed.

Not having had any previous experience in this type of work, I sorted out the mass of drawings store by store, put them in files and arranged them by districts in Western, Central and Eastern Divisions. Then I obtained the buildings and lands file for each post and checked them against my drawings. In several cases, the records weren't up-to-date so I drew up a master plan of each store to scale, showing the exact position for each building as we knew it and indicating each parcel either sold or leased, according to our records with the appropriate lease or sale number. Copies were forwarded to each division office requesting that the district managers have each store manager delete any buildings destroyed and add any new buildings built; and that they check all leases and sales and report any discrepancies. I didn't require accurate drawings, just dimensions of buildings and approximate distances from each other.

A photographic record was kept of all buildings, contained in about a dozen large black books and maintained by Miss Harris. I requested a new set of photographs -- one overall view of the post and a separate picture of each structure. The district managers were most co-operative; the job took about a year after which our records were up-to-date.

The issuing of leases or sales documents was simple. When a request was received from the district manager, he attached a rough plan which I checked against my master plan. If there were no impediments or objections, a new scale plan was drawn up. After receiving the General Manager's okay, the request and new plan were forwarded to Rupertsland Trading Company where Cliff Rogers or Morley Headlam prepared the legal documents.

An interesting request came from the Alberta Provincial Government in the mid-1960s. The highway from Edmonton to Lac la Biche had been extended to Fort McMurray and they wanted to build a bridge across the Athabasca River to extend the highway to the new tar sands development. The Company owned twenty-seven acres of land at the junction of the Athabasca and Clearwater Rivers and the Government asked if we would sell this parcel so that they could bridge the river and build the road approaches to it. Prior to bringing it to the General Manager, I discussed it with Cliff Rogers, Manager of the Land Department. He figured that the Alberta Government probably had the power to expropriate the land if they wished and that we should set a pretty stiff price as a basis for bargaining. He named a figure. Mr Sutherland agreed and I fired off the reply to the Alberta Government. They certainly didn't beat around the bush. Back came a wire: PRICE ACCEPTABLE. STOP. CHEQUE IN MAIL. STOP. WILL ARRANGE LEGAL DETAILS LATER.

One request gave me a lot of fun. A government department wished to purchase a small piece of land at one of our posts to build a dwelling house for their field officer. The accompanying sketch showed a small square of land, neatly ruled off and totally within the boundaries of our property. The district manager had agreed with the request and when I informed him that we could not comply with it, he was quite upset. 'Why not?' he asked.

'Look at your sketch. There's no exit from the proposed sale property to the outside of our land. How's he supposed to get in...by helicopter?'

The manager looked at the sketch again. 'What are you talking about?'

'If the field officer wants to get to the house, he'll have to cross our property. There's no legal entrance or exit. The land behind is a steep hill covered with trees and this other side is too low and wet.' It took a great deal of convincing before he finally pencilled in an exit and I was able to go ahead with the necessary documents.

When the Temagami store was closed in September 1970, I had the sad duty of arranging the sale and land transfer. Sad because I spent four happy years, 1937-1941, in charge of Temagami.

On January 22, 1964, the Company's public relations department issued a press statement that we were inaugurating a U-Paddle Canoe rental service. Directed to experienced canoeists, the service would rent canoes to be picked up at any store in northern Canada and turned in to any other store at the conclusion of the trip. For further details, contact: U-Paddle Canoe, Northern Stores Department, Hudson's Bay House, Winnipeg. The press release received coverage in newspapers all over Canada and the United States as well as radio and television. Everyone at Hudson's Bay House was talking about it but no one, especially in the Northern Stores Department, seemed to know anything definite. Then Normie Simpson, the controller, came into my office and dropped a very slim file on my desk. It was headed U-Paddle Canoe. 'I heard about this on the radio. You're handling it, are you, Norm?' I asked.

He grinned from ear to ear. 'Nope. It's all yours.'

'Mine! What do I know about canoe routes? I did run a canoe rental system at Temagami but that was more than twenty years ago,' I protested, 'and they were just local routes.'

'All I know is Mr Sutherland said that you could handle it,' and he left me with the benediction, 'It's your baby now. Good luck.'

I picked up the file. On top was an invoice from Grumman Ltd. showing that twenty-eight 17-foot aluminum canoes had been shipped and would be arriving by freight. There was a copy of the original press release and a letter from Eric W. Morse of Ottawa requesting three canoes to be picked up at Norway House and two more at Yellowknife that coming summer. The name Morse rang a bell.

During the winter of 1954-55, Bill Cobb had asked me to obtain all possible information regarding portages and rapids on the the Churchill River for a party of canoeists calling themselves 'The Voyageurs'. They proposed to make the trip in the summer of 1955 from Isle a la Crosse, east along the Churchill River via Patuanak and Stanley to Trade Lake where they were to portage over the 300-yard Frog Portage into the headwaters of the Sturgeon-Weir River (the Riviere Maligne of the Fur Trade Voyageurs of old), down past Pelican Narrows and Beaver Lake to Cumberland House and thence to The Pas. I obtained the information from various post managers who quizzed the local Indians and later, I arranged for food orders to be shipped to the posts en route to be picked up by the travellers.

In a few weeks, I had twenty-eight canoes on my hands. The Depot staff were not amused; they took up valuable space. Two were shipped immediately to Yellowknife and three to Norway House and I distributed the rest across the country to such points as Waterways, Isle a la Crosse, La Ronge and Hearst. Since I hadn't a clue where they would be required, I guessed. We kept the balance in the depot basement, slung from the rafters, awaiting further inquiries.

I was swamped with applications. Fortunately I had the assistance of an excellent secretary, Dorothy Soutter, who handled all my correspondence and indeed, when I told her to 'give them the usual reply' would write the letters without my having to dictate them. A good secretary can make even the worst boss look good. Inquiries from amateurs were easy to pick out and they were turned down courteously and diplomatically with the suggestion that they get in touch with our post at Temagami, Ontario which catered to the type of canoe trip they were planning.

Applications from experienced canoeists were handled differently and the first requirement was that they establish the fact that they were experienced. Having been satisfied on that score, the requested number of canoes were shipped to their starting point. Each party was asked to supply us with a copy of their proposed itinerary and to lodge a copy of same with the Royal Canadian Mounted Police in the area. Post managers were advised to expect them and to wire me confirming the parties' safe arrival at the end of their trip.

The disposition of the canoes took a lot of organizing. Some posts had winter freight and some had only summer freight, so it could get quite complicated. Year after year, the inquiries kept coming in and pretty soon our twenty-eight canoes were booked a year in advance. The original rental rate was $25 per week but after a couple of years, I raised it to $30. Without taking my wages into consideration the U-Paddle Canoe managed to at least break even every year. In addition, the provisions and other goods purchased at the posts and the enormous publicity the Company was receiving, made the venture most successful.

After a few years, the odd canoe was so badly banged up it had to be removed from service and replaced. The old bangers were sold to the staff at Hudson's Bay House, many of whom had spent many a summer paddling at some northern post. I always had a list on hand of eager buyers-to-be.

Supplying data on portages, rapids and waterfalls across the country was a problem at first. I had the information on the Churchill River as far as northern Saskatchewan, and I knew of the other rivers in the northern part of that province but not much else. Offices of Tourism in the various provincial governments were most co-operative and supplied me with the details of all canoe trips which they advertised. Eric Morse made available his detailed notes on the trips the voyageurs had taken since 1955.

I found a wealth of information on the shelves of the Company's library at Hudson's Bay House. Shirlee Anne Smith, now Keeper of the Archives of the Hudson's Bay Company introduced me to the printed diaries and journals of old fur traders and explorers of the Canadian North. Furthermore, she allowed me to borrow these books to read and make notes. Slowly files were built up and I always asked for and usually received further comments from canoeists on the completion of their journeys.

During the seven summers I looked after the U-Paddle Canoe service, we lost only two canoes. A party of three Americans and their sons made the trip along the Churchill River from Isle a la Crosse to South Indian Lake where they left the canoes. On their return home, they wrote asking that the canoes remain at South Indian Lake over the winter, as it was their intention to continue their trip down the Churchill River from South Indian Lake to the port of Churchill. I was very much against the idea and told them so. We kept up a running correspondence through the winter. I pointed out how dangerous the river was, being a series of rapids and waterfalls from South Indian Lake north. The Hudson's Bay Company had tried and given it up as a trade route when they were looking for a route into the interior, in the early eighteenth century.

First the Churchill River was tried, then the Nelson River, before they settled on the Hayes River. The more I protested the difficulties, the more adamant the Americans became. Finally they wrote, 'We're going to run the Churchill River. If your company won't rent us the canoes, we'll find someone else who will.'

At my wit's end, I took the matter to my General Manager. 'Well, Hugh, you've done your best to dissuade them. You've certainly pointed out all the dangers in these letters.' He spread them out on his desk and said, 'If anything goes wrong, they can't say they haven't been warned. We may as well rent them the canoes.'

That was the only party I really worried about. Their estimated time of arrival at Churchill was on a Friday. I didn't receive a wire from Churchill confirming their arrival that evening, but I didn't think too much about it. It might have been late when they arrived. I figured I'd get a wire over the weekend. On Saturday afternoon, I got a frantic telephone call from the mother of one of the boys from Tacoma, Washington. Her husband always wired her promptly and she had heard nothing, and that was when I really started to worry. I phoned our Churchill manager but the canoe party had not checked in.

'Call the RCMP and check with them and call me right back.

I'll be waiting by the phone.' In twenty minutes I got a reply. The Police had nothing to report.

'Hire a float plane immediately, and have them search the river. Let me know as soon as you have any news.' I sat beside the phone, waiting.

The pilot spotted the party on one of the few quiet stretches of the river. The going had been tougher than they expected despite my many warnings and, as they were behind schedule, they decided, foolishly, to run a series of rapids. Two of the canoes were almost swamped and the third disappeared entirely after capsizing when it hit a rock. Luckily the two occupants were wearing life jackets and were able to make it to shore. When they were spotted by the pilot the doleful band were drying themselves out before a fire and trying to salvage the remains of their water-soaked provisions. They were flown out to Churchill in relays that evening with the remaining canoes strapped to the pontoons of the plane. I don't know who was the more relieved that night when I passed on the good news to the waiting mother in Tacoma, but I was certainly glad they had arrived safely.

The second canoe was badly damaged by a party of Boy Scouts who travelled from Waterways to Inuvik. All I got was a rather vague and garbled story from the scoutmaster about how a strong wind had blown the canoe onto a still-smoldering campfire during the night and it wasn't discovered until morning.

Fortunately, Vic MacKay, then in charge of Inuvik was able to dispose of the damaged canoe to an Eskimo customer who thought he could repair it and use it when trapping muskrats in the Mackenzie River delta.

For many years, I wondered how and why the U-Paddle Canoe service was started in the first place. It wasn't until late 1985 that I got the answers. When collecting data for this book, I was able to contact Eric Morse, then living in retirement in Wakefield near Ottawa, and through him, Major General N.E. Rodger, also retired and living in Ottawa. I am deeply grateful to these gentlemen for giving me permission to quote from their letters.

Eric Morse wrote, 'The names and titles of the original Voyageurs were Denis Coolican, President, Canadian Banknote

Company;   Blair Fraser, Ottawa correspondent of MacLean's magazine; Toni Lovink, Netherlands Ambassador and Dean of the Diplomatic Corps; Eric Morse, National Director, Association of Canadian Clubs; Sigurd Olsen, President, United States National Parks Association; Omond Solandt, Chairman, Defence Research Board; Major General N.E. Rodger, Vice-President of General Staff, Canadian Army; and Tylor Thompson, United States Minister to Canada.

'Yes, I recall that the idea (for U- Paddle Canoe) was originally mine. When we took our first trip down the Churchill from Isle a la Crosse in 1955, we ordered three Peterborough 'Prospector' canoes from the HBC and the Company then moved these each winter to be ready at our next starting point. We kept these until 1962 and I took two of them from Yellowknife to Baker Lake across the Barren Lands. In 1963, knowing we should need the Hudson's Bay Company to help us again, I got Elliot Rodger to arrange with a friend for me to attend a Board Meeting of the HBC in Winnipeg and I told them of the rising spread of canoeing into the North and what a help it would be to canoeists if they could institute, with canoes, some sort of Hertz system of rental, whereby canoes could be picked up at any HBC post and left at another post at the end of the journey. To my surprise, the Board took to the idea, pointing out that the service could be set at a rental price that would be self-supporting and also that it would tend to make canoeists buy all their provisions from the Hudson's Bay Company when they picked up their canoes.'

Eric Morse continued. 'I was asked to advise what make and size of canoe should be provided'...he tells how he contacted various outfitters for their opinions...'All replied that the Gruman aluminum standard seventeen-foot was the most durable and would stand up to rental use. I so advised the HBC who promptly bought a fleet of twenty-eight and the U-Paddle was instituted in 1964. I was paddling from Clinton-Golden Lake down the Snare River to Fort Rae and took the first two canoes, leaving them with the Hudson's Bay post at Rae.'

In General Rodger's letter he says, 'What Eric Morse told you would be close to the mark. My memory believes that I happened

A.R.C. Jones

A number of the original Voyageurs camping at Crooked Chute campsite in Algonquin Park. Left to right: Jack Goering, Omond Solandt, Pierre Trudeau, Turk Bayly, Pamela Morse, Angus Scott, Jim Bayly, Eric Morse, Blair Fraser. c.1967.

to see Dick Murray (J.R. Murray, Managing Director, Hudson's Bay Company) and mentioned to him that Eric was in Winnipeg and would like a chance to expound to Dick on the idea of the HBC renting canoes to canoe trip parties. I believe Dick called Eric and asked him to come and tell it to the Canadian Committee at a Board Meeting.

'One of my best memories of those trips was the thrill on arrival by Bellanca (!) at Norway House to find three Grumman canoes, *brand new*, in their burlap wrappings and unpacking them and being the first ones to take to the water in them. That must have been in 1964 when we (Olson, Solandt, Lovnik, Blair Fraser, Coolican and myself) went down to York Factory and, under your excellent system, merely left the canoes at the old warehouse.'

And that was the beginning of the U-Paddle Canoe Rental.

In another letter, Eric Morse says, 'Names of people we canoed with after 1964 include Dr Bill Mathers; Jack Goering; Professor Arch Jones; Pierre Elliott Trudeau; Turk Bayly, Deputy Minister of Ontario Lands and Forests; Jim Matthews; Angus Scott and Bill Shephard. They were all a younger generation of voyageurs. I couldn't get any of the original group to paddle in the Barrens.'

The late Eric Morse, M.A., F.R.G.S. -- he died in 1986 at the age of 81 -- made it his life's work to travel and explore the old fur trade canoe routes and waterways of Canada. His book, *Fur Trade Canoe Routes of Canada/ Then and Now*, is a masterpiece of its kind -- required reading for all serious canoeists.

The Government of the Northwest Territories named a river in the Barren Lands, flowing into Lake Garry on the Back River, the Morse River. It was an honour that he cherished.

The U-Paddle Canoe rental service was maintained until 1984 when it was discontinued. At that time, there were approximately eighty canoes in use and I believe the weekly rental rate was $125 per week.

On February 1, 1964 I received a new contract for $8,000 per annum and a new title 'Administrative Assistant'. In that year, H.W. Sutherland was promoted to Deputy Managing Director of the Company and his place as General Manager of the Northern Stores was taken by D.H. Pitts, whom I had first met eighteen years ago in the back of the store at Yellowknife, busily filling orders for prospecting companies.

At home, things were going smoothly. With my increased salary, the mortgage was paid off and we were able to afford a few of the luxuries of life. I joined Elmhurst Golf and Country Club, became a member of the Board of Governors and served for two years as Secretary and four years as President. Bea and I enjoyed all the social functions of the club and each winter, bought season's tickets for the Celebrity Concert series and the Winnipeg Symphony Orchestra.

One by one, the girls married -- Barbara in September, 1959 to Denis Fletcher; Jennifer in June, 1964 to Dr Lawrence Husbands, and in March, 1966, Dorothy married Jerry Hollins. Ian entered the University of Manitoba in 1964 and courted red-haired Jacqueline Delaney.

In due time Bea and I became proud grandparents as Barb and Denis presented us with Anthony Charles in 1961, Colin Wayne in 1962 and Donna Lynn in 1965.

That summer we took a trip to see Ian who was working as a waiter at the Banff Springs Hotel. We planned to continue on to British Columbia but Bea wasn't feeling well. We headed home and I took her to see the doctor at once.

Then the blow fell. My wife had cancer. After a long courageous battle, Bea died on October 9, 1966.

I could not comprehend it. For thirty-one years, we had been partners in marriage, facing life together. Full of love and compassion, she was always there to celebrate my successes and to provide a shoulder to lean on whenever I encountered setbacks. Her advice was always logical and forthright. Bea was a gentle person and everybody was her friend.

I found it impossible to continue staying in the house -- there were too many memories. After giving the family their choice of furnishings, I sold the house and its contents and moved into a small bachelor apartment at Sussex House on the Assiniboine River and Ian went into digs with a few of his university pals.

For a long time I didn't know what to do with myself. I ate the wrong things and put on weight, visited my family, played golf at Elmhurst in the summer and, outside of a weekly workout at the 'Y' in the wintertime, I huddled in my flat, reading and watching television. Time crawled but I was too apathetic to even be bored. I missed talking over the events of the day with Bea and the companionship we shared. It wasn't living...merely existing.

And then I met Jane Allyn Farrell. Although born in Toronto, she had been reared in New York City. Married but separated from her husband for some years, she had decided that New York was no place to bring up her three children:, Jeff,13; Lisa,10; and Janis,7. Her original plan was to go to Alaska but she only had enough money to take them halfway and since she had a brother living in the city, Winnipeg became her destination. Her brother, Gren Marsh, was a respected radio personality with the Canadian Broadcasting Corporation and he helped her get established.

'Gren was delighted when I decided to come to Winnipeg.' Jane recalls. 'He sent the local newspapers, arranged the rental of a house and every letter brought endless reminders that Winnipeg was *cold* in the winter. So I bought wool socks and flannel pyjamas for the kids and figured we were all set. Little did we know what 'cold' meant.'

Up to now, I had avoided the many widows my friends and relatives had attempted to pair me with but Jane -- I always call her Jeanie -- was different. A petite redhead, she was a blithe spirit with an absolutely ghastly New York accent, but in spite of it, her courage in raising three children alone, and her slightly eccentric turn of mind captivated me.

Just as I had to learn the Canadian lingo after I arrived from Scotland in 1930, so did she. She called soft drinks 'soda' and listened with raised eyebrows when a Salisbury House waiter suggested she might like a 'nip'. She discovered that Winnipeg didn't serve sauerkraut on hot dogs but heaped a myriad of toppings on pizza.

The thing that delighted her most about Canada were baby bonuses. 'Imagine,' she said. 'Paying people to have babies. What a great idea!'

She had learned to weave her way through the heavy traffic on the busy streets of New York and tried to continue that reckless practice on Portage Avenue until she was advised by a buffalo-coated Mountie to wait for 'the little green man.'

I suppose if circumstances had been different I would never have met Jane. If Gren's wife hadn't been the vocalist at the opening dance at Elmhurst, if Jane hadn't brought her colour television up from New York and invited half of Charleswood to watch the Stanley Cup playoffs and if she hadn't suggested that Gren and Lorraine bring me over to her house too, my life might have continued on its dreary way.

Mind you, the relationship was almost over before it began. The following day, I invited her for a ride in my brand new Jaguar E-type of which I was extremely proud. Nothing like an exotic car to lift the spirits. Daffodil yellow, it was. But when Jane got into the car, she looked around and said, 'This is nice. What is it? A Mustang?'

Gren introduced her to Don and Lynn McFarlane and he offered her a job with their public relations firm. Some of her observations of the Winnipeg scene caused much amusement -- like the time she commended the ladies of the city for keeping Winnipeg so clean. She'd seen several carrying corn brooms and had never heard of curling.

If my nights were lonely and my meals taken in silence before, all that now changed. My life took a 180 degree turn and something was always happening. Part of her job was arranging interviews for celebrities appearing in Winnipeg. Besides the soloists and guest conductors with the Symphony, she escorted a bear named Victor and a small group of penguins to the *Winnipeg Free Press* for interviews; accompanied Mayor Steve Juba down the Red River on an experimental hovercraft and once, she even brushed the teeth of a killer whale at a trade show. The kids loved all those crazy activities and conversations around the dinner table were sometimes hilarious.

Life with Jane Allyn Farrell was never dull and I proposed. She refused. I was patient and persistent and when I proposed for the tenth time, she accepted. She sued for her divorce and we set a date -- March 25, 1969. We went looking for a house and after much searching found one we both liked. Built in Tudor-style, it stood at the far west end of Wolseley Avenue with a large, well-treed garden in back stretching down to the Assiniboine River. We arranged for our wedding licence, had the blood tests, and moved into the house, which raised a few eyebrows at Hudson's Bay House.

In February, 1969, I dropped Jane off and continued on to the office. As I got to the parking lot, I suddenly felt very ill. There were a couple of bricks on my chest and I broke out in a cold sweat. 'Flu', I thought and turned the car round and drove back home very slowly. Once in bed and thoroughly unwell by now, I called Jane. She asked a few questions, rang off and immediately called Dr MacLean. I had suffered a heart attack. After three weeks of undergoing all kinds of tests in Misercordia Hospital, Dr MacLean said, 'Did you know that you have had heart attacks before?' When I shook my head in dismay, he added, 'Then you are a very lucky man. You've had a massive coronary infarction and you'll have to spend the next three months in bed.'

We had a very large tree in the back yard and the floor-to-ceiling windows looked out on it. Jane bought me a pair of red binoculars and a bird book to while away the time. For the next three months -- with one exception -- I reclined in a white four-poster bed that was Jane's pride and joy, keeping a bird count and re-reading everything in our extensive library.

As I have said, Jane and I had our blood tests but they were only good for one month and, while I've seen her brush a killer whale's teeth and go up in a hot-air balloon, the thought of another needle made her a basket case so we agreed that we wouldn't postpone our wedding date.

But first there was the wedding ring. Obviously I couldn't go out and buy it, so once again my prospective bride went out and bought her own -- just as Bea had done in 1930. But Bea was accompanied by her mother and Jane took along Jeff, Lisa and Janis. They came home laughing. 'You should have seen the saleman's face, Dad,' said Jeff.

'We looked at all the rings and then we decided which one we wanted,' said Jane, 'and the salesman said "A very good choice, Miss". I don't think he knew what to make of us. So I looked him right in the eye, put my arms around the kids and said, "We've decided to make it legal." '

On March 25, 1969, I got up, dressed and slowly made my way downstairs where Jane and I were married by the Rev. Walter Spence, a former minister of the Norwood United Church and a

friend. Jeff proudly gave his mother away and Ian was my best
man. I had one glass of champagne, we cut the cake and I made
my slow way upstairs again while the family had a grand party!

The three months in bed passed very slowly, and the next three
I spent walking -- slowly at first -- then as my strength grew, Jane
and I took leisurely walks along the elm tree-lined Wolseley
Avenue. In August, the doctor gave me permission to return to
work but for half-days only. The Company was very good to me
during my six months' absence from the office. Although I was
only entitled to three months' salary in one year due to illness, my
regular pay cheque went into the bank once every month for the six
months I was absent and I received my full pay while I worked
half-days.

At the office, everyone was very considerate but the work had
to be done. Enquiries were coming in for U-Paddle Canoe rentals
and had to be handled. In a short time, I found myself working full
days most of the time which left me very weak and dragged out and
Dr MacLean gave me hell. 'Take a holiday, man. You'll kill
yourself at this rate.'

So Jane and I planned our long-overdue honeymoon for the
following August.

The 300th anniversary of the signing of the Hudson's Bay
Company Charter was celebrated on May 2, 1970 throughout
Canada by Company staff.

In Winnipeg, the celebration took the form of a costume ball
in the Civic Auditorium and all staff from Hudson's Bay House and
the retail store were invited. The Northern Stores Department had
our own private little celebration first, which was arranged by Jim
Winter, the senior district manager. We met in the Norwood Hotel
for dinner, then piled into our cars and drove to a parking lot near
the auditorium where we all lined up. We must have been a grand
sight. I went in full Highland dress, wearing the two feathers of a
chief in my bonnet and Jane was lovely as the Laird's lady.

Led by Jim Winter, wearing a Sioux feathered warbonnet and
carrying a Union Jack, we followed the kilted piper up to the
entrance, marched into the auditorium and circled the hall three

H.M. Ross Collection

Hugh and Jane Ross in costume for the Tercentenial Ball.

times. A magnificent entrance, but after all, we *were* the Company.

Later in July, 1970, Queen Elizabeth II, accompanied by Prince Philip, Prince Charles and Princess Anne visited Winnipeg and, in accordance with the terms of the Charter of 1670, were paid rent by the Company -- two elks and two black beavers. On this occasion, however, the Company varied the payment by presenting two moose heads and two black beaver, alive and swimming in a pool set up for the occasion.The ceremony took place on the lawn at Lower Fort Garry and, as invited guests, we were most impressed.

Once the formalities were over and the Queen and her family were enjoying the antics of the live beaver, the press rushed forward to capture their candid pictures of this unprecedented event. 'Go on up there, honey. You'll never get another chance like this,' I urged.

'But I'm not an official photographer. Look, they're all wearing I.D. tags. I won't be allowed.'

'Nonsense, you know all the press people. Go on.'

When the film was developed, it was completely blank. Jane

hadn't inserted the film correctly and not one shot of the Royal Family came out.

By now, I had seven children and seven grandchildren. Dorothy and Jerry were living up in Pine Falls where he was the golf pro and had recently celebrated the arrival of their second child, Robbie, in 1970. Stephen, born two years earlier, was a favourite of Lisa and Jan.

Jen and Larry were in Ontario with their two daughters, Lesley who was born in 1968 and Karen in May 1970.

Denis was working for the *Winnipeg Tribune* and both he and Barbara were involved in the Boy Scouts and Girl Guides.

Ian married his high school sweetheart Jacqueline Delaney in May, 1968 and continued his position with the opposition, T. Eaton & Company.

Jeff was in his junior year and Lisa in Grade 10 at Gordon Bell High School, while Janis was at Isaac Brock. She and Jeff were both athletic and involved in sports, while red-haired Lisa constantly drew pictures of horses and said she was going to be a veterinarian. We bought Jeff his first car and Ian taught him to drive.

In August, 1970, we took our delayed trip to Scotland leaving the children and our Cairn Terrier, Misty, in the charge of friends who moved into our home to look after them.

Jane fell in love with Scotland just as Bea had. She loved the lush green of the countryside and the deep purple of the heather. Having been brought up in New York, she had never seen live sheep and kept snapping pictures until she realized that there were thousands of them in the country. I took her to Rothes to see the house where I was born. Alas, it was now a Ford automobile agency.

We spent a few days visiting friends and took side trips from the Rothes Glen Hotel where we were staying. It was very impressive, having been built by the same architect who built Balmoral Castle, the Royal Family's Scottish home.

For the next three weeks, we toured all over with Jane doing all of the driving. We stayed in bed and breakfast homes during the week and at small inns on the weekends. One night we stayed at a forestry worker's cottage and he took us to watch some old-fashioned sheep shearing the next day. We were invited to a ceilidh at Achnasheen, and at Invershin we had fresh herring dipped in oatmeal and fried in butter. I think we saw every castle -- ruined or not -- in Scotland, and there are about 1,500 of them. We went to the Highland Games in Skye where the weather was kind. There was so much to see that we never did more than 125 miles a day, preferring instead to spend more time at each place. Some of the accommodation was homey and comfortable and the odd place was, indeed, odd.

When we reached Edinburgh it was Festival time and we had to look long and hard to find a place for the night, but we found it. It was a large lovely Georgian style house situated between the United States Embassy and another legation. The landlady looked like Elsa Lancaster on a bad day, with a drippy nose and a front tooth missing. Our room was massive and next to the bathroom which seemed to be permanently occupied by someone or something named Alistair. All we ever heard as we walked by was 'Splash, splash.' Breakfast was inedible: cement-like porridge and eggs and sausages swimming in grease. The living room was filled with dead things -- stuffed birds and animals everywhere. Alfred Hitchcock could have used it as a movie set. We were glad to leave.

One of the things we planned to do was to purchase a stud dog. We had spent much time in a fruitless search for a mate for our still-a-maiden Misty. Twice a year, we had to put up with amorous Alsatians, lovesick Labradors and Chihuahuas with high hopes, and we now decided to find her a husband, even if it meant a mail-order groom. We made arrangements with a small kennel in the Cotswolds in England, so a week prior to our return to Winnipeg, we stopped and bought a silver Cairn, grandly christened Gayclan Wandering Star, more commonly known as Lee Marvin. He travelled as excess baggage on our plane.

As we were nearing Canada, Jane sighed. 'Thanks, love. That

was a marvellous trip. Scotland is just beautiful.' She paused. 'I could live there quite happily.'

'Could you? A city girl like you?'

'Yes. I don't think I'm really a city girl at all.' She turned to me and took my hand. 'What do you think of the idea of moving to Scotland when you retire?'

I was surprised. I knew she loved the country and had enjoyed the people we met but this was a big step. 'You're sure about this? What about the kids?'

'I m sure. When we get home, we'll talk to the kids. I'm afraid they've inherited my gypsy feet. We can show them the films and see what they think.'

When all fifteen rolls of film came back, we spent many happy hours watching the slides and introducing three New York-born kids to Scotland.

I returned to work but in a short time, all the benefits of the holiday were gone and I soon began feeling unwell again. Dr MacLean finally said, 'It's no good, Hugh. You can't go on like this. If you continue working you will be dead in five years. If you retire now and take things easy, you could easily live for another twenty years. It's up to you.' I was really shaken. I was only fifty-nine and still had six years to go until I retired. I stuttered that I had a new wife and three step-children to take care of. I couldn't possibly retire. The doctor cut me short.

'Frankly, you can't afford *not* to retire now. You can collect on the disability portion of the Canada Pension Plan and I believe the Company also has a medical disability retirement provision. You'd better think about it seriously,' he warned.

I must have been more sombre than usual because Jane looked at me anxiously during the evening. After the kids had gone to bed, I said to her, 'Were you serious when you said you'd like to live in Scotland when I retire?'

'Of course I was. Are you thinking about retiring?' I told her about my interview with Dr MacLean. 'I don't think you should think about it, honey. I think you should do it, period.' She rummaged around in the desk drawer and came back with a pencil and pad. 'Let's do some figuring and see if we can swing it. I can always get a job over there to help out, you know.' And we started making lists of things to do and facts that needed clarification.

I wrote to my two sisters in the Old Country and their replies gave us detailed figures on the cost of living, including food and utilities which showed that we could live much more cheaply in Scotland in 1971. A transatlantic call to an old school chum confirmed that rural properties in northeast Scotland could still be purchased very reasonably. Chuck Wilkins was now a well established solicitor in Elgin and when I explained that we were looking for a croft -- a small farm -- of about ten acres, he replied that there were several available and the price was gradually rising due to the influx of Americans arriving almost daily to work in the oilfields in the North Sea.

'You should have come home last year, Hugh, you could have bought a croft for a pittance - £500 to £1,000. Now I'm afraid it'll cost you a wee bit more.' He advised us to make our minds up quickly and he would keep an eye out for a suitable property for about £1,500, which would mean about $3,700 Canadian.

I investigated pension plans. A Canadian living abroad could not have his old age security cheque mailed to him unless he returned to Canada one year prior to reaching the age of 65 and re-established his residence in the country. I paid a visit to the local federal pension offices, told them my story and gave them proof that I was a Canadian citizen. I qualified for Canada Pension Plan disability payment which could be mailed abroad.

The Old Age Pension could only be mailed outside of the country if I was more than eighteen when I arrived in Canada and had resided here continuously for forty years. Again the answer was yes. I had come in July, 1930 which was forty-one years ago, at the age of eighteen years and three months. So there would be no difficulty. When I became sixty-five, my cheque would be mailed to me in Scotland. All I had to do was send a reminder to Ottawa six months prior to my birthdate, and they gave me a form to fill out.

Our financial fears allayed, we wondered what the kids would think about moving to yet another country. Over the years of being both father and mother to her children, Jane devised the fair method of a family conference. So she called a meeting, gave them our reasons for the move and presented our plans. The girls were delighted. Fifteen-year-old Lisa and twelve-year-old Janis were both mad about horses and on learning that we planned to have at least ten acres, asked if they could have a pony. When the answer was yes, they immediately voted to go. Jeff wasn't quite so enthusiastic. He was in his final year at Gordon Bell High School and would graduate in June. He had dozens of friends; played hockey, football and baseball. He had been in organized baseball since he was six and was a talented athlete. But initially he agreed to come too. Another hurdle was overcome.

Next I tackled the question of my eligibility to retire on the Company's disability plan. I approached Norman Simpson, the controller, but he said that Dick Phillips, the personnel manager was the only man who could answer that question. He was firm in his response. A heart condition was not considered by the Company to be grounds for medical disability pension and, in my case, he was sure the Canadian Committee would turn down my request. In his opinion, I couldn't collect Canada Pension Plan payments unless I remained in Canada; and to collect Old Age Pension cheques, he assured me firmly that I would have to return and stay here a year before my sixty-fifth birthday. 'I don't think you have a hope in hell and anyway, you'll never be able to manage over there. The cost of living is too high.'

I knew that three of his answers were dead wrong and wondered if he could be wrong in the fourth so I went downstairs to the Canadian Committee to talk with Bill McColl who was in charge of the Company's pension plan. He listened quietly, then asked, 'Can you supply a medical certificate?'

'Yes, Bill, I can. Dr MacLean, the Company's own doctor will give me one.' Bill wasn't sure whether I would qualify or not but there was only one way to find out.

'Get me the doctor's certificate and I'll request a decision from the Company's insurers.'

During the next few weeks, we made inquiries to overseas

movers, the passport office, travel agents and various other firms that could help facilitate the move.

Then I received a call from Bill. My request had been approved and a confirming letter was on its way to the General Manager. Des Pitts called me into his office. Dick Phillips was sitting by his desk. 'I've just received a letter from the Canadian Committee giving you permission to retire early on July 1st on medical grounds.' He quoted from the letter, 'For your information, you will receive half pay until you become sixty-five when you will be eligible for full retirement. While you are on a medical disability pension, the Company will continue to pay your portion into the Pension Fund, enabling you to get your full pension when you officially retire in 1977.'

I could see that Mr Pitts was annoyed. He slapped the letter down on his desk, looked up at me and said, 'Why is it that a member of this department is retiring and the first notification I have is a letter from the Canadian Committee?'

'A good point, Mr Pitts. Perhaps you should ask Mr Phillips,' and I made a tactful withdrawal.

We put our house on Wolseley Avenue up for sale and it sold almost immediately. Since our electrical appliances would not work in Britain, we advertised them along with our furniture. 'Let's take the four-poster bed,' said Jane. I pointed out that they were made overseas too so it went along with the rest. But she was very careful about who bought it. She wanted it to have a good home. Sometimes she was so Irish!

As the leaving day drew nearer, Jeff decided he would rather stay in Canada and, on reflection, it was the best decision. The only jobs we saw listed in the local Scottish papers were for fishermen or farmers and he was neither. There was no point in his moving all the way to Scotland if he then had to go to Aberdeen or Edinburgh for work. So we gave him his suite of furniture and enough utensils to get him started. He was already a fine cook so Jane didn't worry about his nutrition.

Darcy Munro, the manager of the Winnipeg Merchandise Depot was very helpful. He sent some of his staff to pack and inventory all our silverware, china, crystal, pictures and books, as well as bedding and clothing and had them shipped by sea from Montreal to Scotland.

What was left was laid out on tables in the garage and what wasn't sold was either donated to the Salvation Army, distributed among the children or bagged separately for the rubbish man. When the truck arrived on garbage day, they took one look at the dozen well-packed bags and balked. 'You should have called the office. They'll give you a special pickup. We can't take all this stuff,' he grumbled. So we opened a couple of bags and when they saw the almost new ice-skates and dishes their frowns turned to smiles. I'm afraid the garbage pickup was very late in our neighbourhood that day. The three garbagemen emptied all the sacks, picked over everything, made their choices and repacked them. As the truck went up the road, their hearty 'good luck' calls startled many of the neighbours.

The house was empty except for our suitcases and the lawn furniture we were leaving for the new owners. Even Misty and Marv were gone, which caused a great deal of distress to Jane and the kids. But they would have had to stay in quarantine for six months in England and would have pined away so we found them good homes.

Jeff got himself set up with a chum and we spent the last day or so making the rounds to say farewell. On June 30, 1971 the Northern Stores Department held a luncheon and presented me with a beautifully inscribed watch. As I prepared to leave my office for the last time, the girls in the Northern Stores Department gathered round and made their own presentation -- a pewter beer mug filled with licorice all-sorts and bearing the Company's coat-of-arms. It was inscribed 'From your N.S.D. Girl friends'.

As I walked out the front door of Hudson's Bay House, I took off my tie -- that badge of office respectability -- and ceremoniously deposited it in a wastepaper basket.

That same evening, Jane, Lisa, Janis and I were on a plane bound for a new life in Scotland.

But that's another story!

Don Ferguson

Hugh and Jane Ross in retirement on their croft in Scotland.

EPILOGUE

During the forty-one years in which I served actively with the
Hudson's Bay Company, I had the privilege of working under three
great men who were keen businessmen. They had to be to occupy
their high positions. But to me, they all had one common bond.
They were humanitarians.

The legendary Ralph Parsons, last Fur Trade Commissioner,
was reputed to be a stern man and a strict disciplinarian, qualities
he required to pull the fur trade out of the lethargy into which it had
fallen and to make it a viable business. To me, he showed another
side with his complete understanding of the cares and worries of a
young post manager taking his city bride to a rundown bush post.

When I think of R.H. Chesshire, General Manager, Fur Trade
Department, two events come to mind. When Mr Chesshire met
Mrs Skinner at Fort McMurray in 1945 after her husband's transfer
from Fort Chipewyan, he said, 'My God, Mrs Skinner, what is
wrong with you? The last time I saw you, you were the picture of
health.' When Mrs Skinner explained that she had been in poor
health for some time, he said, 'Well, you are coming right out to
Winnipeg with me for a proper medical checkup and you are not
returning to Fort McMurray until you are well again.' It took
several months and the Company assumed all the costs.

The second picture was in 1947 when my wife Bea was ill at
Nakina. Mr Chesshire wrote me, 'Forget about the business. Bring
your wife and family to Winnipeg and don't worry about the cost.'

H.W. Sutherland, General Manager, Northern Stores
Department can best be described as a man who never lost the
common touch. He had the happy knack of putting everyone at
their ease, whether it was a district manager or a first- year
apprentice clerk. He gained the full confidence of his staff at the
posts and they worked for him. Mind you, he could also call a man
down in no uncertain terms and sometimes in pretty salty language
if it was deserved. But at the end, he would say, 'Well, you have
had your bawling out and you deserved it. Now let's both forget
about it and get on with the job.'

HBCA photograph: 1987/363-S-375

H.W. Sutherland, General Manager, Northern Stores Department with J.W. Anderson and R.H. Chesshire, General Manager, Fur Trade Department on the occasion of Mr Anderson's retirement as District Manager, Eastern Arctic, 1958.

On Saturday morning, January 31, 1987, the *Winnipeg Free Press* carried the following headline: *Hudson's Bay Company Sells Northern Stores.* A few terse paragraphs stated that the Company had sold its 178 northern stores for about $180 million to a group of Bay management personnel and the Mutual Trust Company of Toronto effective March 31st, 1987; the new company to be called Hudson's Bay Northern Stores Inc. The deal included the right to use the Hudson's Bay name for two years. It was further stated that the Division had sales of about $400 million in 1986.

The Bay's executive vice-president was quoted. 'The move is part of the Toronto-based Bay's program of concentrating its financial and managerial resources on its core business of department stores and real estate. The assets being sold represent only five percent of the total Company assets.'

I could not believe my eyes! Thus was more than three hundred years of history, including the making of western Canada, wiped out by a stroke of a pen, and the Hudson's Bay Company was out of the fur trade, the basis on which the Company was built. Where now was the great Company of Adventurers of England Trading into Hudson's Bay? Reduced to just another retail store chain selling merchandise in city suburban malls?

In my years of service with the Bay, I saw the Land Department closed -- no more land to sell. And the Mackenzie River Transport wound up. I saw the Red Ensign with the letters HBC on the fly abandoned, and the Fur Trade Department renamed the Northern Stores Department but never in my wildest imaginings did I think I would see the day that the Fur Trade would be abandoned completely.

There are still a few fur traders left, men who joined the Company fifty and sixty years ago, who travelled by canoe and by dogteam and traded with the natives in their own language, mostly in remote areas where the creature comforts were conspicuous by their absence.

Fur Traders are a unique breed of men, the like of whom Canada will never see again. I salute them, one and all!

HMR, June 1989

BIBLIOGRAPHY

Anderson, J.W., *Fur Trader's Story,* Toronto, 1961
Archer, John H., *Saskatchewan History,* Saskatoon, 1981
Benoit, Barbara, 'The Mission at Ile-a-la-Crosse', *The Beaver*, Winter 1940.
Brooks, Maurice, *The Life of the Mountains*, New York, 1966
Calder, Ritchie, *Men Against the Frozen North*, Toronto, 1951
Rue, Leonard Lee III, *Pictorial Guide to the Mammals of North America*, New York, 1967
Lloyd, Trevor et Al., 'Oil for the Planes of Alaska', *The Beaver*, September 1943.
McGregor, James G., *A History of Alberta*, Edmonton, 1981
McKay, William, 'HBC Pioneers No. 5', *The Beaver*, December 1924.
McKenzie, N.M.W.J., *The Men of the Hudson's Bay Company*, Fort William, 1921
Price, Ray, *Yellowknife*, Toronto, 1954
Williams, Glyndwr, 'The Hudson's Bay Company and the Fur Trade 1670-1870', *The Beaver*, Autumn 1983.
Wuorinen, Richard, *A History of Buffalo Narrows*, Buffalo Narrows, 1981

INDEX